A Curriculum of Peace

A Curriculum of Peace

Selected Essays from *English Journal*

Edited by

Virginia R. Monseau
Youngstown State University

National Council of Teachers of English
1111 W. Kenyon Road, Urbana, Illinois 61801-1096

The cover image is a revised version of the artwork captioned "In any language, PEACE" by Richard A. Williams first published in the May 2000 issue of *English Journal.*

Staff Editor: Bonny Graham

Interior Design: Doug Burnett

Cover Design: Pat Mayer

NCTE Stock Number: 10061

Library of Congress Cataloging-in-Publication Data

A curriculum of peace : selected essays from English journal / edited by Virginia R. Monseau

    p. cm.

  Includes bibliographical references.

  ISBN 0-8141-1006-1 (pbk.)

1. Peace—Study and teaching (Elementary)—United States. 2. Peace—Study and teaching (Secondary)—United States. 3. War in literature. 4. Peace in literature. 5. Conflict management—Study and teaching (Elementary)—United States. 6. Conflict management—Study and teaching (Secondary)—United States. I. Monseau, Virginia R., 1941– II. National Council of Teachers of English. III. English Journal.

  JZ5334.C87 2004

  303.6'6'071—dc22

                              2004000673

To all who teach for peace

Contents

II. Peace and the Arts

Objectifying people as "other" is often used as a justification for violence. Gorrell demonstrates how poetic responses to great works of art that depict violent acts can teach students the value of empathy and result in better understanding of others different from themselves. (May 2000)

III. Peace and Our Schools

explain how their reluctant students latched onto Hip-hop as a
means of expressing themselves and how reading, discussion,
and freewrites served as inspiration. Their primary goal in this
article is to help prepare teachers to work with students different
from themselves as they teach for peace. (May 2000)

Introduction

Virginia R. Monseau

When we think of the word *peace,* we often think of it in concert with its opposite, *war.* So much of history, both ancient and modern, has been shaped by the wars that have taken place between peoples fighting for territory, freedom, and power. Not much has changed even today, as our most recent war in Iraq was fought, according to military and government leaders, to liberate the Iraqi people from the tyranny of a dictator. Some suspect that power and territory also may have been issues, but freedom from oppression has been touted as the driving force behind the invasion of Iraq by primarily British and U.S. forces.

Peace has long been sought by many civilizations and cultures, from the references to peace in the Old Testament; to the "Peace on Earth" anthem sung by the angels at the birth of Jesus; to the ancient Hindu prayer for peace, "Om, shantih, shantih, shantih"; to international attempts to institutionalize peace through the United Nations and the League of Nations. Peace in the Middle East has been the goal of the United Nations since the founding of Israel in 1948. Yet, in spite of the best efforts of some of the most effective diplomats, peace in that part of the world has been elusive. Looking at our most recent conflicts, the peace the United States sought in Vietnam was never fully realized in spite of the thousands of soldiers who died for the cause, and the peace between North and South Korea has been jittery at best, recently erupting in a nuclear threat from the North Korean government. We must go back to the aftermath of World War II to see peace in action, with the development of the Marshall Plan to aid in the reconstruction of Europe and reestablish relations between European countries formerly at war.

It seems paradoxical to *fight* for *peace,* yet that is the image most of us have of the struggle. There must be a conflict before there can be a peaceful resolution. Whether the fight is physical, emotional, or intellectual, two forces must be at odds in order for the "good guy" to win. This is certainly the perception most of our students have as they view world events and the conflicts in their own lives. The horrific tragedy of September 11, 2001, is a good example. The death and destruction wrought by nineteen Middle Eastern terrorists who managed to infiltrate the United States and use its airplanes as weapons against its people resulted in the kind of hatred by some that may be beyond reason or understanding—hatred for anything and anyone Middle Eastern. Lacking a historical perspective, many of our young people have bought into this hatred as a result of the fear and helplessness they feel about the future.

Add to this the increase in teenage violence around the country, and it's apparent that military wars aren't the only kind of war on the minds of adolescents today. Gang wars on the streets and peer violence in the schools make being a teenager much more frightening than it was twenty-five or thirty years ago. No longer can school be thought of as a safe haven for students and teachers. Studying in the library or eating lunch in the cafeteria can be risky, as these are places where large numbers of students and teachers gather—proverbial sitting ducks for someone with violent intentions who has managed to smuggle a weapon into a building. The streets are even less safe. Drive-by shootings, abductions, and sex- and-drug-related crimes create an atmosphere of terror and frustration.

In our concern for our students, we sometimes forget that teachers too are profoundly affected by these events. In addition to fear for their personal safety, they wonder about their professional responsibility. How do they confront the issues of war, terrorism, and school and neighborhood violence with their students? How can they comfort and reassure these young people when they are so fearful and uncertain themselves? Just what is a teacher's responsibility in this time of terror? How do teachers respond when they are sometimes the victims of school violence?

This collection of articles from the *English Journal* aims to help teachers answer some of these questions. Most of the essays are taken from the May 2000 issue, also titled "A Curriculum of Peace," since that is the most comprehensive and diverse collection of articles that *EJ* has ever published on the subject. But several pieces are taken from earlier and later years, as well. Though some of the resources cited in the earlier articles may seem dated, the ideas they generate help to expand and enrich the development of a curriculum of peace in the secondary school. As these essays address the myriad ways in which educators can teach for peace, they also offer teachers the comfort of knowing they are not alone in this endeavor.

In her book *The Peaceable Classroom*, Mary Rose O'Reilley asks, "Is it possible to teach English so that people stop killing each other?" (9). The question was presented to her and other teaching assistants by a distinguished professor years earlier, and though they thought he was kidding at the time, for O'Reilley the question would not go away. With apologies to O'Reilley and her professor, I borrow the question as a unifying device for this collection, for it has haunted me ever since I read her book. Can we, indeed, teach English so that people stop killing each other? And, if so, how do we put into action such a huge leap of faith in the secondary classroom?

Our professional forebears such as James Moffett, Louise Rosenblatt, Donald Murray, and others have taught us that, in order to learn, students must be engaged in their work, must care about what they are doing, and must see some connection between what they are learning and what they already know. Applying these three criteria to a curriculum that promotes understanding of others in relation to ourselves in diverse realms of life seems a wise and potentially successful way to teach for peace. In these days of state standards and mandated testing, it is more important than ever to remember our shared humanity as we plan our curriculum. In examining the ideas and activities contained in the chapters of this book, teachers may discover that many of the standards to which they must teach are being addressed. As for testing, the ability to think critically is one of the most essential skills students must possess in order to pass any test. Teaching for peace in the ways suggested here encourages the kind of thought and insight that will serve students well. Developing a curriculum of peace need not be at odds with a teacher's concerns about standards and testing because the wise teacher will find ways to incorporate relevant content into the pursuit of these goals. While no academic curriculum is a panacea for the world's ills, and there is no guarantee that any amount of education will result in the desired outcome, teachers must begin somewhere, and the articles in this collection are a good place to start for those who believe that we truly can "teach English so that people stop killing each other."

Part I: Peace and War

This section sets out to establish the idea of physical conflict and how it affects combatants on both sides, their countries, and innocent civilians. Beginning with a piece by Larry R. Johannessen that focuses on teaching literature, this section concentrates heavily on the human aspect of war. By its very nature, young adult literature reaches adolescents in a way not always possible with more difficult, often distancing, texts, providing more opportunities for students to, as Rosenblatt says, "seek through literature an enlargement of our experiences" (40). Understanding this, Johannessen discusses four types of young adult literature that have emerged since the Vietnam War, pointing out three major devices the authors use to convey meaning. Looking closely at

The Combat Narrative, The War At Home, The Refugee Experience, and The Next Generation, he offers detailed explanations of titles that fit these categories and suggestions for "unlocking meaning" through teaching these novels, debunking the distorted "Rambo myth" that is sometimes the extent of student knowledge of this war. Indeed, Johannessen's insights are invaluable when discussing any war, as we are often caught up in military statistics and television sound bites, making it easy to forget the human cost of combat. Some students may have parents or grandparents who fought in the Vietnam War, and many certainly have friends or relatives who served in either the Gulf War or the most recent war in Iraq. Reading this literature, seeing the horrors of combat, and reflecting on the human element of war can be the starting point for discussing peaceful resolution of conflict.

Further emphasizing the human toll of war, Carolyn Lott and Stephanie Wasta illustrate their use of children's and young adult literature to help students see the difficulties experienced by people involved in fighting a war on their own country's soil. By reading actual Civil War letters as well as historical fiction, and by keeping journals in the voices of teens experiencing the war, students can gain a valuable perspective on why civil wars are fought and how they might be prevented. Lott and Wasta's efforts are a good example of how teachers can use reader response and firsthand engagement to advance understanding of a distant and abstract concept such as war. By beginning with their own emotional and physical conflicts with peers and possibly examining the territorialism of gang violence, students can be led to understand the concept of civil war and see that it is not always military in nature. What kinds of forces cause otherwise peaceful, friendly people to turn on one another and fight to the death? How can these forces be dealt with before it's too late?

To most adolescents today, World War II seems like ancient history, but Joan Ruddiman makes it immediate in her unit on this war in a multicultural suburban school. Giving her students the opportunity to view the war from the perspective of their countries of origin, she has them interview parents and grandparents while doing extensive reading and research. She encourages her students to think critically about the consequences of war and how events of long ago still affect our world today. Historical accounts are nicely balanced with human recollections, making for a richer and more interesting learning experience. Perhaps more than any other war, World War II was a turning point in our history. Why? This is an intriguing question for students to investigate. Most everyone has heard of Adolf Hitler and the Nazi Party, and to the free world they are truly the "bad guys." But Hitler and his soldiers were not always torturers and murderers. They too were once children. What forces made them what they became? What can we do to prevent such forces from reemerging?

Offering a slightly different perspective, Randal W. Withers argues for the inclusion of the contemporary antiwar novel in the high school literature canon, pointing out that such works as *The Red Badge of Courage* and *All Quiet on the Western Front* have long been staples of the curriculum. Reasoning that more recent antiwar literature such as Tim O'Brien's *Going after Cacciato* and Don Delillo's *End Zone* will help students "better understand the impact of war on a variety of social issues" and "educate them so that the tragedy of war is not repeated," Withers offers several titles and describes how they might be used in the classroom. As he points out, Arthur Applebee's 1993 research on the teaching of literature in the secondary school reveals that the classics still prevail and little contemporary literature, especially antiwar literature, is being taught. If we are ever to create a curriculum of peace, we must certainly offer students the most compelling, and the most relevant, literature to read as part of that curriculum. We must become informed ourselves about the possibilities by reading widely in our professional literature and in the literature we might use in our classrooms.

Moving away from the idea that war and peace can be studied successfully only in English and social studies classrooms, Rita Bornstein believes that peace studies must be interdisciplinary to be effective. She describes a unit taught by teachers in the language arts, social studies, art, music, and science departments that resulted in high enrollment and great success in helping students "focus forward" rather than backward as they study war and peace. She lists seven major goals for this unit, which include examining personal values and beliefs about war and peace, looking at the nature of human aggression, analyzing conflict and various models for peacekeeping, and examining the relationship of the individual to the state. Countless books and articles in our professional literature have shown us that an interdisciplinary approach to learning provides rich opportunities for our students, but they haven't said much about the value of this kind of learning to teachers. Through working with colleagues in other disciplines, we gain knowledge that we might otherwise not have access to. As our students see us learning, they realize that the acquisition of knowledge is a lifelong process, a lesson we can teach them by "showing" rather than "telling."

An article on the Middle East is the final piece in this section. Though it focuses more on group investigation of the 1991 Middle East conflict than on the conflict itself, it is still valuable in its interdisciplinary method and satisfying results. Challenging their students to answer the question "How can we achieve peace in the Middle East?," Jack Huhtala and Elaine B. Coughlin launched an interdisciplinary project in their tenth-grade English and government classes. Using a method of instruction called "group investigation," developed by Shlomo Sharan of Tel Aviv, Huhtala and Coughlin used a six-stage process to help their students learn more about the Middle East and its people. While at first their students reacted unthinkingly when confronted with the dilemma of how to handle hostile nations, with remarks like "Just nuke them," they gradually began to see that the conflict was not that easily resolved. Through listening to speakers, conducting interviews, and reading various books and articles, the students learned to work together democratically to arrive at an answer to the focus question. While many books and articles have touted the benefits of cooperative learning, this promising account of interdisciplinary success demonstrates that collaboration among teachers and students, though not without its problems, can be a valuable part of the peaceable curriculum.

As all of the pieces in this section demonstrate, examining the concept of war can enrich our students' understanding of human conflict and how it might be resolved. Teachers might broach the subject of motivation and consequences by asking questions such as the following: Is there such a thing as a "good war"? Are antiwar proponents unpatriotic? Is peaceful negotiation the answer to all problems? What has been the public reaction to war during the past century and into the twenty-first? In fiction, many young men go to war because they see it as glamorous. Does this hold true in life as well? The possibilities for discussion, and insight, are many.

Part II: Peace and the Arts

The arts have always been a medium for expressing our response to war and conflict, from Pablo Picasso's *Guernica,* to Wilfred Owen's "Dulce et Decorum est," to the seventies song "War, What Is It Good For?" This section of the book offers three essays that demonstrate how poetry, music, dance, drama, and personal story can work to reduce the covert violence of name-calling, rudeness, racism, sexism, and psychological intimidation among students.

Nancy Gorrell's "Teaching Empathy through Ecphrastic Poetry" demonstrates how poetic response to great works of art that depict violent acts can teach students the value of empathy and result in better understanding of others different from themselves. Objectification of an "other" is often used as a justification for violence, and responding to images of violent acts through poetry writing provides a means of examining our own biases and prejudices. As Gorrell points out, it's important that we *teach*, not *preach*, empathy by giving students the opportunity to "'*enter into*' the feeling and spirit of others." To do this, she uses an ecphrastic poem of address titled "To the Little Polish Boy Standing with His Arms Up" by Peter L. Fischl, written in response to a photograph of a little Polish boy that was published in *LIFE* magazine in November 1960. After much discussion about the similarities between Fischl's life and that of the little boy in the photo, Gorrell invites her students to write their own poetic response to the photo. The results, as she demonstrates in the article, are thought provoking.

Though Gorrell's unit focuses on teaching about the Holocaust, her method of using ecphrastic poetry as a vehicle for understanding others can be expanded and refocused in many different ways. Students can write ecphrastic poetry in response to any work of art. Taking them to a museum and allowing them to respond to any piece that moves them can be a starting point to showing them works that focus more on human difference or unjust or inhumane treatment of others.

In addition to using poetry as a means of understanding others, Mary F. Wright and Sandra Kowalczyk delve further into the arts by employing music, dance, drama, and printmaking to help their students "hear, read, think, and feel the message of peace in the world." We know that we learn best when we can use all of our senses in the process, and this project taps that potential. Not only do students learn about the Holocaust, but they also examine, among other things, the events of Hiroshima, the horror of slavery, and the importance of cultural identity, using their minds, hands, and bodies in the learning process. Young people do not soon forget what they experience, and using the creative and performing arts as a means of understanding can indeed help build bridges between and among cultures.

The last piece in this section serves as a segue to the next, perhaps summing up the reasons why peace education is so important in our schools. As G. Lynn Nelson points out in "Warriors with Words," metal detectors, surveillance cameras, and armed guards may be common in U.S. schools today, but such methods can never reduce the covert violence of name-calling, rudeness, racism, sexism, and psychological intimidation. Using examples from his students, Nelson demonstrates how the power of personal story can go a long way toward promoting peace and well-being in the classroom and beyond. "Why personal story?" he asks. "Because without that nothing else matters." Paraphrasing Rollo May, Nelson reminds us that violence "is itself a form of communication," something that we teachers tend to forget. In our zeal to instruct students in the skills of expository and argumentative writing so that they can pass state proficiency tests, we forget where our students' souls reside. Nelson beautifully reminds us what it means to write meaningful prose. Using as an example a student in his Native American first-year composition class, he lets us hear Kyle tell his story in a poem titled "Broken Arrows, Broken Hearts: I Will Fight No More." Nelson won the NCTE Hopkins Award for this piece, an essay that so touchingly demonstrates the power of story to heal and comfort. It may prompt us to wonder: If Eric Harris and Dylan Klebold had been encouraged to tell their stories, would the horror of Columbine have happened? And it might certainly encourage us to make room for the personal story in our writing curriculum.

Part III: Peace and Our Schools

Achieving peace in our schools seems like the first step toward a peaceful world, for our students have the opportunity every day to interact with others different from themselves in race, gender, culture, and class. Though we wish for a positive result from this interaction, the seeds of conflicts that occur worldwide on a larger scale are frequently sown in the school years: territorialism, mistrust, envy, alienation, hatred born of misunderstanding. With such a golden opportunity to teach for peace, why have we teachers failed so miserably? Or is achieving peace through classroom experience and instruction an impossible goal?

Sara Dalmas Jonsberg tells us that we must begin by making "a place for every student." She believes that loneliness and fear are at the root of the alienation students often feel, which sometimes has self-destructive and far-reaching consequences. The visible curriculum, she says, doesn't matter very much. It's the hidden curriculum we must pay attention to. The competition for grades, the conformity required for social acceptance—these are matters that work against a peaceful classroom, and they are matters that teachers must deal with. Building a sense of community in the classroom is essential, as Randy Bomer and others have pointed out. In discussing school violence, Jonsberg's question, "Why does our gaze always linger on the victims, refusing compassion or empathy for the perpetrators?," may offend some, but it is an honest question that deserves scrutiny. How can we ever achieve peace if we don't try to understand those who would destroy it?

Marsha Lee Holmes gets right down to business in her piece "Get Real: Violence in Popular Culture *and* in English Class." Holmes stresses that educators cannot and should not try to keep the "real world" out of their classrooms, as some administrators have tried to do as a result of school violence. Using examples from popular culture such as magazines, newspapers, music, and film, Holmes teaches critical inquiry by encouraging students to report on current violent events or review certain violent films. Giving convincing reasons for her direct approach, she cites Paulo Freire's concept of a "problem-posing education" as part of her rationale, emphasizing that this kind of student inquiry is active, not passive.

Popular culture is an area often neglected in the English class, where literature is usually queen and grammar instruction eats up much of the curriculum. Yet here is a research base for students that can be far more instructive than answering study questions or analyzing sentences. As part of a peaceable curriculum, popular culture can be research heaven, as Holmes so expertly points out. What is happening in the world now is of primary interest to our students. Examining behavior, motivation, and consequences in real-life situations makes for the kind of learning that John Dewey called for many years ago, learning that taps the world students live in and brings it into the classroom.

Barbara R. Cangelosi is another educator who believes in real-world learning. As a teacher at an alternative high school for at-risk students, she often observed students taunting one another. Seeing that these students often communicate inappropriately, she devised an assertive communication unit to demonstrate to them that they can take control and get what they need without aggressive communication. Using activities that reveal that meaning is shaped by interpretation and past experience, Cangelosi teaches students to respect individuality, use precise language, and refrain from making assumptions about others.

State and national standards require teachers to address reading, writing, speaking, and listening in their lessons, but speaking and listening are sometimes "covered" by having students answer questions orally or assigning them to work in small groups. The kind of communication that Cangelosi talks about really *teaches* students how what we say and how we say it can mean the difference between a peaceful or a combative situation.

A companion to lessons on assertive communication is instruction in conflict resolution. Emphasizing that the English classroom is the perfect place to integrate anti-violence teaching into the curriculum, Rosemarie Coghlan demonstrates how teaching conflict resolution strategies through the study of literature and encouraging "academic controversy" through cooperative learning can help students discover nonviolent ways of handling conflict that will translate to their personal lives. In "The Teaching of Anti-Violence Strategies within the English Curriculum," Coghlan explains how she teaches students to live peacefully in a violent world and how they can work to improve it. Determining whether a literary character's response is submissive, aggressive, or assertive helps students make connections to the conflicts in their own lives, and role-playing responses to specific conflicts brings the realization that people have choices in their mode of response. Having students formulate "peace contracts" based on the conflicts of literary characters is another method that Coghlan uses to achieve her goals. To those who would complain that this kind of teaching takes time away from the academic curriculum, Coghlan responds with a firm "not so." Integration is the key, and though this takes work on the teacher's part, the instruction is vital to students trying to cope with a violent world.

The kind of role playing that Coghlan describes is similar to Daniel Mindich's method of using simulations in his classroom, though his is a more concentrated approach. In "The Ada Valley Simulation," Mindich creates a society, the Ada Valley, where students are confronted with the issue of differences among various groups. Through role-play they are forced to deal with a society in which no groups are clearly good or bad and political correctness and racism do not exist. Yet the groups have disparate lifestyles that put them in conflict with one another, and they must deal with these problems. The simulation is followed by a debriefing in which students and teacher discuss what happened and why, making connections to real-life situations.

Using simulations to illuminate the real world can put a human face on difference, as Linda W. Rees describes in her piece, "A Thousand Cranes: A Curriculum of Peace." Using as her example a young Japanese girl who transferred to the private school where Rees teaches, Rees describes both the acceptance and the rejection of this student by her peers and the examination by Rees and her students of the reasons for this behavior. Concluding that sometimes peace is taught *to* us rather than *by* us, she demonstrates the value of students as peacemakers. Like the other teachers whose pieces are included in this section, Rees understands that peace must begin at home and that students learn best through authentic experience. Examining their behavior in a real-life classroom situation taps the same critical thinking skills required of students in the analysis of literature, but the learning is so much more meaningful.

Writing, too, has an important place in a curriculum of peace. Colleen A. Ruggieri shows how carefully constructed writing assignments can give students a voice and promote better understanding of differences. Instead of just "studying works written by others," she suggests providing students opportunities for growth through personal research and enriched writing assignments. She tells of a student who, on being disciplined by her for injuring another student in class, threatened to murder her, chop her body parts into pieces, and mail them to each of her family members. "Teens are screaming—and killing—in an effort to be heard by society," she says. In an effort to teach tolerance and understanding, she gives students multiple opportunities for personal writing, much like G. Lynn Nelson describes in "Warriors with Words."

But Ruggieri goes further with creative writing assignments of various types, including a personal research paper. Ken Macrorie is well known for writing about the I-Search paper back in the 1980s, and Tom Romano has published several recent books touting the value of the multigenre paper, which allows for personal exploration and multiple voices. Ruggieri builds on these ideas by giving her students opportunities to explore their lives, resolve personal issues through research, write about these issues, and share their discoveries with others in the class. She is quick to point out that she knows she can't save the world through her efforts, but she also knows that what goes on, however briefly, in the English classroom can extend far into the community and the world.

Like Colleen Ruggieri, David Gill experienced a situation in his school that started him wondering how to teach for peace. The number and severity of student fights had increased, and teachers could no longer break them up without risking attack themselves. After one particularly vicious fight that resulted in vandalized classrooms and a computer being thrown down a crowded hallway, Gill was shocked that students took it all in stride and barely talked about the melee the next day. It seemed they had become accustomed to violence, and some of them even enjoyed watching it occur.

After doing extensive research, Gill came upon some teaching materials that used the works of Martin Luther King Jr. and Mahatma Gandhi to teach adolescents about the philosophy behind nonviolence. He describes these materials extensively in his piece and also gives an example of a Bill of Rights for Students that his class designed as a culminating project, which included such things as "the right to be safe" and "the right to not be afraid." If such teaching can prevent even one student from being involved in a violent act, or prompt a student to prevent a violent act from occurring, it's worth all the time and effort required. Gill ends his piece with an anecdote that illustrates this observation exactly.

As we consider the role of popular culture in our curricula, we can't ignore the presence of Hip-hop in our students' lives. Heather E. Bruce and Bryan Dexter Davis share their attempt to develop a Hip-hop-influenced slam poetry unit that teaches for peace. They explain how their reluctant students latched onto Hip-hop as a means of expressing themselves and how reading, discussion, and freewrites served as inspiration. Their primary goal in relating their experience is to help prepare teachers to work with students different from themselves as they teach for peace.

Some critics see Hip-hop as a _source_ of violence, with its sometimes crude lyrics and dangerous exhortations, but Bruce and Davis make clear what is acceptable and what is not while still allowing for the essence of the genre itself. They work with students to help them express their emotions verbally rather than acting on violent impulse. The authors note that while emotional development is usually supported for girls, it is discouraged for boys, and that research has shown "a high correlation between lack of facility with verbal expression and aggression and delinquency." Of special note is the authors' admission of the difficulties they encountered working together across cultural boundaries with few models for accomplishing their goals. Paulo Freire's _Pedagogy of the Oppressed_ and Geneva Smitherman's publications on language rights, as well as Mary Pipher's _Reviving Ophelia_ and Mary Rose O'Reilley's _The Peaceable Classroom_ are just some of the underpinnings of their work.

After the events of September 11, 2001, many teachers struggled with the issue of how to continue teaching while still acknowledging and honoring their students' grief, fear, and frustration in the face of an appalling act of violence. Vasiliki Antzoulis, who on that day was a student teacher at Manhattan's Stuyvesant High School, describes how her students, who witnessed the horror, "ran for their lives up the West Side Highway." Later, once they were relocated to a school in Brooklyn, she wondered how she could teach through this tragedy. "How could I go in and teach alliteration to students who had just witnessed people jumping out of the 110th story of the World Trade Center?" she asks. But teach she did, creating a poetry unit that allowed her students to express their fears and examine their feelings. In her piece

"Writing to Heal, Understand, and Cope," Antzoulis shows us how she turned a horrific experience into an opportunity to deal with pain through reading and writing poetry. As we confront another kind of war—terrorism and counterterrorism—teachers will continue to seek ways to help students cope with violence.

The final piece in this section, and indeed in this entire collection, may be surprising in its content. Marion Wrye's "The Silent Classroom" suggests a possible antidote to the violence with which students must live every day. In an effort to combat the external power on students of often-violent forces such as technology and the media, Wrye rationalizes and describes her efforts to allow her students the silence they need to gradually realize the shift from external to internal power. Likening her technique to that of the horse whisperer, she attempts to ease the weight of our culture on students' psychology and spirit, helping them realize a more peaceful existence. "We strain at the gnats of scores and standards and curricula and methodologies," she says, "and swallow the camels of wholesale demoralization and alienation." Wrye notes that when she allowed students their silences, they appreciated one another's work more and developed a deeper sense of classroom community. How often do we allow our students to be silent in our classrooms—other than when they are reading an assignment or taking a test? What role does silence play in a curriculum of peace?

At this writing, a fragile cease-fire in the Middle East has once again been shattered by terrorists who prefer death and destruction over peace. Two disgruntled employees in different states have killed several co-workers because they felt alienated and mistreated. A drive-by shooting has killed a three-year-old child in a neighborhood troubled by gang fights. And thousands of children are heading back to school for a fresh start to the new academic year. We want them and their teachers to be safe, just as we want the killing in our neighborhoods and other parts of the world to stop. We can wring our hands and lament the sad state of the world, or we can decide to take a step toward peace, however small, by making a difference in our classrooms.

Works Cited

Applebee, Arthur N. *Literature in the Secondary School: Studies of Curriculum and Instruction in the United States.* Urbana, IL: National Council of Teachers of English, 1993.

Bomer, Randy. *Time for Meaning: Crafting Literate Lives in Middle and High School.* Portsmouth, NH: Heinemann, 1995.

English Journal. 89.5 (2000).

O'Reilley, Mary Rose. *The Peaceable Classroom.* Portsmouth, NH: Boynton/Cook, 1993.

Rosenblatt, Louise M. *Literature as Exploration.* 5th ed. New York: Modern Language Association, 1995.

| Peace and War

If we ignore contemporary antiwar literature and its applications in today's classroom simply because such works have not yet been labeled "classic," then we run the risk of allowing students to graduate into adulthood without having heeded important lessons from the not-so-distant past, of which they are, at least partially, ignorant.

Randal W. Withers,
"New Wars, Old Battles:
Contemporary Combat Fiction
for the High School Canon"

1 Young-Adult Literature and the Vietnam War

Larry R. Johannessen

A few days after the end of the Persian Gulf War, former President Bush proclaimed, "We've kicked the Vietnam syndrome once and for all." Since making this proclamation, the war that won't go away has returned once again. For example, the POW/MIA issue has resurfaced several times since the end of the Persian Gulf War and seems to be as powerful as ever. Most recently, young people who lost parents in the Vietnam War met at the Vietnam Veterans Memorial in Washington, DC, for a ceremony that suggests that the legacies of the Vietnam War are still with us. In fact, the sorrow, grief, and loss expressed by these young people serve as a poignant reminder that despite what the former President or others might say about having buried the ghosts of Vietnam, the legacies of the war continue to haunt the nation. Further, the voices of these young people remind us that the war and its aftermath continue to shape society and the lives of the children of those who came of age during the Vietnam War.

As N. Bradley Christie points out, students come to us with very little real knowledge of the war, but a strong desire to learn more (1989, 35). Unfortunately, their knowledge of the war does not go much beyond Hollywood's *Rambo* series, various adventure novels, such as the Saigon Commando or Night Fighters series in which Vietnam is merely a backdrop, or the romantic novels, such as those by Ellen Elliot, Della Field, and Evelyn Hawkins—all called *Vietnam Nurse*—that Kathleen M. Puhr says are "little more than Harlequin romances set in Vietnam" (1988, 174). Ironically, most of our students know more about the Civil War than they do about the war that was the defining experience for their parents and continues to shape society and their lives.

Fortunately, our students' desire to learn more about the Vietnam War is matched by a diversity of fine adolescent literature that deals with war and its aftermath. In fact, with our national amnesia about the war finally over, a number of these works, such as Bobbie Ann Mason's *In Country* (1989) and Walter Dean Myers' *Fallen Angels*

This essay appeared in *English Journal* 82.5 (1993) on pages 43–49.

(1988), have received considerable critical attention. Having our students study some of these works can help them better understand the war, their parents, and how the legacies of the war continue to have an impact on their lives. Ultimately, studying these works may help students to deal with the world they will encounter outside of school and, as Fred Wilcox argues, "empower [them] to take responsibility for issues that affect their lives and the future of our planet" (1988, 40).

Four main types of adolescent literature have emerged in response to the Vietnam War: works that deal with the experience of Vietnam or the combat narrative; literature that focuses on the war at home; novels that deal with the refugee experience; and works that focus on the legacies of the Vietnam War, particularly the impact of war on the children of the generation that came of age during the Vietnam War. Many authors of this literature also tend to use one or more of three major devices to convey meaning: the Vietnam Veterans Memorial, or "the Wall," in Washington, DC; letters; and the adolescent experience as told through the voice of a young narrator.

The Combat Narrative

The combat narrative is perhaps the best known type of war literature. A number of authors have written works that attempt to portray the experience of fighting in Vietnam. Like some of the texts we already teach *(The Red Badge of Courage, A Farewell to Arms, All Quiet on the Western Front,* and *Catch-22)*, these works demand that students think about what it really meant to live and fight in a war. For example, Myers' novel *Fallen Angels* focuses on seventeen-year-old Richie Perry's tour of duty in Vietnam in 1967. Looking for a better life than he had in Harlem, Perry joins the Army and is sent to the war zone. Despite his loneliness, confusion, fear, and at times, his guilt for having lived when his fellow soldiers have not, Perry survives and comes to trust and care deeply for several of his companions. They give him courage and reason to live. Myers skillfully integrates the themes of innocence, courage, initiation, and mortality in this compelling novel. Readers will emerge feeling that they have experienced 'Nam.

Another combat narrative that has a great deal to offer young readers is Tim O'Brien's memoir, *If I Die in a Combat Zone* (1987). First published in 1973, this new-journalism style narrative is now regarded by some as one of the classics of the war. This is the story of one foot soldier's journey from safe, middle-class America to the center of the nightmare of the Vietnam War. O'Brien emphasizes the fear and hardships faced by soldiers fighting the war. Readers are pulled along as

O'Brien wrestles with the moral issues he faces. For example, O'Brien comes to Vietnam regarding Frederic Henry, the hero of Ernest Hemingway's *A Farewell to Arms,* as one of his heroes. However, when O'Brien tries to apply Hemingway's definition of courage to his own situation, he has trouble making it work. In the end, he rejects Hemingway's definition and decides that true brave men are those who do well on the average and have perhaps a moment of glory. Readers learn what it was like to fight in Vietnam and, if the book is taught in conjunction with other war literature, they clearly see how this literature is part of a literary heritage.

Dear America: Letters Home from Vietnam edited by Bernard Edelman (1986) and *In the Combat Zone: An Oral History of American Women in Vietnam, 1966–1975* by Kathryn Marshall (1988) are two other adult books of interest to young-adult readers. Edelman's book is a collection of letters home from those serving and working in Vietnam during the war. From soldiers to "donut dollies" (Red Cross workers), readers gain a clear sense of what the war was like for those who lived it. Their letters show readers what the war was like for "cherries" (new soldiers in country), as well as what it was like on patrols in the "hush." There are letters from wounded soldiers and those who cared for them that explore the physical, mental, and spiritual wounds of the war. Finally, readers find themselves rejoicing with those who made it home, agonizing with those who were prisoners of war in North Vietnam, and weeping for those who never made it.

In recent years more and more women are telling what the war was like for them, and Marshall's oral history is one of the best and most accessible for teenage readers. Based on Marshall's interviews with twenty women who served in Vietnam, the work delves into their motives for going to Vietnam, their experiences, and the impact that the war has had on their lives. These women include army nurses, Red Cross workers, and civilians living in Saigon. Readers are struck by the idealism that led many of these women to go to Vietnam and the dramatic impact that the war has had on them.

The War at Home

As the war in Vietnam escalated so did the fragmentation and polarization of people at home. Unfortunately, our students have very little knowledge of the events that took place at home during the Vietnam era. Adolescent fiction writers have responded to this need with some excellent offerings that examine the effects of the war on the homefront. Meg Wolitzer's novel *Caribou* (1986) takes place in 1970 and focuses on eleven-year-old Becca Silverman. The family, including her nineteen-year-old brother, Steve, gather around the television set to watch the draft lottery. When Steve's birthdate is drawn first, the family's orderly life is plunged into tension and disorder. Eventually, Steve flees to Canada to avoid the draft, and Becca's father can't forgive him. Becca also speaks out against the war as she comes to understand herself and others.

In Cynthia Rylant's *A Blue-Eyed Daisy* (1987), the war comes home to eleven-year-old Ellie Farley and her family in a very different manner: Ellie's Uncle Joe visits the family right after he comes home from Vietnam. Young Ellie is confused about wars and killing and is surprised when Joe and her family are silent about the subject. While war is only one of the themes in this novel, it does examine how the main characters must confront its meaning.

Bob Greene's oral history, *Homecoming: When the Soldiers Returned from Vietnam* (1990), is an adult book appropriate for young-adult readers. This book is a collection of letters by Vietnam veterans who wrote to author and syndicated columnist Greene in response to a question he asked his readers. Greene had heard stories about Vietnam veterans claiming that when they returned from the war, they were spat upon by people at home. He asked veterans to write him and tell him if the stories he had heard were true. He received hundreds of letters from veterans in response to his query, collecting them in a book that examines the connection between the war in Asia and the war the veterans faced on American soil when they came home.

The Refugee Experience

Since the fall of the Saigon government to the Communists in April 1975, more than one-million Vietnamese people have fled Vietnam. More than half a million of these "boat people" have immigrated to the United States. Our increasingly multicultural classrooms are filled with Southeast Asian students who are part of this still continuing refugee experience. In *A Boat to Nowhere* (1981), Maureen Crane Wartski does an admirable job of describing some of the many hardships and dangers the first "boat people" confronted escaping from Vietnam. This novel details the adventures of Thay Van Chi, his family, and an orphan boy, Kien, during their escape from Vietnam. Kien suddenly appears in a tiny fishing village. Thay protects the orphan whose parents were killed in the war. When the Vietcong arrive in the village, Kien uses his survival skills to help the family escape in a fishing boat. Once at sea, they are attacked by Thai pirates, receive a hostile reception in a coastal village in Thailand, are betrayed by other refugees at Outcast Island, and are rejected by the crew of an American tanker. Eventually, the family and Kien are rescued by an American freighter with sailors sympathetic to their plight.

Norma H. Mandel (1988) reports that when she had one of her multicultural high-school English classes read Wartski's *A Boat to Nowhere,* she was able to foster a positive exchange of cultural information and personal feelings among her students that until she taught the novel had been suppressed (40).

Jack Bennett's *The Voyage of Lucky Dragon* (1985) is similar to Wartski's novel. A Vietnamese family is sent to a Communist reeducation camp after the fall of Saigon. They endure many hardships in the camp and decide that their only hope is to escape and flee the country. Eventually, they end up on a fishing boat bound for Australia and survive many dangers before finally reaching their destination.

Jamie Gilson's *Hello, My Name Is Scrambled Eggs* (1988) examines some of the difficulties refugees experience once they reach the United States. This novel centers on Tuan Nguyen, a Vietnamese refugee who arrives in America to live with the Trumble family in a small town in the Midwest. Harvey Trumble is a seventh grader who tries to mold Tuan into an "American kid." Tuan has many difficulties adjusting, and conflicts develop between Tuan and Harvey. Ultimately, the boys become friends, and they both learn and grow as a result of their experiences.

The Next Generation

Since the mid-1980s, the nation has at last been willing to remember the experience of Vietnam. Memorials to Vietnam veterans have been built, ticker-tape parades to honor Vietnam veterans have been held throughout the country, popular films dealing with the war have been released, and popular books about the war have been published. Despite our willingness to remember the war, we have not been so willing to consider some of its many legacies. An obvious example is the fact that Vietnam veterans account for more than one-third of all homeless people in America. This is an astonishing statistic, and what is even more astonishing is that few seem willing to address this issue. However, a number of authors of young-adult literature have addressed this problem and other legacies of the Vietnam War. Mary Downing Hahn tackles the issue of homeless veterans in her novel *December Stillness* (1990). Kelly McAlister is thirteen years old and bored with the routine of school when she encounters Mr. Weems, a traumatized, homeless Vietnam War veteran. Despite warnings from her family and friends, Kelly attempts to befriend Weems. In the process of helping him, Kelly grows emotionally and acquires social awareness and responsibility.

A number of novels attempt to deal with the impact of the war on the family, particularly on the children of those who served in Vietnam. Premier among these works is Mason's *In Country*. Shortly after graduating from high school, Samantha Hughes, the protagonist of Mason's novel, at last confronts Vietnam. Her father was killed there before she was born. Sam's Uncle Emmett, with whom she lives, returned from the war, but he has never been able to hold a job, start a family, or adjust to the mainstream of American life. Sam suspects that his headaches and skin rash are symptoms of Agent Orange. She queries the adults around her for answers about the war and her father. Her quest culminates in a trip from her small town in Kentucky to the Vietnam Veterans Memorial in Washington, DC. Sam is united with her father and Emmett, and is reconciled with herself in a moving final scene at the Memorial.

While *In Country* ends at "the Wall," *Park's Quest* by Katherine Paterson (1989) begins there. The Memorial sustains Park's search to learn about his father, who was killed in Vietnam. The summer after "the Wall" is dedicated, Park travels to his grandfather's farm to learn more about his father. What he finds is a Vietnamese American girl named Thanh. She is a survivor of war and the refugee camps. She is tough and fears that Park may disrupt the family and the good life she and her mother have found in America. As the plot unfolds, Park learns that Thanh may be his half-sister, and they both discover that they have more in common than reasons to fear and distrust one another. The novel gives readers a second generation to help heal the wounds of the war.

Larry Bograd's *Travelers* (1986) is another offering that focuses on children who lost a parent in the war. In this novel, a high-school student is haunted by the image of a father he never knew. When the boy tries to find out more about him from adults, they avoid his questions. Ultimately, the teenager learns about his father, the war, and how much pain the war has caused his family and others in the community.

Candy Dawson Boyd's *Charlie Pippin* (1987) tackles some other legacies of the war. This novel focuses on eleven-year-old Charlie and her family. Her father came home from Vietnam a bitter, rigid man. Charlie tries to understand him by studying about the Vietnam War. In doing research on the war, she is shocked to learn that African Americans did more than their share of the fighting in the war. This helps her understand why her father is so bitter. She also discovers that her father is a decorated war hero. Charlie comes to understand her father and the war. In the end, "the Wall" is a symbol of understanding and reconciliation.

Kathryn Jensen's *Pocket Change* (1990) focuses on the devastating effects of Post-Traumatic Stress Disorder on veterans and their families. Young Josie's life begins to crumble when her father's increasingly erratic and violent behavior threatens the family. In trying to help him, Josie pieces together clues from his past and becomes convinced that his strange behavior is the result of experiences in the Vietnam War that still haunt him. When she confronts him with her suspicions, the result is a chilling climax that leads to a satisfying ending.

One book that deals directly with the many lessons of the Vietnam War is Bill McCloud's *What Should We Tell Our Children about Vietnam?* (1989). McCloud is a Vietnam veteran and a junior-high-school social-studies teacher. He wondered what to tell his students about Vietnam. He wrote to the people who directed, fought, and protested the war: soldiers, anti-war protesters, politicians, writers, and journalists. McCloud asked them what he should tell his students. The book is a collection of 128 of the letters he received, which form a remarkable and readable historical record. The book contains letters from the likes of McGeorge Bundy, Jimmy Carter, Clark Clifford, Barry Goldwater, Tom Hayden, John Hersey, Henry Kissinger, Timothy Leary, Country Joe McDonald, Dean Rusk, Oliver Stone, Kurt Vonnegut, and William Westmoreland.

Keys to Unlocking Meaning

While the Vietnam Veterans Memorial serves as a symbol of understanding and reconciliation in many novels that deal with the aftermath of the war, many works on Vietnam rely on letters as important keys to unlocking meaning. For example, in Mason's *In Country*, Sam finds and reads some letters her father has written to her mother from Vietnam before he was killed. The letters provide Sam (and the reader) with some of the first real clues to understanding in her quest to learn the truth about the war and her father. In *If I Die in a Combat Zone*, O'Brien corresponds with his friend Eric in an attempt to maintain his sanity amidst the horrors of combat. As O'Brien attempts to sort out the issues and understand the war in his letters, the reader comes to understand what the war means. Other works rely entirely on letters: *Dear America: Letters Home from Vietnam*, *Homecoming: When the Soldiers Returned from Vietnam*, and *What Should We Tell Our Children about Vietnam?* convey the meaning of the war through letters. Terry Farish suggests that the books themselves might be viewed as "letters [that] attempt to communicate and help children and teenagers understand" (1988, 53).

Adolescent literature that focuses on the Vietnam War has tremendous appeal to young people. Since 1989 a number of works dealing with the war have ranked in the top selections of Young Adults' Choices in the International Reading Association's annual national survey of middle-school, junior-high, and senior-high students (1989, 1990, and 1991). Besides the fact that young people want to learn more about the Vietnam War, one reason for this may be that one of the most compelling ways in which this literature speaks to students is through the voice of the narrator. Another reason may be that much of this literature focuses on the adolescent experience (Johannessen 1992, 7).

Take the case of the combat narrative: at first glance this type of work might appear to be far removed from the experience of most teenagers. However, as Jacqueline E. Lawson (1988) points out, most scholars now recognize that Vietnam was "our nation's first teen-age war." The average age of the American combatant in Vietnam was nineteen years as compared with twenty-six years for the soldier in World War 11 (26). As a result, many of the combat narratives of the Vietnam War, unlike those from World War I and II, focus on the adolescent experience—that of naive youths who are transformed by their experiences—viewed through the eyes of someone not much older than most high-school students. In other words, in many ways this literature seems to students to speak with the voice of someone much like themselves, exploring some of the same kinds of struggles they are facing. For example, the narrator and main character of Myers' *Fallen Angels* is seventeen-year-old Richard Perry. As with our own students, one of his concerns is to determine what it means to be a friend, to really care deeply about another human being. As Richie Perry confronts this issue, he and another soldier, Peewee, find themselves cut off from their platoon and surrounded by Vietcong. It is night. They are both terrified, and as they decide what they will do and prepare for an expected attack by the enemy, Peewee reaches out and puts his hand on Richie's wrist. Richie asks Peewee what is wrong. "'Nothing,' he whispered back. He kept his hand on my wrist. I moved my hand and took his. We held hands in the darkness" (1988, 285).

This moving scene, told from the viewpoint of seventeen-year-old Richie, represents Richie's final step in understanding what it means to be someone's friend. They are caught in the absolute worst of circumstances, and in this situation they reach out to help and comfort one another. In terms of the combat narrative, this is certainly the theme of brotherhood in war, but for our teenage students this is an important lesson in friendship—a lesson that is taught to them not by a twenty-six-year-old adult soldier landing on the beach at Normandy in World War II, but rather by another teenager who is fighting in a confusing jungle war which seems to be much like their own confusing world.

The adolescent experience, in the voice of a narrator much like our teenage students, is clear in many of the novels and nonfiction narratives that deal with the war. For example, seventeen-year-old Sam Hughes (in Mason's *In Country*) and eleven-year-old Charlie Pippin (in Boyd's *Charlie Pippin*) struggle to understand the war, their fathers, and themselves. Like other teenagers, they want and need to understand the past, their parents, and themselves.

Beyond Hollywood's Romanticized Vietnam War

Despite presidential proclamations to the contrary, the nation has not buried the ghosts of Vietnam. The legacies of the war are still with us. In fact, as Mason and other writers make clear, the legacies of the war are now being felt by the children of the Vietnam generation. Yet, our students come to us knowing little about the war, and what little they do know is full of distortions and misconceptions acquired from the media and elsewhere. In fact, W. D. Ehrhart (1988) is concerned about the possible consequences of this generation's distorted views of the Vietnam War. He argues that in the absence of teaching about Vietnam, of studying the literature of the war, students' knowledge of Vietnam, of history, and of the world they live in is largely determined by Sylvester Stallone's John Rambo and other distorted media images (26). Having our students study YA literature of the Vietnam War may help them to move beyond their romanticized views. Once students have read one or more of these works, they may have a much more sophisticated understanding of the Vietnam War and of the literature dealing with the war. War, too, will no longer be a vague abstraction, a Ramboesque, shoot-'em-up adventure, or a Harlequinesque, nurse romance, but rather a very real possibility, with consequences that they had never before imagined.

Works Cited

Bennett, Jack. 1985. *The Voyage of Lucky Dragon.* New York: Prentice-Hall.

Bograd, Larry. 1986. *Travelers.* New York: Lippincott.

Boyd, Candy Dawson. 1987. *Charlie Pippin.* New York: Puffin.

Christie, N. Bradley. 1989. "Teaching Our Longest War: Constructive Lessons from Vietnam." *English Journal* 78.4 (Apr.) : 35–38.

Edelman, Bernard, ed. 1986. *Dear America: Letters Home from Vietnam.* New York: Norton.

Ehrhart, W. D. 1988. "Why Teach Vietnam?" *Social Education* 52.1 (Jan.): 25–26.

Farish, Terry. 1988. "If You Knew Him, Please Write Me: Novels about the War in Vietnam." *School Library Journal* 35.7 (Nov.): 52–53.

Gilson, Jamie. 1988. *Hello, My Name Is Scrambled Eggs.* New York: Simon.

Greene, Bob. 1990. *Homecoming: When the Soldiers Returned from Vietnam.* New York: Ballantine.

Hahn, Mary Downing. 1990. *December Stillness.* New York: Avon.

Jensen, Kathryn. 1990. *Pocket Change.* New York: Scholastic.

Johannessen, Larry R. 1992. *Illumination Rounds: Teaching the Literature of the Vietnam War.* Urbana: NCTE.

Lawson, Jacqueline E. 1988. "'Old Kids': The Adolescent Experience in the Nonfiction Narrative of the Vietnam War." *Search and Clear: Critical Responses to Selected Literature and Films of the Vietnam War.* Ed. William J. Searle. Bowling Green, OH: Bowling Green State UP. 26–36.

Mandel, Norma H. 1988. "The Use of a Novel to Discuss Vietnamese Refugee Experiences." *English Journal* 77.5 (Sept.): 40–44.

Marshall, Kathryn. 1988. *In the Combat Zone: An Oral History of American Women in Vietnam, 1966–1975.* New York: Viking.

Mason, Bobbie Ann. 1989. *In Country.* New York: Harper.

McCloud, Bill. 1989. *What Should We Tell Our Children about Vietnam?* New York: Berkley.

Myers, Walter Dean. 1988. *Fallen Angels.* New York: Scholastic.

O'Brien, Tim. 1987. *If I Die in a Combat Zone.* New York: Dell.

Paterson, Katherine. 1989. *Park's Quest.* New York: Puffin.

Puhr, Kathleen M. 1988. "Women in Vietnam War Novels." *Search and Clear: Critical Responses to Selected Literature and Films of the Vietnam War.* Ed. William J. Searle. Bowling Green, OH: Bowling Green State UP. 172–83.

Rylant, Cynthia. 1987. *A Blue Eyed Daisy.* New York: Dell.

Wartski, Maureen Crane. 1981. *A Boat to Nowhere.* New York: NAL.

Wilcox, Fred A. 1988. "Pedagogical Implications of Teaching Literature of the Vietnam War." *Social Education* 52.1 (Jan.): 39–40.

Wolitzer, Meg. 1986. *Caribou.* New York: Bantam.

"Young Adults' Choices." 1989. *Journal of Reading* 33.3 (Nov.): 199–205.

"Young Adults' Choices." 1990. *Journal of Reading* 34.3 (Nov.): 203–09.

"Young Adults' Choices." 1991. *Journal of Reading* 35.3 (Nov.): 231–37.

2 Adding Voice and Perspective: Children's and Young Adult Literature of the Civil War

Carolyn Lott and Stephanie Wasta

When a small, multigraded, rural school wanted to examine the effects of an integrated approach on seventh and eighth grade students' understanding of voice in the Civil War, we suggested children's and young adult literature that focused on different perspectives of people involved in the war. We focused on both the processes and outcomes of our integration of two subject matters, language arts and social studies; introduction of team teaching between two professionals in the classroom; and evaluation of student outcomes as measured against the initial objectives (McMillan and Schumacher 23).

Naturally, language arts can be integrated with social studies, since language "permeates every part of people's lives and itself constitutes a major way of making meaning" (Moffett and Wagner 34). As Moffett and Wagner strongly suggest, we decided to make literature about different Civil War perspectives the focus for evoking an understanding of war, suggesting issues for students to research and evaluate, and prompting students' discussions in the literary communities they formed in their social studies classes (Standards for the English Language Arts 3).

Action in the Classroom

How can we make sure that students recognize that a civil war involves real people with honest motives? What are the worst aspects of a civil war? Can reading a piece of literature bring to life people who

---

This essay appeared in *English Journal* 88.6 (1999) on pages 56–61.

lived 150 years ago at the time of the Civil War and still teach historical facts? To address these questions, our students examined Eli Landers' letters in *Weep Not for Me, Dear Mother* by Elizabeth Roberson. Amy, Jennifer, and Jerrod found specific places on the wall map that followed Landers' movement from Lilburn, Georgia, just outside Atlanta, to the Virginia battles at Richmond, Fredricksburg, and Chancellorsville, and to his death at the battle of Gettysburg in Pennsylvania. When Christie drew a circle around the geographical area where the battles were fought, students realized that Eli fought Yankee soldiers very close to his own home. When they examined Eli's picture and a letter in his own handwriting, he actually became a nineteen-year-old person, a real live statistic from the era. They concluded that war and its repercussions might be worse when fought on home turf. They also related part of Eli's story to that of Pinkus Aylee in Polacco's *Pink and Say,* since he, too, was close enough to seek shelter at his own home for the wounded Sheldon Curtis. Students discussed how civil war affects civilians at home as well as soldiers in battles, from Mo Mo Bay's death at the hands of marauders to Eli's family scrounging for food after he joined the army. Doug, an eighth grader, later wrote, "A war isn't fought just good guys against bad guys. Both sides have plenty of reason behind them, and that is what makes them fight. Beliefs, tradition, and religions all tie in as causes. And usually there are [sic] more than one cause." That same day, Sam and Cissy, two students whose attendance in class was sporadic at best, gleaned from Eli's letters reasons why he joined the Confederate Army. Cissy pointed out that he did not own slaves himself and was not interested in protecting slavery, but that he was more concerned with "southern rights." Leanne and Nicole immediately contrasted Eli's reasons for fighting with those of Pink and Say by pointing out that the latter were fighting for personal rights and freedoms. Perspective—voice—permeated the thinking of these seventh and eighth graders about both literature and the history of the Civil War.

Students connected pieces of literature they had read, stories from fiction and nonfiction, and added to their understanding of the horrors of a civil war. By viewing the actual letter in Eli's own handwriting, they realized statistics represented "real people" in the war and revisited their own generalizations about why some southerners and northerners considered civil war an option. And they learned that looking at different perspectives on an issue can help them better understand why people assume firm stances for their beliefs.

Excitement at how students can make leaps in understanding about perspectives caused us to exclaim in our reflective journals,

"Thursday's class was the best one we have had so far at Woodman." When we saw students who had expressed no interest in studying the United States Civil War, who thought that the only reason for the war was to abolish slavery, and who seemed to have limited capacity to view history from a personal perspective get involved in and take responsibility for their own learning, it's no wonder we were excited.

Overview of the Unit

As we developed the unit, we discovered that we could integrate content and skills across English language arts and social studies relatively easily, without changing students' schedules or inconveniencing other teachers. Assignments could seamlessly flow from one class period to another. Student grades could apply to either subject area, and emphases in assignments could be determined by student need or curricular topic. This combination of classes was a natural way to show students the connections between the two subject areas, and this combination fit our *perspective* emphasis in literature and social studies.

Questions we wanted to study during the Civil War unit included the following:

1. Would students identify with the literary characters in Civil War literature enough to aid in their understanding of the Civil War itself?

2. Would reading various voices in literature enable students to "know" Civil War people?

3. Would literature aid in getting students to look at the different perspectives of the Civil War and in understanding the complexities of those perspectives, as well as help students learn basic Civil War historical facts?

4. Would students be able to connect or transfer those understandings of the United States Civil War to examples of current civil wars in the world?

As we said, a major emphasis of the Civil War unit was "voice": of the historical figures, of the various perspectives, of the literary characters, and of our own students. Literature here was defined as both fiction and nonfiction, children's as well as young adult. *Across Five Aprils* (Hunt), *A Separate Battle* (Chang), *The Boy's War* (Murphy), and *The Day Fort Sumter Was Fired On* (Haskins) were some of the titles used in the past. We wanted to broaden the genres and the voices of those books, incorporating some different assignments that would enable students to try out their voices in discussions, writings, and presentations.

We had to remain cognizant at all times of the skills and concepts students needed to have at the end of the unit. Students verified information in *Pink and Say;* they practiced and modeled taking on voices of the different perspectives in *Bull Run* (Fleischman); they extracted important information from *Lincoln: A Photobiography* (Freedman); and they kept research notes, outlined, and learned to reference resources in their expert group searches using *The Boys' War, When This Cruel War Is Over* (Damon), and *Who Was Who in the Civil War* (Bowman), as well as many other nonfiction resources. Expert groups were small groups of students who researched topics such as the home front, youth in the war, and major battles, acting as knowledge sources for the other class members. As the unit progressed, students more readily searched for the voice and the perspective in their readings and could complete their assignments more easily and with more accuracy. Their skill in asking questions improved after we worked with them to refine their expert group research questions—from more specific to broader concepts, and vice versa.

For example, the group that studied leaders of the Civil War began their investigation by focusing on general characteristics of the people under study—e.g., their "job" in the Civil War, the side they were supporting, the battles they fought. They needed prompting to explore other dimensions of these people's lives—e.g., the qualities that made them "leaders," their specific roles in the war. Another group researched Civil War battles, seeking specific information such as the number of casualties, wounded, and missing persons, but needed guidance to explore more general information about what took place at the selected battles and their significance to the outcome of the war. Throughout the process, we all learned about asking the right questions.

A Typical Class Period

On one particular expert group day, students began the period by reviewing the *Bull Run* activity they had participated in during the previous class session. We wrote on the chalkboard, "What new understandings about the Civil War did you gain from participating in the *Bull Run* presentations: (1) from "being" your person, and (2) from listening to others?" We engaged in a full group discussion to recap the experience and to review some of the *Bull Run* characters. A number of students readily chimed in about their character's viewpoint of the war. Tim felt quite comfortable describing Shem, a southern white soldier, while Lynn described Gideon, a northern black man who passed as white to join the army. Lisa spoke truthfully about Nathaniel Epp, a photographer who epitomized the capitalistic spirit and took photos to make as much money as possible. And Kathie eloquently described Carlotta, a slave woman, capturing the hardships of her life and the tough decisions she had to make to become "free."

The students then were instructed to write for ten minutes in their journals, reflecting on the new understandings that resulted from their "becoming a person from the Civil War" and listening to the other Civil War characters. They wrote diligently and were extremely focused. The majority captured not only the experiences of their characters, but also their emotions and viewpoints. Lynn wrote of Gideon Adams:

> My character helped me realize that a majority of the men went to war because they felt that it was their duty. My character went to war for this reason and for revenge as well. I learned some of the feelings of the men fighting in the war such as when the Northerners were retreating, a grave disappointment set in. They had failed and were almost ashamed. I learned from others more feelings. Some were frustrated because there was [sic] shortages of everything. Some were excited because of the chance to prove themselves, and others were sad and happy all at once because the outcome of the war determined if they were slave or free.

Alice also highlighted emotions when she wrote:

> I learned that the war was more emotional, not just people ruthlessly fighting. Dietrich Herz, my character, helped me realize that each soldier was an individual. In a lot of stories and descriptions of the Civil War, it seems as though the soldiers are just fighting tools, not real, unique people. Dietrich Herz was in love with a woman he'd never met. He thought of her as he lay dying on the battlefield. This helped me realize that the war wasn't just plain fighting and killing; it was harder than that, more complicated.

After these two students read their entries to the class, their conclusions became an effective full class discussion starter about what the *Bull Run* experience meant to them. Students mentioned that they had learned facts about the Civil War, but through the voices of the characters, they also learned about individuals' feelings. A number of students commented that the war was more real to them now. The students also described the patriotism exhibited by their characters' actions and thoughts. No matter which side they were fighting on, their "people" were fighting for their country and because of their strong beliefs.

After writing in their journals and discussing their writing, students moved to their expert groups. We gave them some suggestions about what they might want to consider: (1) to research their remaining questions (students had generated at least ten to twelve questions they wanted to research about their selected topics); (2) to research other important information that may not have been reflected in their questions; (3) to share their information with group members; and (4) to begin to categorize their information in preparation for developing outlines. We also reminded the students to cite their references, as some had failed to do this when taking notes during previous class sessions.

Most students made a smooth transition and eagerly began working in their groups. Alice, Mary Ruth, and Cissy, who researched women of the Civil War, had divided their readings, each focusing on a different famous woman. The "battles" group used the textbook to guide them in determining influential battles to research and were busily using books and CD-ROM resources to answer their questions.

However, the "famous leaders" group was having difficulties with focus. Two members, Leanne and Jennifer, had been absent during previous expert group sessions and were struggling to catch up. They were unclear about their responsibilities and what they were to research. Instead of trying to solve their problem, they decided to chat about personal matters. They needed firm but clear guidance to get back on track. Another group member, Sam, was frustrated because he could not find the answers to his questions, some of which were opinion and not fact (e.g., Who was the most famous general?). He needed guidance in changing some of his questions, deleting from his list those that were inappropriate.

Sam was not alone; a number of students needed help in reevaluating their questions. Both of us moved from group to group, assisting the students as best we could. Just at the time we thought they were making progress, the period ended. There was no time for closure and no time to assess each group's progress.

So went the typical class: There were moments when the students were deeply engaged in learning and other times when they seemed scattered and unclear about what they were doing.

The Role of Journals

An important aspect of the project was the reflective journals that each of us kept about the actual teaching process. Reflections on student growth, successes in the classroom, problems in presentation and reception, and comments on what we would do differently next time were incorporated in our teacher journals. We shared these journals daily via e-mail to help "keep us on the same page."

We were not the only ones to learn from and engage in journal writing; our students also kept journals. In a preunit writing assignment to assess their understanding of the Civil War and its "voice," we asked students to become a thirteen- or fourteen-year-old in 1861, from any state of their choice. They wrote on what that teenager knew and thought of the Civil War, any facts they could add about the war, and any preknowledge they might have of the era. In addition to these writings, students also selected entries for their journals from assignments given throughout the semester on their readings and activities. One of the first prompts was to choose either Pink or Say (*Pink and Say*) just at the moment the two boys were separated for the last time and write the thoughts that might have gone through the minds of either. All but three students chose Pink, since he was courageous and willing to fight for his beliefs, even though his actions put him in grave danger. A postunit writing assignment for their journals again asked students to become teenagers in 1865 and write their reflections on the Civil War. "Voices" became more obvious and distinct, and students demonstrated more understanding of the Civil War perspectives than they did in the preunit writing assignment. Jennifer wrote:

> The war is over. Land is ruined, people are dead, and people are free. Was it worth it? As I ask myself I wonder. Was it worth losing thousands of men for free black slaves and state's rights? Maybe yes, maybe no. But I believe if it didn't happen now it would have happened later. So, now after four years, it's over. The killing's stopped, the nation's one again and our hearts and souls are at rest.
>
> I walked through town seeing happy faces, hearing laughter and delight, but feel sadness and sorrow because now I have no one in the world to share rejoicing of the end of the war. My only brother, my only family member, is now dead.

Student Reflections

In post unit interviews, we asked students which assignments they liked best and from which they learned the most. Generally, they liked the shorter assignments best: the "bio minutes" of famous personages in the Civil War time period, the voice in the diary *Weep Not for Me, Dear Mother,* and the sharing of characters' stories from *Bull Run.* The activities they learned the most from, however, were the expert groups and the reading of *With Every Drop of Blood* (J. and C. Collier). Students became familiar with the different perspectives of the Civil War: black and white in *Pink and Say,* north and south in *With Every Drop of Blood,* civilians and soldiers in *Bull Run,* young and old in *The Boy's War.* They also learned about the importance of primary sources in *Lincoln: A Photobiography* and *Weep Not for Me, Dear Mother* and in the reproductions of the newspapers from the Civil War era. In addition, students also viewed Hunt's *Across Five Aprils* on videotape to compare voices and perspectives from the two sides of the war. To learn the importance of details in settings and to give them an artistic outlet for their presentations, we had students create a mural that covered the room, representing the major events in *With Every Drop of Blood.* The variety of activities helped to maintain a high level of enthusiasm for the study of the Civil War and provided a diverse array of assessment focuses as well.

In those same interviews, students also told us they liked working in groups, interchanging group members (the only consistent group assignments were for the expert groups), varying assignments with each literature selection, and choosing their own expert group topics as well as questions to research in these groups. They also liked the *Bull Run* assignment, where we assigned characters for them to read about and later "become." They assumed the identity of the character, brought an object to represent that character, and then shared their stories in small groups. At first, the assignment presented difficulties with reading the stories in the voice of the era, but once over that hurdle, they buzzed with excitement. Later in the unit students researched and presented a first person account of someone from the Civil War. Because they had the skills of assuming voice, knowing how to extract information and synthesize it, and understanding the Civil War background to help with connections, these biographical minutes were completed in two days and became one of their favorite assignments.

Teacher Reflections

Looking back over our daily journal entries, we can now see patterns in student learning, kinds of assignments that needed refining, and ways we could better become facilitators for learning. Students responded more to lessons that covered two or three days of class. The expert group projects, which involved research, notes, and cooperative groups for most of the unit, needed to be shortened. Most every week expert groups worked together at least one time, but much of that time was spent catching up and redefining what they wanted to research. The end product of the expert groups was to create an engaging, creative presentation that incorporated the new information the students had gathered. These expert group presentations should have received more emphasis during the research process. Instead, the students did not consider how to present their findings until almost the very end of the term, when the projects were due. Because students were scrambling, shuffling, and sifting information at the last minute, their oral presentations did not reflect as much new information as we anticipated. Students enjoyed their presentations, but when class members were asked to write three new things they learned about the youth, women, or leaders in the war, the facts were not significant. We learned that we should have either condensed the time frame for the expert groups to explore their resources, or we should have helped more with the student-generated research questions to facilitate the new learning. In addition, we should have continuously helped students focus on how they could incorporate their findings into their oral presentations.

Other changes in our teaching pertained more directly to the content of our instruction. We constantly needed to make clear connections between the various pieces of literature that we read and how each character or "voice" added to the students' background knowledge of the Civil War. We continuously explained and used diagrams to show how each of the assignments fit together and how each provided skills and knowledge to use for future activities. In addition, we altered assignments to include different types of reflections and writing styles from taking on first person, third person, or comparisons between two individuals of the Civil War. Finally, we discovered that having students examine the same literature, primary sources, or other documents several times, but with a different focus for each lesson, was a valuable experience welcomed by the students. In the case of our newspaper activity, students had perused replicas of Civil War newspapers over a period of several days, primarily during their free time. We were wary of involving the students in a structured newspaper lesson, believing they would be bored and uninterested in examining the newspapers again. However, the students responded enthusiastically to a guided examination of articles, illustrations, and ads of that time period. They even requested more time to continue their exploration of the newspapers, perhaps because they had new skills with which to examine them. Middle schoolers, like all other students, benefit from opportunities to explore a piece of literature or a primary source in various ways.

Conclusion

So what did the voices and perspectives from children's and young adult literature add to students' understanding of the Civil War? They discovered that the power of literature could add a new dimension to such an event. They still learned the facts about the War, but facts became attached to deeper understanding and connections to people. They went home and talked about Johnny, and Cush, and the hardships of women and children in the war. With literature in their Civil War unit, they learned to "touch the hand that touched the hand . . ." (Polacco 26).

Works Cited

Bowman, John. *Who Was Who in the Civil War.* New York: Crescent Books, 1994.

Chang, Ina. *A Separate Battle: Women and the Civil War.* New York: Puffin Books, 1991.

Collier, James, and Christopher Collier. *With Every Drop of Blood.* New York: Delacorte Press, 1992.

Damon, Duane. *When This Cruel War Is Over: The Civil War Home Front.* Minneapolis: Lerner Publications Co., 1996.

Fleischman, Paul. *Bull Run.* Illustrated by David Frampton. New York: HarperCollins Children's Books, 1993.

Freedman, Russell. *Lincoln: A Photobiography.* New York: Clarion Books, 1987.

Haskins, Jim. *The Day Fort Sumter Was Fired On: A Photo History of the Civil War.* New York: Scholastic, 1995.

Hunt, Irene. *Across Five Aprils.* New York: Follett, 1964.

McMillan, James H., and Sally Schumacher. *Research in Education: A Conceptual Introduction.* New York: Longman, 1997.

Moffett, James, and Betty Jane Wagner. *Student Centered Language Arts, K–12.* Portsmouth, NH: Boynton/Cook Publishers, 1992.

Murphy, Jim. *The Boys' War: Confederate and Union Soldiers Talk about the Civil War.* New York: Clarion Books, 1990.

National Council for the Social Studies. *Expectations of Excellence: Curriculum Standards for Social Studies.* Washington, D.C.: NCSS, 1994.

National Council of Teachers of English and International Reading Association. *Standards for the English Language Arts.* Urbana, IL: NCTE, IRA, 1996.

Polacco, Patricia. *Pink and Say.* New York: Philomel Books, 1994.

Roberson, Elizabeth Wheatley. *Weep Not for Me, Dear Mother.* Gretna, LA: Pelican Publishing Co., Inc., 1996.

3 World War II: A Research/Presentation Project for Eighth Graders

Joan Ruddiman

World War II was a major event in the history of the world and the defining benchmark for the twentieth century. While in all wars lives are affected and boundaries are changed, it is difficult to think of any aspect of our twentieth-century world that has not been transformed by this event. The beginnings of the blending of multicultural, interracial families began with GIs returning with war brides from far-flung countries. The Civil Rights movement was spurred by the inanity of black GIs being segregated in all but the fighting and dying. The seeds of the women's movement were sown as women wore pants and worked in all manner of "men's" jobs. Communication, like filmmaking and Nazi Joseph Goebbel's development of propaganda techniques, defined "mass media." Radar, sonar, and air warfare changed how war is waged. The creation and use of the atomic bomb created a new type of war—the Cold War.

With the advent of the 50th anniversaries of many World War II and Holocaust events, the retrospective analysis of these years reveals how much our children today are products of those events. Yet, most history curricula do not touch on World War II in the elementary grades. In our district, students will not be introduced to World War II until high school. Middle school students, though, have a fascination and intense interest in what this war was about, particularly the Holocaust.

The Setting

I am in a seventh- and eighth-grade middle school in a multicultural suburban area. Last year we had 52 different languages and dialects represented in our school's population. Our eighth-grade social studies and

This essay appeared in *English Journal* 86.5 (1997) on pages 63–71.

reading curricula focus on global issues. Units are divided by countries or areas of the world, such as Russia, the Middle East, Japan, China, Latin America. Our students become aware of how the world is connected and how history is not static. Thus, the World War II unit is done in conjunction with the social studies unit on Russia. We find, however, that references to World War II are made throughout the remainder of the year in order to understand situations in other countries.

I first used World War II as a unit with my reading classes five years ago. I was teaching eighth grade, using Nancie Atwell's Reading Workshop approach (1987, *In the Middle,* Portsmouth, NH: Heinemann). In keeping with my goal to have a variety of titles for students to choose from, I took novels from the established curriculum on Russia, Japan, and a "dystopia" unit to create a World War II reading unit. I used Anne Frank's *Diary of a Young Girl, The Endless Steppe, The Upstairs Room,* and *Farewell to Manzanar,* of which we had multiple copies. With the support of our media specialist, I pulled another twenty titles from the media center and have since added to this unit a wealth of titles and materials.

Making the Subject Manageable

World War II is an immense topic of which my students know very little. Therefore, I set the stage with a one-class period overview. We get the key players—Allies and Axis—and who was who. ("What do you mean, Russia was our ally?" students asked incredulously.) We look at the world map and get some idea of places and dates. I answer questions students have as they begin to put the facts together.

The students then are assigned to find out if someone in their family had been part of the World War II era, in what way, and whether they would be willing and able to answer some questions. In each class, at least one third of the students (six or more) have someone to interview. We then analyze what stories we have available to us; e.g., a nurse on Iwo Jima, an infantryman at Normandy, a factory worker in a munitions plant, a survivor of Auschwitz. We call these people our primary sources and form groups around that student who has access to a source.

Because of the global nature of World War II, all students can find connections in their personal histories. My students from lands such as India, Taiwan, Sweden, Korea share their families' experiences from a point of view that American history courses can't offer.

Each class has four to six different teaching groups. The focus of their lesson is taken from the aspect of the World War II era which their primary source (the interviewee) shares with one member of their group. Because of the diversity of my classes, each teaching group has a very different focus. For example, in one class we learned about the Russian front and the Siege of Leningrad from Kate's Russian family, the blitz on London from Felicity's British grandmother, the life of a German infantryman in France from Chris' grandfather, and the building of the Burma Road from Vehlakki's family.

In the latter case, Vehlakki came to me the day the project was announced and said, "My family is from India, and I don't think the war was in our country. I don't think anyone in my family will have a story to tell about World War II." My reply was that this was a "world" war, so something must have been happening in India. In any case, I told him to ask family members what happened to them during the late 1930s and 1940s. As it turned out, Vehlakki was surprised—and the class and I were enthralled—by his group's account of the Burmese Road and the significance it played in the war.

The goal of this project is not to cover every front or even each theater of the war. Indeed, one year I had no one who covered the Pacific Theater. What is important is that students get a personal account of one area of this watershed moment in the world's history.

Group Responsibilities

Each group is responsible for teaching the class about their specific area or event of the war. The level of research and supplemental information students find greatly enhance what usually are sketchy bits of information initially gathered in the interview. For example, Paul's grandfather was an airman. Paul had the flight jacket and dress uniform his grandfather wore, but very limited stories. When Paul and his group began to research air warfare, they learned how critical this branch of the military was during World War II, and after.

The group is required to provide geographic references (maps), research (done in the media center) to augment the information provided by the primary source, and analysis of the significance of their topic or specific event then and now. Being able to see ramifications beyond just the moment itself demands higher critical thinking. Julie and her group were able to understand the importance of establishing the state of Israel after they researched and presented a Polish family's experiences during the Holocaust.

Everyone in the group is expected to do research and to contribute to the teaching presentation. How and what they contribute is a reflection of what they feel is their particular strength. For example, those with a musical strength gravitate to the songs and dances of the era. According to the rubric, these areas are welcomed additions to the presentation.

Evaluation of Group Presentations

After the groups are formed I go over the rubric for this "Learning/ Teaching Project" (see boxed figure) and allow each group to choose the level of performance they wish to pursue.

Students are asked for self and group evaluations after the research work, the presentation planning sessions, and, finally, after their lesson is presented to the class. Each student in the class also evaluates each lesson, as based on the rubric, for organization of content, what they learned, and how engaging/interesting the lesson was for them.

This is a critical piece in the evaluation because the objective is to teach the class—not me, the teacher. When students of the lesson can respond with specific facts they learned, and, most importantly, what they are considering for the first time, I know the lesson has been suc-

---

World War II Learning/Teaching Project
RUBRIC
OBJECTIVE: To teach the class about one specific aspect of World War II through use of primary sources (interviews), geographic references (maps), research and analysis of significance then and now.

Evaluated by Teacher:
LESSON: A : all *   items covered
                     B : all **   items covered
                     C : all ***   items covered

Evaluated by Class and Teacher:
PRESENTATION is organized, understandable, engages the interest of the class.

Evaluated by Group Members and Teacher:
PREPARATION time used effectively
Group cooperates
All group members contribute

Responsible for in the Lesson
***   Define topic/subject area
***   Map/geographic reference is given
***   Terms and specialized vocabulary defined
**   How this event was significant to the war or during that era
*   Relate how these events impact on the world today

FOR AN A DO 2 OF THE FOLLOWING 4:

FOR A B DO 1 OF THE FOLLOWING 4:
Relate topic to novels or books read
Relate to videos/film (film clips of 1 to 5 minutes can be used) Relate to music/songs/dances/foods/clothing
Media: newsreels/films/radio/newspapers/magazines
Use artifacts: photos/diaries/letters/clothing, etc.

cessful. Through evaluation sheets I provide for class assessment, I know the teaching team has been effective in meeting the objective to teach the class.

It is a valuable lesson for students to experience what teaching is. Some groups have wonderfully creative ideas HOW to teach, but little substance in WHAT they are teaching. Sam, Susan, and Joy, for example, developed a board game that allowed students to move around color-coded desks. Their classmates, however, quickly tired of the game when the questions were superficial and repetitive. More time on the "what" they were teaching would have saved their lesson.

I use the rubric as a checklist and to register my comments as I watch each lesson. Later, the students' evaluations are reviewed and relevant comments noted on the form. After all the lessons have been presented, I conference with each group using the form I've compiled on their group. The three areas, Lesson, Presentation, and Preparation, are evaluated with a compilation for the final grade.

Each student gets a group grade and an individual grade that is based on the self-evaluations and group evaluations. Students are very honest with these evaluations. Students may choose not to contribute to the group, but they then accept their low grade as the consequence of that choice.

The Steps Leading to the Lesson

This past year the unit began right before the week-long December break. Everyone had chosen a World War II novel from our eighth-grade novels as well as an extensive collection from our school's media center (see Appendix 1). I also suggested that when they finished reading, and if they needed something to do, they might enjoy renting a video or two related to World War II. I provided an annotated list for suggested viewing and briefly reviewed—"film talked"—the titles (see Appendix 2).

By now parents and grandparents had been involved with the initial search for a person in the family to interview. With the novels and video suggestions going home, my students came back with tales of enthused fathers, grandmoms, and older siblings who were "into" World War II history. This genuine interest at home is a key reason this unit is so valuable to the students. Students feel connected to a world outside of their own adolescence; they begin the transcendence into adulthood.

After students have collected their interview information, they are ready to fill in the gaps with research. We spend three days in the media center with books and microfiche and computer sources like

Groliers. They use maps, biographies on key generals and leaders, dates, and details of events.

One source that proved to be invaluable was *National Geographic* from the World War II era. Students poured over photos and articles written from the perspective of that time. This is where Paul and his group gleaned most of their information about the early Air Force. Even the advertisements in these old magazines reflect the atmosphere of a nation, and world, at war. This wasn't textbook history; this was primary material.

Another source that was helpful to the students' research was my vertical files on World War II and the Holocaust. The media has been filled with retrospectives in the past several years due to the 50th milestone. Students also accessed stories on D-Day, Hiroshima, etc. through newspaper microfiche or film and, more easily, the Internet.

The class had the remainder of the week to organize materials and begin making their lesson plans for their presentations. At the beginning of this assignment, I ask them what is their least favorite way to be taught. Unanimously, lecture and note taking wins this dubious honor. Therefore, I suggest they NOT use lecture when they teach the class.

The rubric also gives them ideas on how they can stimulate interest with the use of video clips, music, dance, clothing, and diaries, as well as excerpts from the novels they've read. The only limitation was that they use no more than one class period (40 minutes).

The Results

The resulting presentations were remarkable: unique in style, rich in information, and delivered with obvious group effort and pride.

The group that gathered information on Russia from research sources, and from Kate, who came to the U.S. from the USSR, created a "Jeopardy"-style game called "Russia-dy." The key events and facts were taught through classmates' interaction with elaborate "Jeopardy"-styled categories on the board. For example, for $100 the answer was, "It was Russia's secret weapon." The question was, "What role did winter weather play in Russia's defeat of the advancing German army?" The group then explained through photos and anecdotes how the German army was ill-prepared to cope with the intensity of Russia's winter snows and bitter cold. The class was fascinated.

The group for the Battle of Britain, based on Felicity's grandmother's stories of being in the London Blitz as a child, used outstanding video clips from the PBS series "World at War." Students who had read Robert Westall's novels such as *The Machine Gunners* offered anecdotes about the Blitz and asked questions to clarify historical points.

To share what life was like in Germany throughout the war, Chris enacted the role of a teenaged German writing in his personal diary. His diary entries changed from initial excitement and patriotic fervor to despair and disillusionment. Interspersed with Chris' narrative were relevant details about the war in Germany given by the other members of the group, including maps and explanations of terminology.

One group used the talents of a group member to compile a series of clips from the film *A League of Their Own.* Adam is a spatially talented young man who watches a lot of television and movies and who works easily with video equipment. He is not strong verbally, strongly resists writing, and does not like to present, though he does enjoy attention as the class clown. The group developed a skit where Chantelle comes to visit "Gramps" (Adam), who acts deaf and a bit senile; "Grandmom" does all the talking for him as she shares with her "granddaughter" what life was like on the homefront. After sharing some artifacts and anecdotes, "Grandmom" turns on the tape (Adam's editing handiwork), which shows the anxiety suffered by those who were waiting at home.

Everything the actors had conveyed in their skit was summed up by the clip where the women in the locker room wait to see which of them will receive the dreaded telegraph from the War Department. It was a poignant moment in class for all of us. I not only was impressed with this informative, dramatic lesson, I marveled how this group worked together, particularly in finding and using Adam's strengths so effectively.

Julie had read Maxine Rosenberg's *Hiding to Survive: Stories of Jewish Children Rescued from the Holocaust.* She had heard firsthand accounts from Holocaust survivors in her Hebrew classes. This group wove these stories into a character Julie portrayed in an effective skit. This was followed by a brief explanation of Nazi policies and tactics used against the Jews throughout the 1930s into the 1940s. They concluded with two clips from *Schindler's List,* one where Schindler is challenged by his Jewish bookkeeper to take a stand, and then, from the end of the film, where Schindler is bid farewell by his grateful people and sobs because he did not save more of them.

Going beyond the Subject

There is a concern today about incorporating values education in the classroom. I see evidence that this unit on World War II helps my students delve into important issues. Asking students to critically think about the consequences of war and to relate those events to today encourages awareness of human behaviors, both heroic and evil.

Before the presentations began, I wondered if these students could, or would, deal with how these events during World War II affect the world today. Only two out of the twenty groups did not address this question. Their insights on how events over 50 years ago affect our world today showed strong critical thinking ability. For example, the group that presented on the air war tied in the strategies used in the recent Gulf War conflict using technology first developed in World War II. Kate and her group reflected on how the USSR could have so callously invaded and taken over countries like Czechoslovakia when they had fought so hard to resist a German invasion.

The students' comments on the self-evaluation forms confirmed what I had seen demonstrated in class. This unit expanded their knowledge of a particular era and of their world today. They connected with family members in a new and very positive way. They took responsibility to learn information in order to teach it to others.

Students learned the facts and what is beyond the facts. Carina's observations filled a page: "I learned that the Burma Road was used to get needed supplies to soldiers, and that elephants were used to build it. . . . soldiers gave their medicine for small pox to children . . . in the Homefront lesson I learned about victory gardens and 'victory speed' for cars (35 miles per hour)." She concluded, "I learned about Hitler and Schindler, and more about Roosevelt, and this is just one hundredth of what I've learned."

Conclusion

The unit on World War II was rewarding for students and for me as the teacher. We all were aware that this unit had made a difference in our lives. Students went from knowing little to nothing to being well versed in several areas and quite expert in one. They were able to relate history to their families and to their world today. Most continued to read from the World War II list of novels, as well as nonfiction, after the project was over. Many commented in their reading journals that they read more than in prior units, and without prompting. "This was the best unit, so far, in Reading" was a typical refrain.

The research component, coupled with a teaching presentation, integrated important skills. Assessment of the projects was not difficult and allowed for students' self-reflection.

For the teacher, this is a most satisfying unit. The subject is of high interest to middle level students. Because we are not held accountable for "teaching World War II," students could be offered ownership of what aspect of the war they learn and choose to teach to the class. No class learned everything; none even touched on all theaters of the war. But the topics that were researched and presented were initiated by contacts with real people who had been part of these historic events, and thus had a relevance that is usually difficult to establish.

My eighth graders reached out to an older generation to learn how life more than a half century ago shaped their world today. In the process, they explored ideas that ultimately can make them better people.

Note

The author gratefully acknowledges the support of media specialist Suzanne Manczuk in the compilation and annotation of the book list.

Appendix 1: Book Suggestions for World War II

Note: The following are listed alphabetically by author. Titles can be regrouped by theme, such as children of war, post-war effects, the Holocaust, or regrouped by a particular venue, such as Japan's war, the resistance movement in Denmark, etc. All the titles are suitable for middle school (fifth grade through ninth grade). Age appropriateness is noted where necessary. Nonfiction and/or memoir are specifically noted.

Aaseng, Nathan. 1992. *Navaho Code Talkers*. New York: Walker and Company. Nonfiction. Little known story of the Navaho marines who helped win the battles in the Pacific Theater by using an unbreakable code—their own Navaho language.

Aline, Countess of Romanones. 1987. *The Spy Wore Red: My Adventures as an Undercover Agent in World War II*. New York: Random House. Autobiography. American woman married to European royalty assumes espionage role for the Allies.

Armor, John and Peter Wright. 1988. *Manzanar*. New York: Times Books. Photographs by Ansel Adams. Commentary by John Hersey. Nonfiction. Authors found and fully documented the photographs which Adams had given the Library of Congress in the 1960s. Many had never been published. Some were only recently declassified. A worthwhile companion piece to the Jeanne Houston *Farewell to Manzanar* memoir.

Attema, Martha. 1995. *A Time to Choose.* New York: Orca Book Publishers. A boy must choose between his Nazi-sympathizer father and the resistance movement.

Ayer, Eleanor H., Helen Waterford, and Alfons Heck. 1995. *Parallel Journeys.* New York: Simon and Schuster. Nonfiction. A Jewish woman and German man—Holocaust survivor and former Hitler youth—share memories of their experiences in Nazi Germany.

Bachrach, Susan. 1994. *Tell Them We Remember.* Boston: Little, Brown. Nonfiction. A publication of the U.S. Holocaust Memorial Museum. Photographs and documents of children who did not survive the Holocaust.

Bawden, Nina. 1989 [1973]. *Carrie's War.* New York: Yearling Press, Dell. Twelve-year-old British girl and her brother are evacuated from war-torn London to Wales.

Besson, Jean-Louis. Trans. by Carol Volk. 1995. *October 45: Childhood Memories of the War.* New York: Harcourt Brace. Memoir. Seven-year-old Jean-Louis and his family are not Jewish nor are they Communists, yet the war finds them anyway. Unfiltered view of France's war as a child experienced it. Illustrated by the author.

Bitton-Jackson, Livia. 1997. *I Have Lived a Thousand Lives.* New York: Simon and Schuster. Memoir. 1944–45. A Hungarian Jewish teen lives through Auschwitz, labor camps, the "liberation" train at the end of the war. Well-told story of survival and the power of love.

Boas, Jacob. 1995. *We Are Witnesses: The Diaries of Five Teenagers Who Died in the Holocaust.* New York: Henry Holt. Nonfiction. Evocative written legacies.

Carter, Peter. 1994. *The Hunted.* New York: Farrar Straus Giroux. The war is over for Italy in 1943. An Italian corporal finds himself responsible for the welfare of a small Jewish boy who is being hunted by the Gestapo.

Choi, Sook Nyul. 1991. *Year of Impossible Goodbyes.* New York: Dell. North Korean family suffers Japanese occupation during the war and longs for peace only to find themselves under Russian communist rule after the peace accords.

Colman, Penny. 1995. *Rosie the Riveter: Women Working on the Homefront in World War II.* New York: Crown. Nonfiction. Eclectic mix of what happened at home.

Cormier, Robert. 1992. *Tunes for Bears to Dance To.* New York: Delacorte. A boy struggles with the moral decision whether or not to destroy a Holocaust survivor's recreation of his Holocaust village.

Dillon, Ellis. 1992. *Children of Bach.* New York: Charles Scribner's Sons. Budapest is not safe for young Jews, even if they are musical prodigies.

Drucker, Olga L. 1995. *Kindertransport.* New York: Henry Holt. Nonfiction. Memoir of a girl sent from Germany to England in 1939 and the reunion of these children 50 years later.

Dwork, Deborah. 1991. *Children with a Star.* New Haven, CT: Yale University Press. Nonfiction. Based on hundreds of oral histories of survivors who were children in the Holocaust. Wide range of primary documentation and photographs. For older readers and for use in research.

Fluek, Toby. 1990. *Memories of My Life in a Polish Village.* New York: Random House. Memoir in words and pictures. Original miniatures, from watercolors to charcoal, done by the author as a young woman during the Holocaust.

Frank, Anne. 1994 [1947]. *Diary of a Young Girl.* New York: Pocket Books. *The Definitive Edition* (1995, New York: Doubleday) includes 30% more material expurgated from the original by Anne's father.

Friedman, Carl. 1994. *Nightfather.* New York: Persea Books. Postwar trauma. Children come to know about the war through their father's nightmares.

Friedman, Ina R. 1990. *Other Victims: First-Person Stories of Non-Jews Persecuted by the Nazis.* New York: Houghton Mifflin. Nonfiction. Includes stories of homosexuals, mentally defectives, and gypsies who were targeted by the Nazis.

Gee, Maurice. 1993. *The Champion.* New York: Simon and Schuster. Wounded American GIs are invited into homes to convalesce. The guest is black, and racial tensions, tragedy ensue.

Green, Bette. 1986. *Summer of My German Soldier.* Toronto: Bantam Books. Twelve-year-old Patty Berger opens her heart to a German prisoner-of-war who escapes the camp outside her small Arkansas town. Patty is Jewish, which further complicates a dangerous situation.

Greenfeld, Howard. 1994. *The Hidden Children.* New York: Ticknor and Fields. Nonfiction. The children who survive by changing identities or being closeted away and their survivor guilt.

Hahn, Mary D. 1991. *Stepping on the Cracks.* New York: Houghton Mifflin. The war at home. Trouble with a bully and a crazy man in the woods who is a deserter.

Hamanaka, Sheila. 1990. *The Journey: Japanese Americans, Racism, and Renewal.* New York: Orchard Books. Nonfiction. The story of a mural that depicts the Japanese experiences as immigrants to internees.

Hamanaka, Sheila, ed. 1995. *On the Wings of Peace: Writers and Illustrators Speak Out for Peace, in Memory of Hiroshima and Nagasaki.* New York: Orchard Books. Nonfiction and Fiction.

Poems, stories, essays, art works in memory of the atomic bombing victims of 1945.

Hautzig, Esther. 1974. *The Endless Steppe.* New York: Scholastic. Author's own story told from the point of view of a teenager of her family's exile to Siberia.

Hersey, John. 1944. *A Bell for Adano.* New York: Knopf. Pulitzer Prize-winning account of the impact of American soldiers occupying an Italian village.

————. 1985 [1946]. *Hiroshima.* Toronto: Bantam Books. Nonfiction account of the atomic bombing of the Japanese city.

Higa, Tomiko. 1991. *The Girl with the White Flag: An Inspiring Tale of Love and Courage in War Time.* New York: Kodansha America. Nonfiction. Memoir. The author's story of her surrender on Okinawa in 1945 and the reunion 40 years later with the American soldier who took her picture.

Holm, Anne. 1987 [1963]. *North to Freedom.* San Diego: Harcourt, Brace, Jovanovich. David has spent most of his life in an Eastern European prison camp. Given the chance to escape, this twelve-year-old has to make it to Denmark.

Houston, Jeanne Watasuki with James D. Houston. 1983. *Farewell to Manzanar.* New York: Bantam. Nonfiction memoir of Japanese internment camp with glimpses of life before and the consequences after.

Howard, Ellen. 1996. *A Different Kind of Courage.* New York: Atheneum. Paris in June of 1940. Based on the exploits of American Martha Sharp who organized a plan to save French children from German occupation and bring them to the United States.

Ippisch, Hanneke. 1996. *Sky: A True Story of Resistance During World War II.* New York: Simon and Schuster. Nonfiction. Memoir. The author's story of how she became a courier for the Danish underground.

Kerr, M. E. 1978. *Gentlehands.* New York: Harper Row. A rebellious teen seeks out his grandfather, long ostracized by the family. Moral conflict ensues when the boy learns his grandfather was a Nazi.

Krull, Kathleen. 1995. *V is for Victory: America Remembers World War II.* New York: Random House. Nonfiction. Colorful pages full of archival photos, postcards, posters, letters. Lots of primary sources with captions that capture the mood of the times.

Laird, Christa. 1990. *Shadow of the Wall.* New York: Greenwillow. In the Warsaw ghetto of 1942, Misha and his two younger sisters live in the Orphan's Home and struggle to survive. Based on the heroic efforts of Dr. Janusz Korczak to save Jewish children.

_____. 1995. *But Can the Phoenix Sing?* New York: Greenwillow. Told in letters and flashbacks, a modern day teen's alienation from his stepfather is juxtaposed with the older man's accounts of his life as a freedom fighter in Poland during the war.

Levine, Ellen. 1995. *A Fence Away from Freedom: Japanese Americans and World War II.* New York: Putnam. Memoir. Comprehensive history of internment camps told in voices of those who were young.

Levoy, Myron. 1977. *Alan and Naomi.* New York: Harper and Row. Post-war consequences. Jewish New Yorker Alan attempts to befriend war-traumatized Naomi who has arrived from France.

Lindwer, Willy. 1992. *The Last Seven Months of Anne Frank.* New York: Doubleday. Nonfiction. The testaments of six women who knew Anne in the concentration camps.

Lingard, Joan. 1990. *Tug of War.* New York: Puffin Books. Latvia, 1944. Teenage twins are separated while escaping the advancing Russian army.

_____. 1991. *Between Two Worlds.* New York: Puffin Books. Sequel to *Tug of War:* the war and its aftermath from the perspectives of the twins who have had very different experiences.

Lowry, Lois. 1989. *Number the Stars.* New York: Dell. Newbery Award winner. Based on the events of how the Danes saved 3,000 Jews from occupying Nazi forces.

Matas, Carol. 1989. *Lisa's War.* New York: Charles Scribner's Sons. Copenhagen in 1940. Twelve-year-old Lisa is caught up in the Danish resistance movement.

_____. 1990. *Kris's War.* (formerly, *Code Name Kris*) New York: Scholastic. Sequel to *Lisa's War.* Lisa's love, a non-Jewish resistance fighter named Jesper (code name Kris) continues to battle Nazi occupation of Denmark.

_____. 1993. *Daniel's Story.* New York: Scholastic. Based on a display at the U.S. Holocaust Memorial Museum. Depicts how the lives of Daniel and his Jewish family are changed forever.

_____. 1995. *After the War: The Story Behind Exodus.* New York: Simon and Schuster. Polish Jewish girl finds her way home after surviving the concentration camp only to discover there is no place for her there. She joins an underground group that takes survivor children to Palestine. (Over 67,000 Jewish children were smuggled into Palestine after the war.)

McKissack, Patricia and Frederick McKissack. 1995. *Red-Tail Angels: The Story of the Tuskegee Airmen of World War II.* New York: Walker and Company. Nonfiction. Story of African American pilots flying in World War II.

Morpurgo, Michael. 1991. *Waiting for Anya*. New York: Viking. French Gentile boy heroically battles Germans in defense of Jews.

Nolan, Han. 1994. *If I Should Die Before I Wake*. New York: Harcourt Brace. Present day skin-head is cared for in a Jewish hospital after a motorcycle accident. Flashbacks to the war through hallucinations. Note: strong language; for mature teens.

Orgel, Doris. 1988. *The Devil in Vienna*. New York: Puffin. Child's point of view of impact of war on school culture; textbooks rewritten, Jewish friends disappear.

Orlev, Uri. Trans. by Hillel Halkin (from Hebrew). 1984. *Island on Bird Street*. Boston: Houghton Mifflin. Boy left behind in Warsaw Ghetto. Survival story of a child alone.

_____. Trans. by Hillel Halkin (from Hebrew). 1991. *The Man from the Other Side*. Boston: Houghton Mifflin. Boy's stepfather smuggles for the Jews in the Warsaw Ghetto. Boy's anti-semitism is tested when he discovers the identity of his real father.

_____. Translated from the Hebrew by Hillel Halkin. 1995. *The Lady with the Hat*. Boston: Houghton Mifflin. Two years after the concentration camp, Yulek returns to Poland to honor his father's dying wishes. But his world there is no more, and he turns to Palestine for a new home and identity.

Pearson, Kit. 1995. *The Sky Is Falling*. New York: Puffin Books. British children are sent to Canada to avoid the war.

Perl, Lila and Marian Blumenthal-Lazan. 1996. *Four Perfect Pebbles: A Holocaust Story*. New York: Greenwillow. Nonfiction, some memoir. Blumenthal family's experiences in Bergen-Belsen and more.

Poynter, Margaret. 1990. *A Time Too Swift*. New York: Atheneum. The attack on Pearl Harbor changes fifteen-year-old Marjorie's world forever.

Ray, Karen. 1994. *To Cross a Line*. New York: Puffin. Seventeen-year-old Egon can't get a driver's license because he is a Jew. This becomes the least of his worries when he must flee his home in Germany to escape a Nazi round-up.

Raymond, Patrick. 1990. *Daniel and Esther*. New York: Macmillan. Daniel, a gifted but troubled musician, falls in love with Esther, whose Viennese parents are fighting fascism in Austria. World War II brings fear and uncertainty into already troubled adolescent lives.

Reiss, Johanna. 1984. *The Upstairs Room*. Toronto: Bantam. Memoir. Author's story from a child's point of view of hidden children in Holland.

Reuter, Bjarne. 1994. *The Boys from St. Petri.* New York: Puffin. Sons of the minister commit acts of resistance against Nazis in Denmark.

Rochman, Hazel and Darlene Z. McCampbell. 1995. *Bearing Witness: Stories of the Holocaust.* New York: Orchard. Compilation of stories and excerpts of poems that convey the emotions of those in the Holocaust.

Rosenberg, Maxine. 1994. *Hiding to Survive: Stories of Jewish Children Rescued from the Holocaust.* New York: Clarion. Nonfiction. Memoirs of fourteen survivors. Belgium is the most frequent setting. Complements *Hidden Children.*

Salisbury, Graham. 1994. *Under the Blood Red Sun.* New York: Delacorte. Pearl Harbor through the eyes of a Japanese American boy as he and his family experience the backlash from their neighbors after Japan's surprise attack.

Serraillier, Ian. 1974. *Escape from Warsaw.* New York: Scholastic. (Originally published in 1959 as *The Silver Sword.*) Gentile family torn apart when schoolteacher father disrespects Nazi regime. Children left alone must make their way to the safety of grandparents in Switzerland. Based on true accounts, written for upper-elementary aged children.

Schloss, Eva, with Evelyn Julia Kent. 1992. *Eva's Story.* Middlesex, Great Britain: Castle Kent. Memoir. Eva Geiringer, a friend of Anne Frank, survives Auschwitz and, in a twist of fate, becomes, with her mother, Otto Frank's new family.

Spiegelman, Art. 1991 [1973]. *Maus I: My Father Bleeds History.* New York: Pantheon. Cartoon format of author/cartoonist Spiegelman's father's Holocaust experiences.

_____. 1991 [1986]. *Maus II: Here My Troubles Began.* New York: Pantheon. Volume two of the profound telling of one survivor's story. *Maus I* and *II* are available on CD-ROM from the Voyager Company.

Stanley, Jerry. 1995. *I Am an American: A True Story of Japanese Internment.* New York: Random House. Nonfiction. For younger readers. Period photos and narratives.

Stevenson, William. 1982 [1976]. *Man Called Intrepid, the Secret War.* New York: Ballantine. Nonfiction account of the British Intelligence and the importance of creating and breaking codes.

Taylor, Theodore. 1995. *The Bomb.* New York: Harcourt Brace. Fourteen-year-old boy on Bikini Island is glad to see the end of Japanese occupation, but what the U.S. government has planned for his homeland is devastation beyond imagination.

Toll, Nelly. 1993. *Behind the Secret Window: A Memoir of a Hidden Childhood.* New York: Dial. Memoir. Poland in 1943. Author, eight years old at the time, and her mother are hidden away. Illustrated with childhood drawings by the author.

VanKirk, Eileen. 1990. *A Promise to Keep.* New York: Lodestar. Teenage girl sent to the country to escape the London Blitz. Love for an Austrian refugee and the plight of a downed German pilot create moral dilemmas.

Van Der Rol, Ruud and Rian Verhoeven. 1993. *Anne Frank: Beyond the Diary.* New York: Viking. Nonfiction. A photo-biography of Anne and her family before the war years.

Volavkova, Hana, ed. 1993. *I Never Saw Another Butterfly: Children's Drawings and Poems from Terezin Concentration Camp 1942–1944, Second edition.* New York: Pantheon. Nonfiction. A reissue, expanded version of primary materials.

Vos, Ida. 1995. *Dancing on the Bridge of Avignon.* New York: Houghton Mifflin. A Jewish family in Holland in 1942 live under the everyday horrors of Nazi occupation.

Watkins, Yoko Kawashimi. 1986. *So Far from the Bamboo Grove.* New York: Puffin. Memoir. Japanese family of a military officer in Korea during the occupation must flee to Japan when Korean forces regain control.

_____. 1994. *My Brother, My Sister, and I.* New York: Simon and Schuster. Sequel to *So Far from the Bamboo Grove.* Mother has died. The three children must overcome discrimination as refugees and terrible poverty.

Wiesel, Elie. 1989 [1960]. *Night.* New York: Bantam. Memoir. Wiesel, a Nobel Prize winner in 1986, tells of the horrors of a Nazi death camp as seen by a young Jewish boy.

Westall, Robert. 1976. *The Machine Gunners.* New York: Greenwillow. The Blitz of England in 1941. Young boys find remains of a Nazi plane with a machine gun which they move to their hide-out. Pretend war becomes real. Winner of the 1976 Carnegie Medal.

_____. 1989. *Blitzcat.* New York: Scholastic. England during the Blitz. A variety of stories woven together by the experiences of a lost cat as she tries to find her home. Authentic war details.

_____. 1990. *Fathom Five.* New York: Knopf. Spy stories from Britain from 1939–1945.

_____. 1991. *Echoes of War.* New York: Farrar Straus Giroux. Five short stories of post-war effects on Britain. The impact of war on those too young to fight.

Yep, Laurence. 1995. *Hiroshima.* New York: Scholastic. Parallel narratives; one by the men on the *Enola Gay,* the second by two children in the city before the bombing.

Yolen, Jane. 1988. *The Devil's Arithmetic.* New York: Viking. Modern day Jewish girl who is unresponsive to her culture and religion finds herself back in time in the midst of Holocaust horror.

Appendix 2: Video Suggestions for Teaching World War II

Note: Most vintage films pre-date a rating system. Due to the censorship guidelines followed in the 1940–1950 era, it may be assumed that these films would be *PG* by today's standards. For further and more complete listings, consult any film guidebook, such as *Video Hound's Golden Movie Retriever,* Gale Research Inc., Detroit, which is updated each year.

Anne Frank Remembered

Directed by Jon Blair, won the Academy Award for Best Documentary Feature, 1995.

Anzio (aka *The Battle for Anzio*)

Historic Allied invasion of Italy. 1968, 117 minutes, VHS.

Au Revoir Les Enfants

Louis Malle's memory of an incident from his childhood in Nazi-occupied France. The headmaster of a Catholic board school hides Jewish boys by giving them false names and backgrounds. 1988, PG, 104 minutes, VHS.

Battle Cry

Based on the novel by Leon Uris. U.S. Marines enter the war. 1955, 169 minutes, VHS.

Battle of Britain

Heroic Lawrence Olivier and those indomitable Brits during the Blitz. 1969, G, 132 minutes, VHS.

The Best Years of Our Lives

A big Academy Award winner. The story of a group of men after they return from World War II and the difficulties they have re-entering civilian life. 1946, 170 minutes, VHS.

Bridge on the River Kwai

Pacific Theater, Japanese prisoner of war camp. Based on an actual event. Unforgettable story. 1957, 161 minutes, VHS.

A Bridge Too Far

Recreation of one of the most disastrous battles of World War II, the Allied defeat at Arnhem. All-star cast. 1977, PG, 175 minutes, VHS.

Casablanca

Humphrey Bogart and Ingrid Bergman. The war in Africa and the resistance movement. Another classic. 1942, 102 minutes, VHS.

Das Boot (The Boat)

An excellent film from the German point of view. Set in a German U-boat. 1981, R, 150 minutes, VHS.

The Dirty Dozen

If you enjoyed *The Great Escape* don't miss this one! 1967, PG, 149 minutes, VHS.

The Enemy Below

Suspenseful sea epic. U.S. destroyer and German U-boat in the South Atlantic. 1957, 98 minutes, VHS.

Empire of the Sun

Steven Spielberg directed, Tom Stoppard wrote the screenplay from the J. G. Ballard novel. Japan's invasion of China at the beginning of World War II as seen by a young British boy who is caught in the fray. 1987, PG, 153 minutes, VHS.

Exodus

The establishment of Israel after the war. Based on the novel by Leon Uris. 1960, 208 minutes, VHS.

From Here to Eternity

Another classic, a real tear-jerker. Pacific Theater, events of war, and the consequences of war. 1953, 118 minutes, VHS.

The Great Escape

Steve McQueen and company. Absolutely a dynamite story! Allied soldiers in a German prisoner of war camp plot their escape. A classic. 1963, 170 minutes, VHS.

Guns of Navarone

British intelligence in the Middle East. Based on the Alistair MacLean novel. A great cast. 1961, 159 minutes, VHS.

Hell is for Heroes

Steve McQueen leads a strong cast in this riveting drama and action film. 1962, 90 minutes, VHS.

Hellcats of the Navy

The mission to sever the link between mainland Asia and Japan. (Ronald and Nancy Reagan's only film together.) 1957, 82 minutes, VHS.

The Hiding Place

Based on a true story of righteous Gentiles who saved Jews in Holland and were sent to a concentration camp themselves. 1975, 145 minutes, VHS.

Hope and Glory

Set in England during the Blitz. Told from a boy's point of view (that of director John Boorman) who thinks the war is thrilling. 1987, PG-13, 97 minutes, VHS.

Inside the Third Reich

A behind-the-scenes view of Hitler and his operation. Originally done as a TV mini-series. 1982, 250 minutes, VHS.

Judgment at Nuremberg

A classic film that does not flinch from examining the issue of individual accountability when acting under orders. Spencer Tracy as the chief justice presiding over the 1948 Nazi war crimes trial. 1961, 178 minutes, VHS.

A League of Their Own

Women invited to play professional baseball to fill the void left by the men who went to war. Good fiction that deals with a little known aspect of sport's history. 1992, PG, 128 minutes, VHS.

The Longest Day

The D-Day story, accurate and epic. 1962, 179 minutes, VHS.

Memphis Belle

A remake by Catherine Wyler of her father's war-era film. 1990, PG-13, 107 minutes, VHS.

Memphis Belle: A Story of a Flying Fortress

The experiences of this famous plane and crew. Produced by William Wyler. 1944, 43 minutes, VHS.

Mrs. Miniver

Lots of Oscars including Best Actress for Greer Garson as the gentle, courageous mother of a middle-class British family which is struggling to survive the war. Recognized for contributing to the Allied effort. 1942, 143 minutes, VHS.

Objective Burma

A great World War II-era production. 1945, 142 minutes, VHS.

One Survivor Remembers

Directed by Kary Antholis. Won the Academy Award for Best Documentary Short Subject, 1995.

Patton

George C. Scott in a powerful performance as the brilliant and controversial general in the European Theater. 1970, PG, 171 minutes.

PT109

Cliff Robertson as JFK. The story of Kennedy's heroics as a young commander of a PT boat. 1963, 159 minutes, VHS.

Schindler's List

Steven Spielberg's award winning film based on the facts surrounding a non-Jew, Oskar Schindler, who uses his influence with the Germans to save Jews from death. It is an excellent film, but very tough emotionally. 1993, R, 195 minutes, VHS.

Swing Kids

Not a great movie, but it does show Nazi persecution of anything not deemed acceptable to Hitler's ideal society. In this case, German teens are harassed when they openly embrace American swing music which is strongly influenced by black musicians. 1993, PG-13, 112 minutes, VHS.

To Hell and Back

From Audie Murphy's autobiography; Murphy plays himself as the most decorated U.S. soldier. 1955, 1016 minutes, VHS.

A Town Like Alice

Pacific Theater, forced marches, abuses of civilians, and, in Australia, what happens to these people after the war. Made by PBS. Based on the novel by Nevil Shute. Originally done as a PBS mini-series. 1985, 301 minutes, VHS.

Where Eagles Dare

Clint Eastwood in an action-packed suspense thriller. 1968, PG, 158 minutes, VHS.

Why We Fight

Frank Capra's response to Germany's propaganda films. Capra turns the propaganda back on the source by using actual German and Japanese film footage to reveal the intentions of those totalitarian regimes. Nominated for Academy Awards. 1942 (a series of six, about one hour each), VHS.

Winds of War

An epic (that means VERY long) that follows the lives of one family and how the war involves and affects them. Pearl Harbor, Europe, the Holocaust are incorporated. Originally done as a TV mini-series. 1983, 900 minutes, VHS.

4 New Wars, Old Battles: Contemporary Combat Fiction for the High School Canon

Randal W. Withers

Students need to read accessible, worthwhile, relevant, controversial, and contemporary literature.

Elfie Israel

My title is an homage to a recent *English Journal* issue devoted entirely to the teaching of classic literature (March 1998). I could not agree more with the focus. Challenging students with great literature should be the cornerstone of English studies, whether in middle school or at the graduate level. Classics, after all, have influenced an untold number of writers, who, in turn, have influenced our students, our children, and us.

My argument, however, pertains to one specific arena of literature—the antiwar novel, or "combat narrative," as it is often called today. Does the high school canon typically include a representative sample of the best writing from every war that this nation has faced? Arthur Applebee's *Literature in the Secondary School: Studies of Curriculum and Instruction in the United States* suggests that the answer is no. While novels such as *The Red Badge of Courage*, *A Farewell to Arms*, and *All Quiet on the Western Front* have been staples of the curriculum for years, literature of more recent wars has not. I do not argue that educators should discard the literature of "older" wars as if it is no longer relevant to contemporary society. Rather, I believe that teaching fiction that focuses on more recent wars will enable students to better understand the impact of war on a variety of social issues—from American history, to United States foreign policy, to their own way of life. If we ignore contemporary antiwar literature and its applications in today's classroom simply because such works have not yet been labeled "classic," then we run the

---

This essay appeared in *English Journal* 88.6 (1999) on pages 62–69.

risk of allowing students to graduate into adulthood without having heeded important lessons from the not-so-distant past, of which they are, at least partially, ignorant.

Investigating Alternatives

The fact that a novel has been taught for decades does not guarantee that students will appreciate its value. Conversely, simply because a novel has never been taught before does not mean it won't be popular among students, nor does a contemporary status imply that it lacks literary merit. The three novels I propose as alternatives to the established antiwar canon are all critically acclaimed, though they are rarely, if ever, taught at the secondary level: Kurt Vonnegut's *Mother Night,* Tim O'Brien's *Going after Cacciato,* and Don Delillo's *End Zone.* Two of these three authors have won the National Book Award, and Graham Greene has called the third author, Kurt Vonnegut, "the greatest living American writer."[1] Their novels are as diverse as the individual wars they depict. Their literary styles are various, ranging from dark satire to magic surrealism and allegory. Yet, despite their differences, all three embody a unifying thematic thrust: the changing attitude of writers toward war since the end of World War I, an attitude which has steadily shifted from reverence to contempt.

For centuries, works such as *The Iliad, Macbeth, Julius Caesar,* and *Paradise Lost* have served up romanticized views of combat, and their notoriety has no doubt colored society's perception of war. In the twentieth century, John Wayne movies taught entire generations that battle is slick, exciting, and full of glory. Perhaps this is why *Mother Night, Going after Cacciato,* and *End Zone* have never been accepted into mainstream society. War is not pretty. Sherman went so far as to call it "hell," and these novels have the guts to examine war's often abstract and always horrifying realities.

Contemporary Censorship Issues

Though no foolproof way of teaching a censored text exists at the secondary level, one way to limit trouble is by knowing the appropriate grade level at which to teach it. "The literature of war is appropriate for twelfth grade students," says John Simmons. In his book, *Teaching Literature in Middle and Secondary Grades,* he writes:

> High school seniors face the direct or indirect effect of war and/or the possibility of war as part of their entrance into adult life . . . Furthermore, the cry in the decade of the 1980s for

improved cultural literacy among the nation's youth had made knowledge of America's engagement in major armed conflicts, both from an historical and a literary perspective, a need of growing importance. (231)

The three novels I have chosen address these needs. They also acquaint younger readers with the various issues each war has raised in America's conscience, issues that continue to form our cultural identity and influence foreign relations.

Despite the value of these contemporary antiwar novels, I must offer one caveat: The issues, language, and themes in these works may prove catastrophic for an uninformed teacher. They are unflinching critiques of relatively recent conflicts, and it stands to reason that some students have relatives who fought and/or died in these wars. They challenge American history, values, and ideals with refreshing frankness and wit, and such bold characteristics make easy fodder for the censorship crowd. In the following sections I offer a synopsis of the novels, followed by an exploration of their various themes, inherent obstacles (e.g., profanity, anti-American sentiment, drugs), and most importantly, their applications in the classroom.

World War II and The Evil American: Teaching *Mother Night* by Kurt Vonnegut

> This is the only story of mine whose moral I know. I don't think it's a marvelous moral; I simply happen to know what it is: We are what we pretend to be, so we must be careful about what we pretend to be.
>
> *Mother Night*, Introduction

I hesitated to include a novel about World War II, given that my focus concerns the literature of more "recent" wars. However, it seems to me foolish to discuss the literature of war in the twentieth century and ignore a conflict that saw entire countries decimated, more than six million Jews murdered, the use of atomic weapons, and the birth of "total warfare," in which civilian targets were considered fair game. Furthermore, some rather extensive spin doctoring by Hollywood has given the American people a false impression of the war that killed fifty-five million people—more than half of them civilians. "Adolescents today have only a fuzzy view of World War II," wrote Kathleen Dale Colarusso, in *The ALAN Review.* "They see it as ancient history or an event glorified and romanticized in old John Wayne movies. They do not understand what Nazi Germany was like or why the war was fought" (12).

The same might be said of many educators today, given that the war concluded some fifty-four years ago. Even so, much of the world is still feeling the sting of that global conflict; consider the constant distress in Israel over Palestine, the rise of neo-Nazi groups in Germany, and our own country's wartime internment of Japanese Americans, an act for which President Clinton only recently apologized.

Just as there is no shortage of novels that deal with the war, there is also no shortage of issues that Americans have had to deal with since the deployment of two atomic bombs, Fat Man and Little Boy, over Hiroshima and Nagasaki in August of 1945. While the atomic strikes on Japan are widely discussed across America, the destruction of Dresden, Germany, is often quietly overlooked, even though the attack by Allied bombers on this peaceful city killed more than the Nagasaki and Hiroshima bombs combined. It was this event that prompted Kurt Vonnegut to write the semiautobiographical *Slaughterhouse Five,* an account of his year as a prisoner of war in Dresden and how he survived the attack.

The Dresden bombing is an excellent way to introduce Vonnegut; after all, one could argue that Vonnegut might never have started writing had the city survived the war. "At Dresden," wrote scholar Jerome Klinkowitz, "Vonnegut looked into the abyss, and his sense of shock from that terrifying view has imprinted itself on his writer's personality ever since" (46).

The Dresden bombing, like the use of Fat Man and Little Boy, or the internment of Japanese American citizens, is an embarrassing example of the atrocities committed by the United States government, atrocities frequently overlooked in textbooks. Fortunately, they have not escaped the watchful eye of Kurt Vonnegut. Even though *Slaughterhouse Five* is one of the most banned books in American high schools, teachers can still examine Vonnegut's antiwar writing by teaching his third novel, the relatively obscure *Mother Night.* Often funny and deeply disturbing, it is a satire of nationalism, Nazism, and the evil American who, according to Vonnegut's story, was responsible for the Holocaust.

Briefly, the story is presented as the confessions of Howard W. Campbell Jr., an American-born German playwright who served in the Ministry of Propaganda in Nazi Germany. As the story opens, it is 1961. Campbell has been captured by the Israelis and is writing his memoirs at the behest of the Haifa Institute for the Documentation of War Criminals in Jerusalem. Unbeknownst to the world, Campbell was actually an Allied spy. During his anti-Semitic radio hour, he would broadcast coded messages to the Allies through precise coughs, vocal mannerisms, and inflections in his voice. Unfortunately, he was so good that not only was he never caught, but he was so believable that the entire world considered him a horrible Nazi.

Vonnegut raises a number of complex moral issues in *Mother Night.* Aside from his introduction, in which he warns us to be careful about what we pretend to be, he also lampoons all types of fanatics, from the absurd neo-Nazi characters who worship Campbell in New York, to the zealot Bernard B. O'Hare, a World War II veteran with a personal score to settle. Ultimately, *Mother Night*'s largest target is blind obedience, which Vonnegut sees as a tool of Fascism. "Say what you will about the sweet miracle of unquestioning faith," Howard Campbell writes in his cell. "I consider a capacity for it terrifying and absolutely vile" (120).

Mother Night, like *Going After Cacciato* and *End Zone,* deals with war indirectly, in that the bulk of the story takes place fifteen years after the Germans surrendered. The novel is more concerned with the consequences of faith, the pitfalls of nationalism, and the simple, pervasive tragedy of war. Howard Campbell is a voice through which Vonnegut speaks volumes about the nature of man. His wartime radio show, which we learn from Campbell propelled average German citizens to keep fighting long after they should have surrendered, warns of the power of media, of the hypnotic effect of the spoken word, and of the irony of man's faith. That Germany rallied behind the deceptive words of an American agent is only part of Vonnegut's trademark ironic condemnation. He also suggests that America share some measure of complicity in the death of six million Jews, since it was our agent who inspired such ferocious fanaticism in our enemy. Yet with all this criticism leveled against Campbell, Vonnegut does not allow his readers to hate him. He portrays his hero as a pawn of both countries, a writer of medieval plays whose only true loyalty is to his wife, whom he loses during the war. Fifteen years after his repatriation to New York, Campbell is again used as a pawn, this time by a group of aging neo-Nazis, who want to empower their cause with an infamous personality. Russian agents also want Campbell as a spoil of war. And if that isn't bad enough, the Israelis are after him, too.

Clearly, *Mother Night* stands in stark contrast to the traditional portrayal of America's involvement in World War II, glamorized frequently in popular movies and television shows, which have been a staple of the American film diet since the mid 1940s. Simmons suggests in a personal interview that students today are familiar with only a "romanticized" view of World War II, and for this reason alone, *Mother Night* serves as an excellent way to introduce and examine some uncomfortable realities about that war. In an interdisciplinary approach, an English teacher might coordinate the reading of *Mother Night* with a history teacher's Holocaust unit. Together, both teachers might discuss whether or not blame should be issued solely to the citizens of Germany, or if the potential for genocide resides within all countries. Since *Mother Night* is based in part on actual spies, most notably Mata Hari, a female spy to whom the novel is dedicated, classroom discussion could also center on the pros and cons of such covert activity. A question such as, Were the Allies justified in using Campbell as a spy if it meant the lives of six million Jews, but a victory over Nazi Germany? could prove stimulating and engaging for students whose knowledge of the war is limited to stories their grandfathers have told. Moreover, an English teacher might want to examine the works of purported Nazi sympathizers, most notably the American poet Ezra Pound, who broadcast Fascist propaganda from Rome throughout the war.

In 1996, Fine Line Features released the film version of *Mother Night,* starring Nick Nolte, John Goodman, and Alan Arkin. Screenwriter Robert Weide, a longtime Vonnegut enthusiast, collaborated with the author in order to keep the script as close as possible to the original text. Perhaps the best reason to supplement the teaching of Vonnegut's novel with the film is to show students the visual similarities between Nick Nolte, who plays Campbell, and Kurt Vonnegut. Jerome Klinkowitz, in his insightful article, "*Mother Night* as Film," writes of the widely-held belief that Campbell is Vonnegut's literary doppelganger, and it is fascinating to watch Campbell go from a powerful Nazi to a decrepit old man, weak and beaten by life.[2] This point is reinforced at the film's close, when Vonnegut makes a cameo appearance on a crowded sidewalk and looks into the eyes of a destitute Howard Campbell, who then takes his own life minutes later as a final apology to a world he helped destroy.

As fascinating as *Mother Night* is to read, teachers should be aware that some of the questions raised in the novel might not sit well with some parents. Though it is virtually devoid of profanity and sexual content (despite Campbell's recollection of intimate moments with his wife), *Mother Night* is a challenge to the widely held belief that America was the white knight of World War II. However, besides being an important story and a vintage piece of writing by Vonnegut, the addition of the 1996 film makes it an extremely teachable story, which touches on a variety of hot topics today, including the influence of the media on society and the need to question authority.

Teaching *Mother Night* can also allow the introduction of the Internet to aid homework assignments. Fine Line Features, the company that produced the movie, offers an interactive "study guide" that prompts students to think about a variety of *Mother Night*'s themes. Questions range from multiple choice surveys to more involved short answer responses that ask students to think beyond the text and apply Vonnegut's message to current world issues, from the unrest in Bosnia to the terrorist acts in Northern Ireland. The site is currently located at http://www.flf.com/mnight/guide.htm.

Vietnam Conflicts: Tim O'Brien's *Going after Cacciato*

> It was a bad time.
>
> *Going after Cacciato*

In a paper presented to the Annual Joint Meetings of the Popular Culture Association, author/educator H. Bruce Franklin reminded teachers that we "tend to forget that the [Vietnam] antiwar movement began as an attempt to *educate* the government and the nation" (1). He argues that Vietnam has particular relevance in today's classroom, given that students have grown up in an environment "in which the Vietnam War has been redefined, rewritten, and most importantly, reimaged" (2). Citing revisionist movies such as Gene Hackman's *Uncommon Valor,* Chuck Norris's *Missing in Action,* and Sylvester Stallone's *Rambo: First Blood, Part II,* Franklin argues that educators must offer students a more accurate picture of what actually happened in Vietnam. He specifically zooms in on the "celluloid POW myth," which portrays the Vietnamese as "unfathomably cruel Communists, who for no rational reason have been torturing our heroic POWs for decades" (4). In more recent years, Franklin argues, the enemy has simply been erased from vision, as in the Academy Award winning *Forrest Gump,* which portrays "Vietnam as merely a shadowy jungle that shoots at American soldiers" (4).

"Ironically, most of our students know more about the Civil War than they do about the war that was the defining experience for their parents' generation," says Larry Johannessen, an accomplished teacher of the Vietnam War (11). He has created a way to help solve this problem by using revisionist history to his advantage in the classroom. In a workshop presented at NCTE in 1995, he suggested that the discrepancy between the myths and realities of the Vietnam War can prove extremely engaging in the classroom. The literature of the period and the topic captivate both students and teacher, enhancing the learning process.

One author who has gained considerable notoriety in his attempt to destroy these illusions is Tim O'Brien, perhaps the most highly acclaimed writer about the Vietnam War. O'Brien's works are particularly useful in high school because of his brilliant ability to blend the reality of war with his own imagination and perceptions. Robert Wilson, in *The Washington Post,* wrote that "Tim O'Brien knows the soldier as well as anybody, and is able to make us know him in the unique way that the best fiction can" (E4). Though Johannessen suggests using O'Brien's first novel, *If I Die in a Combat Zone,* a terrific alternative would be his 1979 National Book Award winner, *Going After Cacciato.* It is the story of Paul Berlin, a thoughtful, intelligent soldier whose platoon is ordered to apprehend a deserter named Cacciato (Italian for "the pursued"), who has decided to walk to Paris. Eventually Berlin and the platoon capture Cacciato at the Laotian border, but Berlin seems unable to let go of the incident, returning to it again and again in his dreams. These dreams become the meat of the story, as Berlin fantasizes about the possibilities of actually walking to Paris with the rest of his war-weary platoon.

Just as Gabriel García Márquez used magical realism to transform the fantastic into the ordinary in *One Hundred Years of Solitude,* so, too, does Tim O'Brien in *Going After Cacciato.* The narrative consists of a series of chapters called "The Observation Post," where Paul Berlin spends his nights recounting war stories and imagining a mystical journey from Vietnam to France. Numerous flashback chapters detail the horrors Berlin's platoon have faced during his tour of duty, and through these flashbacks we gain insight into the surviving members and their relationships to each other, the war, and themselves. Finally, O'Brien interweaves the fantastic journey to France in a series of chapters called "The Road to Paris." As all three components merge into one seamless narrative, the reader is given the complex task of determining what is fantasy and what is real.

Dreams are important to Tim O'Brien. In *If I Die in a Combat Zone,* he asks this question:

> Do dreams offer lessons? Do nightmares have themes, do we awaken, and analyze them and live our lives and advise others as a result? Can the foot soldier teach anything important about war, merely from having been there? I think not. He can tell war stories. (31–32)

Going After Cacciato may well be a novel-length answer. Just as Larry Johannessen uses the misconceptions about the Vietnam War to teach the reality, Tim O'Brien uses Paul Berlin's dreams to question the concept of courage and the reality of the war. As Maria Bonn notes in *Critique:*

> Paul Berlin's purpose in creating his elaborate journey . . . to Paris is a way of mentally escaping the facts of war that he cannot confront, [but] the journey is also a way of arriving back at the war . . . this time with a greater degree of moral comprehension and a clear definition of courage. (9)

Going After Cacciato requires students to embrace the fantastic. It also requires exploring the tenuous division between reality and fiction. In the same way Johannessen uses the POW myth as a springboard for discussing the reality of Vietnam, the metafiction in *Going After Cacciato* can also inspire interest from students on everything from the topography of Vietnam to the moral dilemma a deserting soldier like Cacciato must face. Because the impossible trip to Paris requires travel through a diverse array of countries, including Laos, Iraq, Greece, and Italy, an interdisciplinary approach might include a geography lesson that highlights the extreme difficulty of such a trip, not to mention the multitude of customs, languages, and climates students would need to know in order to survive. Furthermore, the arduous task of fleeing Vietnam for Paris invites the reader to question both Paul Berlin's motivation and the concept of courage.

In contrast to the traditional ideals of a novel like *The Red Badge of Courage,* O'Brien's characters are portrayed as cowards for *not* running away. In *The Things They Carried,* he wrote, "I was a coward. I went to war" (63), and this mentality pervades both *If I Die in a Combat Zone* and *Going After Cacciato.* The questions he raises about the nature of courage are perfect for exploratory essays, in which students can express their own thoughts on the subject and how they might react in a similar situation.

Going After Cacciato is a biting protest against a war that continues to shape our society. Having students study it will go far toward helping them reevaluate their current notions of courage and patriotism and will allow them to gain a better understanding of the scope of the Vietnam War and its continuing implications. However, teachers should be aware that even though *Going After Cacciato* deals with the fantastic, O'Brien's use of profanity and his descriptions of death and destruction are very real. As the novel warns us at the beginning, "It was a bad time." Tim O'Brien never allows us to forget that.

A Metaphor for Nuclear War: *End Zone* by Don Delillo

> I'm afraid of my own country. I'm afraid of the United States of America. It's ridiculous, isn't it? But look. Take the Pentagon. If anybody kills us on a grand scale, it'll be the Pentagon.
>
> *End Zone*

Bronx-born Don Delillo is known primarily for his postmodern brand of fiction, but with the recent publication of *Underworld*, he has become a considerable literary voice of the Cold War. His first best-seller was a 1988 Cold War era tale called *Libra*, a fictitious account of the life and times of Lee Harvey Oswald; the novel garnered much critical and popular attention for discounting the theory of the lone gunman. Winner of the International Fiction Prize from the *Irish Times*, *Libra* afforded Delillo previously unknown commercial success. His 1985 novel, *White Noise*, succeeded in winning the National Book Award and is excerpted in the newly published *Postmodern American Fiction: A Norton Anthology*.

Generally speaking, Delillo exists in relative obscurity, in part because he prefers it that way, but also because, as one reviewer noted, his novels "deal with deeply shocking things about America that people would rather not face" (Harris 26). The *South Atlantic Quarterly*, which dedicated an entire issue to the writings and study of Don Delillo in 1990, featured an article by Daniel Aaron, in which he praised Delillo "for his intelligence and wit, his range of reference, vocabulary, energy, and inventiveness, and . . . for the varieties of styles in which he couches his portentous bulletins to the world" (319). I have included Delillo's second novel, *End Zone*, for precisely those reasons.

End Zone is a far cry from the magical surrealism of *Going after Cacciato* and farther still from the satire of *Mother Night*. But then its subject, the Cold War, was a different type of war from Vietnam, and a much different war from World War II. Though it is clear that all three wars have a distinct relationship to one another, the Cold War remains an enigma to today's students, even though its most prominent symbol, the threat of nuclear annihilation, has hung over our nation for forty years. Rather than attempt the arduous task of dissecting the war or its politics, Delillo chose to take an archetypal fear of the Cold War, thermonuclear holocaust, and plug it into an arena of interest that captivates our nation.

In *End Zone*, football really *is* a metaphor for nuclear war. Delillo's protagonist, a running back for Logos College named Gary Harkness, spends his off-hours fantasizing about nuclear annihilation, playing war games with his teammates, and researching the vocabulary of mass destruction- "Blast area. Fire area. Body-burn area" (90)— terms he ponders after an extracurricular interview with an ROTC officer, who enlightens him about nuclear stockpiles, kill ratios, cellular turnover, plutonium 239, and the like. For Gary, the ordered chaos of war is fascinating; he is a running back because football is as close as he can get to war in times of peace. And as his obsession with Cold War tactics and nuclear armament grows, the line between metaphor and reality begins to thin; Gary's teammates suffer grievous injuries on the battlefield; Emmett Creed, the head coach, begins to sound like a military general, and fellow players begin to think of football on a global scale, as the following dialogue between Gary and a teammate illustrates:

> "This whole game could be played via satellite. They could shoot signals right down here. We'd be equipped with electronic listening devices. Transistor things sealed into our headgear. We'd receive data from the satellites and run our plays accordingly."
> "Who sends the data?" I said.
> "The satellites."
> "Who feeds the satellites?"
> "A computer provides the necessary input. There'd be a computerized data bank of offensive plays, of defensive formations, of frequencies. There'd be an offensive satellite and a defensive satellite." (133)

Even Delillo's prose seems affected by Gary's obsession. As the novel progresses and Gary's fascination with nuclear war grows, the story begins to sound less like a football story and more like a combat narrative. "The special teams collided," he writes at the start of Part II, "swarm and thud of interchangeable bodies, small wars commencing here and there, exaltation and first blood, a helmet bouncing brightly on the splendid grass, the breathless impact of two destructive masses, quite pretty to watch" (111). By the novel's close, the aesthetic pleasure of athletic competition is all but replaced by overtones of battle and annihilation, which Gary seems to welcome more than a winning season. Whether or not Delillo is suggesting that man seems to create opportunity for war is an excellent area of discussion in the classroom.

At least two other aspects of *End Zone* would prove quite useful in the high school classroom. The first is Delillo's attention to terminology. As with most postmodern writers, Delillo grasps the tremendous impact that language can have. At one point in the novel, Gary Harkness discusses how abstract terms make killing seem impersonal. Words like *post-attack environment, circular error probability,* and *overkill* are all supposed to mean something awful, he knows, but the vulgarity of their true meanings seems lost in euphemism. A related lesson plan might have students exploring the various euphemisms of war and how they are used to lessen the horror. For example, we can have students cluster the various names soldiers have given to enemies over the years like Krauts, Charlie, and Russkies, to name a few, then have them discuss the reasons a solider might not want to think of the enemy as a person.

The second reason why *End Zone* would be useful in the classroom actually has little to do with war. "Most lives are guided by clichés," (69) Gary tells his audience, and the irony is that Delillo seems to go out of his way to steer his writing away from this idea. The most interesting example is that the football players are all well-read, articulate, and eager to use their brains. A particularly funny scene has two teammates pondering who was the greater man—Sir Francis Drake or the prophet Isaiah. "How can you compare them?" one teammate asks. "They were in two different fields" (75). *End Zone* is replete with such refreshing depictions, which stand in such sharp contrast to the depiction of athletes in the media of recent years. A lesson set for *End Zone* might require students to compare and contrast their ideal athlete with the fictional players of Logos College.

End Zone might also be especially useful for male students who are reluctant readers, given that its content is largely sports related and supplemented by engaging war jargon. Of the three novels I have presented, it is probably the easiest to read and understand, and it reads more like a young adult novel than a convoluted literary text. However, its realistic football dialogue (read: profanity), sports-related violence, and sporadic attention to recreational drugs may warrant a letter home to parents before you attempt to add it to your curriculum.

Conclusion

Recently, The Learning Channel presented an eight volume series called *War and Civilization,* an episodic look at the innate relationship between armed conflict and humanity, ranging from the first organized battles in Greece to the threat of nuclear annihilation today. Watching it with the eye of an educator, I was struck by the symbiotic nature of the subject matter—the documentary would have us believe, correctly so, that our very world could not exist without the wars that have shaped it.

Largely missing from the program, though, was the impact of literature on war. One might argue that so much has been written on World War II and Vietnam that the conscience of the world may never allow these wars to happen again. As Colarusso says, "By reading about others who have dealt with constant fear and anxiety during war, adolescents today can obtain some insights into their own feelings and options for coping with and attempting to prevent situations of conflict" (12). By using *Mother Night, Going After Cacciato, End Zone,* or other antiwar novels like them, educators can not only help today's students understand our world, but can educate them so that the tragedy of war is not repeated.

Notes

1. The origin of this statement is unknown to me. The quote is taken from the jacket of Kurt Vonnegut's *Slaughterhouse Five.*

2. Many scholarly essays, including the aforementioned Klinkowitz review, have theorized that *Mother Night* is actually an "apology" of sorts from Vonnegut, who is a German American and feels that if his mother country could have committed genocide, then he is perhaps just as accountable.

Works Cited

Aaron, Daniel. "How to Read Don Delillo." *The South Atlantic Quarterly* 89.2 Spring (1990): 305–19.

Applebee, Arthur N. *Literature in the Secondary School: Studies of Curriculum and Instruction in the United States.* Urbana, IL: National Council of Teachers of English, 1993.

Bonn, Maria S. "Can Stories Save Us? Tim O'Brien and the Efficacy of the Text." *Critique* 36:1 Fall (1994): 2–15.

Colarusso, Kathleen Dale. "World War II and Its Relevance to Today's Adolescents." *The ALAN Review* 13:2 Winter (1986): 12–14, 70.

Delillo, Don. *End Zone.* New York: Penguin, 1972.

Franklin, H. Bruce. "Teaching the Vietnam War in the 1990s." Paper presented at the Annual Joint Meetings of the Popular Culture Association, Philadelphia, PA. 12–15 April, 1995.

Harris, Robert R. "A Talk with Don Delillo." *New York Times* 10 October 1982, sec. 7: 26.

Israel, Elfie. "What Contemporary Authors Can Teach Us." *English Journal* 86.8 December (1997): 21–23.

Johannessen, Larry R. "Winning Hearts and Minds with the Literature of the Vietnam War." Mini-workshop presented at the Annual Meeting of the National Council of Teachers of English, San Diego, CA. 16–21 November, 1995.

Klinkowitz, Jerome. "*Mother Night* as Film." *The North American Review* 282 September/October (1997): 44–47.

O'Brien, Tim. *Going After Cacciato.* New York: Dell, 1975.

_____. *If I Die in a Combat Zone, Box Me Up and Ship Me Home.* New York: Dell, 1973.

Simmons, John. Personal Interview. 12 May 1998.

_____. *Teaching Literature in Middle and Secondary Grades.* Boston: Allyn and Bacon, 1992.

Vonnegut, Kurt. *Mother Night.* New York: Dell, 1962.

_____. *Slaughterhouse-Five.* New York: Dell, 1971.

Wilson, Robert. "Dreaming of War and Peace." *The Washington Post* 19 Feb. 1978: E4.

Young Adult Library Services Association. *Hit List: Frequently Challenged Books for Young Adults.* Chicago: American Library Association, 1996.

5 An Interdisciplinary Approach to War-Peace Studies

Rita Bornstein

Today's classroom is increasingly becoming a workshop for the examination of contemporary issues and the testing of values and beliefs, and among such topics, "War and Peace" has increased in respectability and popularity in the school system. For instance, in "The Postwar Pursuit of Peace Studies" (*Saturday Review of Education,* May 1973), William A. Sievert and Howard Langer note the "creation of a new curriculum—peace education—at a rapidly increasing number of colleges, some secondary schools, and even a few elementary schools" across the country. The purpose of the new curriculum is to "study seriously why mankind is constantly at war and how war might be erased in the future." According to Thornton B. Monez, whom the authors cite, "Its basic purpose is to help students design strategies of action which can contribute to the shaping of a world order characterized by social justice and absence of exploitation." Alan Geyer from Colgate University, also quoted in the article, says that "the genius of peace studies is that it is not a single discipline. It is cross-disciplinary or better, transdisciplinary."

Until recently, consideration of war-peace issues tended to be confined within a specific academic discipline (English or Social Studies) and organized around a particular focus, such as literature or diplomatic history. While the study of war through literature is illuminating, the nature of a social issue of such import requires something further of teachers and students. A student may be deeply moved by a reading of *Johnny Got His Gun,* for example, and horrified by the devastating effects of war on the individual, but will his behavior be changed? He may become more sensitive to the ravages of war, but he is also frequently left with a sense of helplessness about the repeated and seemingly inevitable occurrence of warfare. Has he researched the causes of war and the possible means of prevention? Is he aware of the

This essay appeared in *English Journal* 63.2 (1974) on pages 64–66.

avenues within which the individual can work to effect change in society? Can he gather his diffused sympathies and energies in a productive effort to achieve his goals? Does he even know what his goals are? Such questions, outside the traditional purview of the discipline of English, have not been dealt with systematically. The study of war exclusively through literature often fails to focus on the possibilities of peace in any world of the future, and it frequently fails to examine alternative sources like the paintings of great artists.

The traditional social studies approach to war and peace, on the other hand, has been primarily an historical approach to international affairs, including such topics as the history of peacekeeping efforts, the history of international law and world politics, and, more recently, an examination of world "trouble spots." This approach, while important, also lacks the breadth and scope required by a major social issue. It concentrates on the past without looking to the future, emphasizing content instead of process, war instead of peace. It fails to raise the questions that must be answered if man is to survive beyond the twentieth century and seldom explores the relationship of the individual to these questions.

War and peace curricula need to become interdisciplinary, combining literature, history, geography, economics, anthropology, psychology, sociology, international relations, physics, and art. They should emphasize process skills: the examination and clarification of values, the generation and simulation of alternative systems or models, and experimentation with modes of conflict resolution. The problem of war itself (along with the other major problems of human survival) is an international one, and it requires international solutions. As we enter the twenty-first century our planet will be increasingly viewed as a single ecosystem (Buckminster Fuller's Spaceship Earth) in which events in one part of the system affect the other parts. In order to reflect the close interaction of forces involved in major global issues, the fierce independence of the academic disciplines must give way to a transdisciplinary approach.

With these ideas in mind, I developed an interdisciplinary course of study, *Man Between War and Peace* (ERIC #SO 002 709), for Dade County in 1971. The course, which I first taught in September of 1972, has been offered at my high school three times. Enrollment has been as high as 370 students in one section, taught by a team of two teachers—language arts and social studies—with occasional input from art, music, and science teachers. Students are offered credit in either or both departments, depending on their needs. With two teachers, the class size is doubled and, using two classrooms, we work out a variety of logistical patterns—large group for lectures and movies, small groups for discussion.

The major goals for this course include the following:

- To examine and evaluate traditional and personal values and beliefs concerning war and peace.

- To analyze and react to war literature and discuss the role of literature in meliorating human problems.

- To investigate various approaches to the nature of human aggression and conflict and project some alternatives to war as an outlet for aggression.

- To analyze alternative models for peacekeeping and predict various outcomes.

- To develop tools for analyzing conflict and apply them on a personal level as well as on a national and international scale.

- To examine the relationship of the individual to the state and consider ways in which an individual can influence decisions affecting international relations.

- To differentiate between constructive and destructive roles in group interaction and analyze one's own role in such situations.

Though this is a partial list of desired outcomes, it implies the variety of experiences such a course can include. Its scope ranges from studying the history of warfare to a clarification of values and an awareness of interpersonal role-playing. This wide range of experiences also dictates diversity in the modes of instruction employed. While a lecture on the history of warfare may be appropriate, game-playing and small group exercises are more suitable for value- and role-clarification. My own experience with the course vividly pointed out the need for a wide variety of activities in order to generate and maintain a high level of student interest and involvement. Following are a few of the activities that were successful:

Students read "The Body of an American," an excerpt from USA by John Dos Passos; the essay "Tragic Conflict," by Herbert Butterfield; the cartoon essay "The Last Flower," by James Thurber. They compared the approaches used in different genres for developing a similar theme and discussed the effectiveness of each in getting across the author's point.

The students read *Johnny Got His Gun* by Dalton Trumbo, a novel which raises the provocative question of whether abstract concepts such as liberty, democracy, and honor are worth fighting and dying for. *All Quiet on the Western Front*, by Erich Maria Remarque, also raises a number of important issues. It is written from the point of view of a German soldier (something which the students tend to forget), and this allows for discussion of "the enemy" and how he is dehumanized during wartime. Students also responded positively to *Cat's Cradle,* by Kurt Vonnegut, which deals with the moral responsibility of the scientist. (Incidentally, almost no one liked *The Red Badge of Courage* by Stephen Crane, although a few exceptionally sensitive students responded positively.)

Among the poems that the students enjoyed were: "War Is Kind," Stephen Crane; "Hiding Place," Richard Armour; "Buttons," Carl Sandburg; "Now We Are Six," Sagittarius; "Hero," Don Lee; "Dulce Et Decorum Est," Wilfred Owen (especially after reading *All Quiet on the Western Front*). We asked the students why artists and writers continually return to the subject of war. Since the earliest civilizations, men of sensibility have questioned the idiocy of war; what difference has such artistic questioning made? If war is ugly and almost universally denounced, why does it persist as a means to resolve conflict? Can literature be an agent of change in human affairs?

Students viewed slides of Picasso's *Guernica,* shown by one of our art teachers, who then discussed its history and the relationship of an artist to his society.

Students collected pro- and anti-war songs and played them for the class. They ranged from "The Yanks Are Coming" to "What Have They Done to the Rain?"

A multi-faceted performance created by one of the drama classes included anti-war songs, a reading from Mark Twain's *The War Prayer,* and a section of *Bury the Dead* by Irwin Shaw.

We asked students to do readings on the nature of aggression, including selections from Robert Ardrey, Konrad Lorenz, Ashley Montagu, and Margaret Mead. Many of these works proved to be too difficult for the average student, and in the future we hope to find some that are easier. Students enjoyed this topic enormously and took passionate sides in the debate over whether man has a "killer instinct" or is culturally indoctrinated into violence and war. Although authorities are themselves in disagreement on this question, the students learned about some of the pertinent historical data and the arguments on both sides of the controversy. At the end of the unit, they played a game called Hawk and Dove (from *Self-Awareness through Group*

Dynamics by Richard Reichert), designed to encourage students to "become more conscious of their own feelings and their own reactions to others in conflict situations." Student participation in this game elicits feelings and discussion that bear directly on this abstract issue, making it far more personal and meaningful.

For a segment on "nationalism," we studied *The War Prayer,* along with the poems "Mending Wall" by Robert Frost and "What Were They Like (Questions and Answers)" by Denise Levertov. These poems supplemented filmstrips and readings on the historical development of nationalism and its implications for the future. Last letters home from kamikaze pilots and German soldiers were read, followed by letters from pacifists and draft card burners, and this led to a heated discussion on the meaning of patriotism.

In small groups, our students debated whether or not the United States should have bombed Hiroshima and Nagasaki. Alternatives available at that time were explored. Preparation for this small group work was made through appropriate readings and a filmstrip. Each group made a report and supported its decision with evidence. Minority reports were accepted as well.

Students read speeches by Kennedy, Khrushchev, Lin Piao, and Pope John (in *"Let Us Examine Our Attitude toward Peace"* by Priscilla Griffith and Betty Reardon), and role played each of these prominent shapers of world opinion in a panel discussion of the topic, "Is it possible to build a climate of trust within which world peace can flourish?" Role playing gave more insight into the perspective of other peoples; the observers filled out observation sheets on which they noted how well the panelists stayed in character.

Students played "An Experiment in Cooperation," a simulation game from *Today's Education* (October, 1969). In general, students found it difficult to obey the rules of the game and became highly competitive instead of cooperative as the game directed. The ensuing discussion of the dynamics involved proved fruitful.

Students investigated several models for world order: the United Nations as presently constituted; the United Nations Association proposal for retaining the present United Nations with additional peacekeeping provisions; the Clark-Sohn plan for a revised United Nations under a new charter. Then they projected their own version of a peaceful world.

Several groups investigated local and national organizations involved in war and peace issues, sharing their information with the class. In future courses, I plan to have students investigate all the avenues within which an individual can operate to influence international affairs, and then plan and execute some action of their own. This could range from letters to the editor to organized group action.

The possibilities for student activities are endless; and more and more ideas and materials are being generated in public schools and universities and by various organizations.* Until now, writes Alvin Toffler in *Future Shock,* the school has been "silent about tomorrow." The student has "focused backward instead of forward. The future, banned as it were from the classroom, is banned from his consciousness as well." It is time, he says, to "sensitize [young people] to the possibilities and probabilities of tomorrow. We must enhance their sense of the future." An interdisciplinary approach to war-peace studies represents a relevant and constructive investment in your students' future.

---

*In particular, the Institute For World Order, Inc., 11 West 42 Street, New York, 10036, is active in setting up workshops and developing curricula in this field for teachers.

6 Group Investigation, Democracy, and the Middle East

Jack Huhtala and Elaine B. Coughlin

What do suburban sophomores in Oregon know about resolving conflict in the Middle East? More than many adults, after being given a chance to investigate the issues. More important, they must know how to learn about such issues if they are going to be active, assertive members of our free society. We were determined to help our students become independent, autonomous learners. To help them take ownership of their learning, we had to teach them a new way to play school. They had to become equal partners with us in determining both the content and the process of their learning—within our guidelines, and meeting or exceeding the objectives of our class, of course.

To create this shared responsibility, we decided in August 1990 to focus on the Middle East for a "group investigation" unit in our interdisciplinary sophomore English and government classes. These classes were one-semester, heterogeneous, untracked classes. We had no idea that by January, Alison, a sophomore, would be writing to President Bush about her brother Tom, who was serving in a marine division stationed in Saudi Arabia.

This six-week unit was highly successful, only partially because it turned out to be so timely. Our students liked the unit, felt they had to work hard and think, and claimed to have learned significantly not only about the Middle East but also about how to learn and how to work in groups. Their grades reflected their learning. They did well on tests related to the content, and perhaps more important, they did their work with commitment. They earned half as many low grades as students in nonteamed classes.

Shlomo Sharan of Tel Aviv and his colleagues contributed to the method of instruction used in the unit, called "group investigation." This model can be used in long or short units, any subject, any grade

This essay appeared in *English Journal* 80.5 (1991) on pages 47–52.

level, but it works best with subjects for which there are no simple answers and which require considerable research, for it provides a structure to harness the energy of a group to learn far more than any individual could alone. We found that the power of group investigation was multiplied, however, when it was linked to a political question, because the method is designed to structure group work and decision-making democratically. At first, our students had simplistic reactions: "Just nuke them." Later, they began to feel they could not support any position: "How can I have an opinion? There's too much to know." Finally, they realized that no one ever knows all the answers, but that they were as informed as they could be in the time available. They were ready to make suggestions, often quite sophisticated ones, to public officials.

Trying Group Investigation

We discovered that group investigation of our topic was different from teacher-assigned group projects or group reports. The method was originally proposed by Herbert Thelen as an attempt "to combine in one teaching strategy the form and dynamics of the democratic process and the process of academic inquiry" (Joyce and Weil 1986, 227). Yael Sharan and Shlomo Sharan refined the method and describe its present form as follows:

> In Group Investigation, students take an active part in planning what they will study and how. They form cooperative groups according to common interest in a topic. All group members help plan how to research their topic. Then they divide the work among themselves, and each group member carries out his or her part of the investigation. Finally, the group synthesizes and summarizes its work and presents these findings to the class. (1989/1990, 17)

Sounds simple? We found it took all our combined efforts to plan, modify, adjust, and create this unit as we taught it and to support and encourage each other. We needed a topic that would help students learn to inquire, to research, to write, to work cooperatively—and to learn about our government. We now realize the enormity of the task we set ourselves and our students when we chose, shortly after Iraq invaded Kuwait, to select the Middle East as our topic. We planned the unit according to the Sharans' stages.

Stage One: Identify the Topic and Organize Research Groups

Our team of four English and four social studies teachers taught seven classes. Each was handled slightly differently, but kept the same topic.

To focus our inquiry, we presented students with this problem: "How can we achieve peace in the Middle East?" We gave a pretest and discovered, not surprisingly in September 1990, that our students knew very little about the politics, geography, or history of the region. Our first task, then, was to motivate students to learn about the region and to provide some initial information to stimulate their interest. We had them read some general background articles from magazines and newspapers, gave a brief overview chapter to study, and brought in two speakers—a Palestinian and a Yemeni. We then had them complete a brief library research project on basic facts about the region as a cooperative activity, intended to teach them library skills and to enhance their cooperative skills as well as to teach them about the region.

They were now ready to plan their initial inquiry. We used various methods in our classes at this step, but a typical lesson involved students' brainstorming questions about the Gulf crisis. These ranged from the amount of oil the United States imported from the region to Saddam Hussein's age. Groups of students wrote their questions on butcher paper; lists were then displayed around the room. Groups went from list to list reviewing, discarding, and ranking questions. The compiled list was then put on the overhead, and a classification lesson followed. As the students grouped similar questions, the teachers checked to see that no significant topics were being overlooked. Finally, six or seven major topics emerged, and students created labels for the groupings.

At this point, two different strategies were used by the teacher teams. Some allowed students to choose their topics individually. Others formed study groups based on student requests—and teacher judgment—and asked each group to make a choice of topic, with second choices in case of overlap.

Stage Two: Plan the Investigation

Once formed, student study teams began the task of formulating their inquiry. This involved stating their topic as a question to be researched and then dividing it into subtopics to be investigated by individuals or pairs within the team. This cognitively demanding task requires thinking, social skills, and considerable time. Some plans had to be changed more than once.

Final plans were posted on a bulletin board. The way each individual's topic related to the group's question and the way that question was linked to the class inquiry were visually obvious. For example, Steve's topic was "How did oil prices influence Saddam Hussein's actions before and during the crisis?" This supported his group's question, "What impact does oil have on the Middle East crisis?" The answer to this larger question was necessary to answer the class problem of how to achieve peace.

Stage Three: Investigate

This stage of the unit took place during the next three to four weeks, while other parts of the curriculum also were being covered in class. Students spent time in the library, interviewed people out of class, or watched the news. They brought in newspaper and magazine articles to share with each other. They often found they had to redefine or completely change their individual questions. When they completed their investigation, they produced individual papers on their findings both for a grade and to share with their study teams.

Stage Four: Prepare a Report

The reports prepared by the study teams were more than cut-and-paste summaries of the individual papers, although some started out as such. Students were encouraged to work together to draw inferences from their individual findings that had bearing on their team's question. As they did so, their report took shape and became a group paper, summarizing their findings and suggesting implications the significance of which exceeded the sum of their parts. These group papers were collated and duplicated so that each class member had a copy to use to study for the test and to use as a reference for the final writing assignment: a letter to some person or organization with political influence related to the crisis.

Stage Five: Make Final Presentation

As the teams completed their work, a steering committee was convened, formed of one representative from each team. This committee planned the presentation to the class of the most significant findings of each team in an interesting and creative fashion. Some teams used skits, others made videos, while others designed charts and maps, or presented cooperative learning lessons based on the "jigsaw" method devised by Elliot Aronson (1978). One class chose to have a local newspaper columnist come in to conduct a "town hall" discussion on the Gulf, based on a local television station's audience-discussion format. By coincidence, the station ran a discussion program on the Gulf during our unit, so a dozen of those students were able to attend the taping, and one was able to participate.

Stage Six: Test and Evaluate

There were many measures of student performance in this unit. One of the most useful was each teacher's monitoring students closely by serving as a guide and coach rather than a whole-class lecturer. Students took a post-test as well as a pretest. They wrote individual reports, group implication papers, and individual letters to politicians or the media. They created team presentations for the class, completed a variety of daily assignments, and kept individual journals.

The final exam for this unit included a teacher-designed post-test, but students also designed an exam. As Sharan and Sharan suggested, we had each study team write two questions on its topic for an essay exam. In a typical class this would total fourteen questions for the exam, twelve to be answered by each student. The study teams then graded the questions they wrote. This procedure provided useful review for the students and additional ownership of the unit. Unfortunately, we did not provide enough time for the teams to develop grading rubrics, so we had to regrade the tests for consistency. With some time and some instruction, however, students could have graded them on their own.

We often asked for informal feedback, in the form of "letters" to their teachers or "exit slips." When the unit was completed, we asked for attitudinal feedback by having students write letters of advice to the next class to undertake a group investigation unit. One of Mary's comments was, "The good part about working in a group is that you can all teach each other things and you make each other work hard." Nick wrote, "I learned that the harder I worked the more I learned, and the more I learned, the more interesting it became." Some of these statements were among our most powerful and most treasured endorsements: "The teachers weren't really teachers. They were there to help us out, but we did most of the learning ourselves."

We also compared grades in these classes with grades of students in nonteamed classes. The results were dramatic. Absenteeism was reduced by a third. Grades of D and F were reduced from twenty to thirteen percent. The percentage of students failing these required classes was cut in half, from ten to five percent. Finally, our district administered an attitudinal survey to the teamed classes to compare with those same classes taught in a traditional, nonteamed approach.

Steering Committee

This group proved to be indispensable. We erred in some classes by not supervising the selection of representatives; our sophomores "elected" male representatives from every group. Nex time we will require some sort of quota system. Even so, the group worked well. Not only did it plan and organize the final presentations, it also helped plan and organize the ongoing investigation. The steering committee facilitated the sharing of information among teams, negotiated with the teachers for revised deadlines, and helped each other problem-solve difficulties in interpersonal relationships within teams.

This representative body served the dual role of modeling democratic institutions and creating the vehicle for students to take ownership of the learning process. There was a noticeable shift in motivation some time in the first week, in the library, when students began to realize that the teachers did not have any simple answers, that there was no answer key, and that problems did not have clean, simple shapes. They first expressed some understandable frustration and then began to accept responsibility for defining their tasks and for accomplishing them. Much of the processing needed to create this crucial transition took place in ad hoc meetings of the steering committee

Problems and Frustrations

Some problems we expected, some we did not. Among those we anticipated were the frustration of teachers teaching a topic which they did not yet know well and which changed daily. We also expected student frustration, especially among those who had learned to play school well. To those used to succeeding by giving the teacher just what was expected, having general—even ambiguous—expectations seemed unfair at first. It is necessary, however, to have some frustration—or disequilibrium—for learning, or change, to take place.

Other problems should perhaps have been obvious but did not occur to us until we were faced with student difficulties. Asked to summarize news or editorials, our students stumbled. We had to regroup and plan lessons to teach close reading, analysis, and summarizing. What we had taught in units on poetry and the short story did not transfer automatically to prose, especially to technical articles or to ironic opinion columns. Our students had trouble with inferences. Again, we were forced to invent lessons in drawing inferences in general, and then applying the skill to issues in the Gulf, until the language and process became familiar. The skill of subdividing topics is not simple, and students needed a few hours and some guidance in doing so. Many needed to refine their subdivisions more than once as they learned more about their topic.

Finally, we had prepared our students by using cooperative learning techniques earlier in the year, as well as various inquiry strategies. As in any organization, however, some conflicts occurred. Some students, for example, felt they were the only ones in their group who could do good work; others felt they were not treated with respect by another group member. They were encouraged to talk to each other to work out their problems, as no one individual could possibly complete the team task alone. The steering committee provided a support group for sharing these problems.

Climate of Change

Group investigation can be incorporated into any class, in units of a few days to several weeks. In our case, however, to implement such a complex topic in several team-planned classes required a special climate. We probably could not have made it work without the previous years of staff development in our building.

The last five years have been significant, as our faculty has become increasingly united behind a goal to increase student success and, specifically, to reduce D's and F's. Our school's dropout rate is about the state average. We knew two things about this rate, besides that it was too high: it was the result of many complicated factors, only a few of which we could affect; and we were doing an award-winning job of teaching and working hard at it. Nonetheless, we were not satisfied with the results. Students were not succeeding as well as we wanted.

We focused on what we could change: the instructional climate. If we could motivate students to learn and to pass our classes, they would have one less reason for dropping out. Therefore, we have studied a variety of methods of teaching. We have become quite intimate with the educational change process. We know from experience that "significant educational change consists of changes in beliefs, teaching style, and materials which can only come about . . . through a process of personal development in a context of socialization" (Fullan 1982, 121). We were fortunate to have learned several new—to us—models of teaching, from inductive classification to inquiry to synectics to concept attainment. We also received training in cooperative learning.

The Ultimate Goal

We anticipated that our students would learn two important skills during the unit. They would get better at team work, and they would get better at the critical thinking skills required of inquiry. We knew these were precisely the skills that will be important to them as they enter the work force of the twenty-first century. We also found later that they expanded their skills in the areas identified by Douglas Heath as important contributors to vocational success:

- Adaptive intelligence skills, such as analytical and organizational abilities and good judgment
- Motivational commitment to work hard
- Understanding and managing interpersonal relationships
- Communication skills, such as empathy
- Disciplined knowledge and competence
- Caring concern for and patience with others
- Adaptive work attitudes and habits: reliability, objectivity, and decisiveness
- Imaginative perspective
- Mature sense of self: self-confidence, mental health
- Ethical sense (1991, 182)

Other people have taken an interest in this unit. Our local media came to look—two newspapers ran articles on the classes, and a local television station inquired about filming a class. Other classes within our building are experimenting with group investigation units, including composition, social studies, and physics classes.

We were pleased with this unit. We were touched by student comments such as Heather's: "I could actually go home and talk to my parents about the crisis. That made me feel pretty good!" But we were most pleased that our original question, "How can we achieve peace in the Middle East?" was answered, at least as far as overt hostilities; we hope for a lasting peace.

Works Cited

Aronson, Elliot. 1978. *The Jigsaw Classroom.* Beverly Hills: Sage.

Fullan, Michael. 1982. *The Meaning of Educational Change.* New York: Teachers College P.

Heath, Douglas H. 1991. *Fulfilling Lives: Paths to Maturity and Success.* San Francisco: Jossey-Bass.

Joyce, Bruce, and Marsha Weil. 1986. *Models of Teaching.* 3rd ed. Englewood Cliffs, NJ: Prentice.

Sharan, Yael, and Shlomo Sharan. 1989–1990. "Group Investigation Expands Cooperative Learning." *Educational Leadership* 47.4 (Dec. Jan.): 17–21.

II Peace and the Arts

In our schools, as in society at large, we rush toward computers and the Internet of the Information Age with open arms, as though toward salvation. We don't seem to understand that we are leaving our hearts, our humanity, our stories further and further behind. We don't seem to understand that our stories will get published, one way or another.

G. Lynn Nelson,
"Warriors with Words:
Toward a Post-Columbine
Writing Curriculum"

7 Teaching Empathy through Ecphrastic Poetry: Entering a Curriculum of Peace

Nancy Gorrell

The most important thing is . . . I want to help people start to think and to educate themselves and to love each other, so no one ever has to go through what that little Polish boy went through again.

Peter L. Fischl, Holocaust survivor

Over a half century ago, Nazi guns pointed at children. Today, children point guns at children—in our homes, in our schools, and in our communities. In this context, Peter L. Fischl's simple but eloquent words get to the heart of any curriculum of peace. They challenge us to define the teaching of peace as one of the "most important things" we do, and at the same time, they challenge us to reflect: How can we teach for peace? How can we teach our students to feel compassion and kindness towards their fellow human beings? If we believe as I do that the first step in justifying violence against another human being is the objectification of that human being into an "other," then it also follows that any curriculum of peace must have at its core the teaching of empathy, "the power to enter into the feeling of others."[1]

But the question still remains: How can we *teach*, not preach, empathy? How can we empower our students to *"enter into"* the feeling and spirit of others? One answer lies in a remarkable teaching tool—ecphrastic poetry—and one particular ecphrastic poem of address written by Peter L. Fischl, "To the Little Polish Boy Standing With His Arms Up" (see page 75).

Ecphrastic Poetry: The Poetry of Empathy

Ecphrasis, the poetry I like to think of as the poetry of empathy, is a little known, technical term used by classicists and art historians concerning

This essay appeared in *English Journal* 89.5 (2000) on pages 32–41.

the long tradition of poetic responses to great works of art. John Hollander, poet and critic, has written a definitive work on the subject, *The Gazer's Spirit: Poems Speaking to Silent Works of Art,* in which he chronicles the history of ecphrasis from ancient to modern times, including ecphrastic poems in response to sculpture, monuments, and photography. By definition, ecphrastic poetry requires the viewer/poet to "enter into" the spirit and feeling of the subject through a variety of poetic stances: describing, noting, reflecting, or addressing.

I first became acquainted with Fischl's ecphrastic poem of address when he sent it to me in response to reading my article, "Teaching the Holocaust: *Light from the Yellow Star* Leads the Way" (*English Journal,* Dec. 1997). From the moment I first read "To the Little Polish Boy," I knew I had in my hands the companion lesson that would open the door to the teaching of empathy. His poem and personal story, in conjunction with fellow survivor Robert O. Fisch's memoir, *Light from the Yellow Star: A Lesson of Love from the Holocaust,* have become the cornerstone of my teaching of peace, prejudice reduction, and Holocaust and genocide literature ever since. As companion lessons, either one may follow the other. I begin with the *Light from the Yellow Star* lesson, followed by the lesson in empathy centering on Fischl's poem of address. Interestingly enough, both survivors, Fischl and Fisch (similarity of names is purely coincidental), grew up in Budapest, Hungary, knew each other at the time, and have remained lifelong friends.

In nearly three decades of teaching English and writing to eleventh and twelfth grade students in a diverse, public high school, I have found no introductory lesson more authentic, relevant, and deeply affecting for both me and my students. In two lessons, one eighty-minute block and a follow-up lesson, students produce mature, serious, and empathetic poetry, entering our curriculum of peace.

A Lesson in Empathy

Historical Background to the Photograph

I begin by displaying a large poster reproduction of the roundup of Jews in the Warsaw ghetto (1943) with Fischl's poem printed beneath (see Figure 1).[2] The photograph immediately captures my students' attention, and a brief discussion naturally follows. I tell them that the photograph of the little Polish boy stands as one of the most powerful photographic images of our century—etched forever in the minds of those who first saw it when it was published in *Life Magazine* on

Figure 1. Instytut Pamieci Narodowej/Institute of National Memory, courtesy of USHMM Photo Archives. Warsaw, 1943.

To the Little Polish Boy Standing with His Arms Up

by Peter L. Fischl

I would like to be an artist
So I could make a Painting of you
Little Polish Boy

Standing with your Little hat
on your head
The Star of David
on your coat
Standing in the ghetto
with your arms up
as many Nazi machine guns
pointing at you

I would make a monument of you
and the world who said nothing

I would like to be a composer
so I could write a concerto of you
Little Polish Boy

Standing with your Little hat
on your head
The Star of David
on your coat
Standing in the ghetto
with your arms up
as many Nazi machine guns
pointing at you

I would write a concerto of you
and the world who said nothing

I am not an artist
But my mind had painted
a painting of you

Ten Million Miles High is the Painting
so the whole universe can see you Now
Little Polish Boy

Standing with your Little hat
on your head
The Star of David
on your coat
Standing in the ghetto
with your arms up
as many Nazi machine guns
pointing at you

And the World who said nothing

I'll make this painting so bright
that it will blind the eyes
of the world who saw nothing

Ten billion miles high will be the
   monument
so the whole universe can remember
   of you
Little Polish Boy

Standing with your Little hat
on your head
The Star of David

on your coat
Standing in the ghetto
with your arms up
as many Nazi machine guns
pointing at you

And the monument will tremble
so the blind world
Now
will know
What fear is in the darkness

The world
Who said nothing

I am not a composer
but I will write a composition
for five trillion trumpets
so it will blast the ear drums
of this world

The world's
Who heard nothing

I
am
Sorry
that
It was you
and
Not me

Poem from the Archives of the Simon Wiesenthal Center, Los Angeles, California
©1994 Peter L. Fischl.

November 28, 1960 (106). I mention that the Warsaw ghetto confined nearly half a million Jews and that nearly 45,000 died there in 1941 alone, due to starvation and disease. When, in April 1943, the Nazis attempted to raze the ghetto and deport the remaining 70,000 inhabitants to Treblinka concentration camp, a revolt ensued that lasted five weeks (*The Betrayal of Mankind* 14). I comment that the photograph we are looking at was taken by Nazi photographers for General Jurgen Stroop, a Nazi official, to document the uprising and the final liquidation of the ghetto.[3] I ask my students if anyone has seen this well-known photograph, as it has been published in many history textbooks and has been reprinted numerous times in popular literature. Despite its historical significance, few of my students can recall seeing it.

Then I ask my students to imagine for a moment a Holocaust survivor seeing this photograph years after the Holocaust. How do you think that survivor might feel? Students speculate that the survivor might be shocked, that the image might bring back painful memories, and that the survivor might not even want to look at the photograph at all. I tell my students that this is what happened to a Holocaust survivor, Peter L. Fischl, whom I have come to know.

Peter Fischl's Personal Story

I share with my students the personal story Fischl related to me. Like the boy in the photograph, Fischl was a child growing up during the Holocaust. At the age of thirteen he wore the Star of David on his clothes and was subjected to harsh anti-Jewish laws. Soon after, the Nazis invaded Hungary. Separated from his family, he went into hiding in a Catholic school with sixty other boys. A few months later, he received a phone call from his father telling him that he had been discovered by the Gestapo. That was the last contact he had with his father. Fortunately, Fischl managed to survive the last weeks of the war in hiding with his mother and sister. In 1957, during the Hungarian Revolution, he escaped to America, where he settled in southern California.

Years later, in 1965, he saw the photograph of the little Polish boy by accident, when he was browsing through old *Life* magazines in a bookstore on Hollywood Boulevard near his home. The effect on him was so powerful that the image of the little boy remained with him every day for four years thereafter, until he woke up one morning at 2:00 A.M. and, although he was not a poet, wrote a poem to the little Polish boy.

Peter Fischl's Poem of Address

At this point I place on each student's desk a smaller version of the poster with a copy of the photograph and the poem printed beneath, and I read the poem aloud as the students follow along.[4] After hearing the poem, my students are visibly moved; a sense of awe and silence permeates the room. I ask them to take out their response journals and pose the following questions for personal reflection: What are you wondering at this moment? Write a list of "wonder" questions. What are you feeling? Write about your reactions to the poem.

After a few minutes of writing, I share with my students what happened after Fischl wrote his poem. As he related it to me, until the moment of writing, he had never before expressed his feelings about his Holocaust experience. After writing the poem, he cried "for a long time," and then he put it in his desk drawer where it sat for nearly a quarter of a century. He was not a poet, and he never thought to publish the poem for fear it would be exploiting the memory of the little Polish boy. Then one day he went with his daughter to see the opening of Steven Spielberg's film, *Schindler's List.* After seeing the film, he sat frozen to his seat, consumed once again with the image of the little Polish boy. At that moment he knew he had to break his silence, and in 1994 he published his poem in lithograph form, where it is on display in the Los Angeles Museum of Tolerance as well as in museums throughout the world.

Student Writing Response: Poems Speaking to the Little Polish Boy Photograph

Without further discussion, I ask my students to turn their attention once again to the photograph before them. I suggest that they write their own poem to the little Polish boy or to anyone in the photograph. Keeping the instructions open and simple, I pose the following questions:

- If you could speak to the little Polish boy, what would you say?
- If you could speak to anyone in the photograph, what would you say?
- If you could imagine any of the subjects speaking, what do you think they would say?
- On a new page in your journals, write any poem reflecting on your viewing of this photograph. You may reread your wonder questions and reflections to help you get started.

In the two years I have been teaching this lesson to students of various ability levels and attitudes towards poetry, I never cease to be amazed at how eagerly students respond. After ten minutes of composing I ask, "Who would like to share their poems in progress?" Sitting in our "sharing circle" format, students readily respond with an array of poetic stances: addressing the subjects, letting the subjects speak, reflecting on the subjects.

At this point in the lesson, I want my students to listen to the power of the poems, "to enter into the spirit" and to reflect upon that spirit. As the students do so, they and their poems reveal mature insights into the nature of genocide, the most extreme form of violence, raising the critical questions so vital for our subsequent study. Since I want my students to process those insights, I ask them to go to a blank page in their journals. I tell them we will listen to the poems without commenting, and after hearing each poem, we will reflect in our journals upon that "hearing." I suggest they write what the poem reveals to them about the nature of violence, genocide, or human behavior, or they may write a wonder question. Without further comment, we proceed around the sharing circle, hearing volunteers who are moved to read, reflecting for a few minutes in our journals after each reading.

Karen "enters the spirit" of the little Polish boy in her poem of address, first describing and then ending with her personal reflection. She reads to us:

To the Little Polish Boy

Looking at you little boy
your arms up in the air
thinking of what you may miss
if one of the demons shoots their guns
ending your already scarred life
looking at you little boy
facing the fear that faces you
how brave you really are . . .
looking at you little boy
seeing the star of David staining your clothes
locked up in this ghetto with nowhere to go
looking at you little boy
and seeing only
how precious
life really is.

What more important lesson can we learn in our study of peace than Karen's last lines leading us to the conclusion of the "precious" value of human life?

Lily addresses the little Polish boy by imagining she is his mother. She takes a speculative stance, reading to us:

Untitled

What if I were your mother
and held you high in the air
in my tall arms
under the warm sun
exalted and kissed by God
on your rosy cheeks,
And the barbed wire and concrete
grayness and cold were a far off
twister of a storm cloud
soon to be swept to sea
never to rain on us
as I hold you high in the air
no pain of a gun piercing your back.

The hearing of this poem poses for us a most provocative question . . . *what if ?* . . . prompting us to reflect upon the issue of moral choice: What if ? . . . What if we/they choose/chose peace, not violence?

John assumes a different stance, taking on the identity/persona of the little Polish boy, by letting him speak. John reads to us only four short lines:

Untitled

How did I get here?
Why am I here?
What did I do to deserve this?
How will I . . .

The sudden break in the poem, indicating either the inability to express in words the unthinkable, unknowable horror about to come—*there are no answers*—or the sudden cliffhanger ending of a vibrant young life—*Was the little boy shot at that moment of questioning?*—enables us to enter into the moment with its inexplicable possibilities. In four remarkable lines, John imaginatively enters the "spirit and feeling" of his subject, *"How will I _____?"* leading us to fill in the blank with our own reflections—*survive*?

Cormisha focuses on the woman in the photograph, letting her address the little Polish boy:

The Woman's Cry

Son, whatever you do keep those hands up.
Soon in time, you will be able to put them down
And let them move freely.
You will be able to play with all the children again.

But son, whatever you do, keep those hands up.
Soon in time, you won't have to think about danger or fear.
You will be able to go out at night without crying your heart out.
But son, whatever you do keep those hands up.
Soon in time, they will see how they hurt my little boy . . .
The gun toward my son is not necessary,
He is just a child.
Son, whatever you do keep those hands up.
Soon in time, the whole world who kept silent
Will come out and help.

Cormisha imagines the mother not thinking of herself, but only how to help her son survive. The mother's assurances affirm the bonds of family and hope for future survival: "Soon in time, the whole world . . . will come out and help." Cormisha's poem reminds us of an important aspect of any curriculum of peace: Goodness, love, and bravery must prevail, even in the most violent and inhumane circumstances.

Several students address poems to the Nazi soldiers in the photograph. Many of these poems express anger, others struggle to understand. Jessica addresses the Nazi soldier with a litany of questions:

The Killing Soldier

There you stand with your big bad gun,
There you stand with all the power,
There you stand with your face as a rock.
Don't you care about that boy?
Don't you care about his mother and father?
Don't you care about his other family and friends?
What did this boy do to you?
Did this boy hurt you?
Maybe you should think
before you pull the trigger.

In contrast to Jessica's poem, Amanda struggles to understand the Nazi soldier's behavior:

Numb

Ignorance
It
          Befalls
      You
              like
                    rain.
Senses shut down.
No longer can you hear
or feel or see.
SEE the troubled eyes
the little fingers and

the tattered clothes.
They call only to you—
salvation!
Senses shut down.
You cannot cry back
nor do you want to.
This Innocence is your enemy.
Remote controls
     move
       your
      body
With the switch of a button
    —Your HEART is turned off—

In her poem Amanda offers an explanation for the Nazi soldier's behavior, "ignorance" and "numbness," for how could anyone be so inhumane and yet possess the feelings that make us human?

Closing Discussion

As a final exercise, I ask students to speculate on what all the poems we have heard in the sharing circle have in common. Students wonder why the world remained silent, what happened to the little Polish boy, and "How can people be so cruel?" We list on the board in brainstorm fashion our collective thoughts, feelings, and insights, framing questions for our subsequent study of peace:

- Why did it happen?
- How can human beings be so cruel?
- What is the nature of violence?
- Why did the "world say nothing?"
- What did America know about the Warsaw ghetto and the little Polish boy?
- What is the nature of good and evil?
- Why do some people choose "good" and others "evil"?

In our discussion I tell my students that the most reliable sources to date contend that we do not know what happened to the little Polish boy; we can only assume that he perished. As far as the question, "Did the world know?" I tell my students about an article recently published in *Newsweek.* In "Word from the Ghetto" *Newsweek* reports that the Polish government-in-exile sent Jan Karski, a courier for the underground resistance, to visit the Warsaw ghetto and other transit camps in Poland. I hold up the March 8, 1999, edition of *Newsweek* with a prominent picture of Karski and the little Polish boy photograph. Karski saw the atrocities and was desperate to tell the world. He did so, but few believed him. When he returned to Washington in June 1943 during the final days of the Warsaw ghetto uprising, he spoke to President Roosevelt. Then I read his words to the class:

> A distinction has to be made . . . The Germans persecute my people . . . they want to make us a nation of slaves. With the Jews, it is different. They want to exterminate them . . . Mr. President, I am going back to Poland . . . Everybody will ask me: what did President Roosevelt tell you? What am I to tell them? (47)

I pause for a moment and then ask my students: What do you think President Roosevelt said? What do you think he should have said? After a few responses, I read Roosevelt's answer:

> You will tell the leaders that we shall win this war! You will tell them that the guilty ones will be punished. Justice and freedom will prevail. You will tell your nation that they have a friend in this house. (47)

As my students reflect on Roosevelt's words, I mention that Karski was given by the state of Israel its Honorary Citizenship Award as a distinguished rescuer. At this point I introduce the term "righteous gentile," pointing out the many who made the moral choice to work for peace in the face of genocide. I read Karski's own words in the foreword he wrote for a book of portraits and stories of Holocaust survivors and their messages of hope and compassion:

> I understand the uniqueness of the Holocaust. I saw it. We cannot let history forget it. The Jews were abandoned by governments, by church hierarchies, and by societal structures. But they were not abandoned by humanity. Thousands upon thousands of individuals, priests and nuns, workers and peasants, educated and simpletons—risked their lives or freedom to help—we cannot let history forget them. (*The Triumphant Spirit* 10)

As class ends, I distribute to my students the *Newsweek* article and Jan Karski's foreword for further reading that evening. I tell them, "If you are satisfied with the poem in your response journal, write a final, edited draft, or, if you are inspired after hearing other students' poems, write a new poem in response to the little Polish boy photograph."

Follow up Lesson: Expanding Our Circle of Empathy

I open the following class period by asking for examples of new or revised poems written in response to the little Polish boy photograph. Without discussion, we hear a few selections. Then I tell my students that the poems we have been studying and writing are a special kind of poetry, ecphrastic poetry, in which the viewer/poet "speaks to" great works of art, sculpture, and photography. I point out that, in that "speaking," the poet "enters into the spirit and feeling of others." I define that "entering" as empathy. At this point I praise my students' extraordinary poems for helping us enter into the spirit and feeling of the little Polish boy, and, by his example, the genocide and Holocaust experience.

Then I tell my students that I want to give them the experience of writing their own poem of address to expand our circle of empathy. In order to do so, I ask them to recall or find a photograph, a work of art, or a monument or piece of sculpture that affected them as profoundly as the little Polish boy affected Peter Fischl. I ask my students to brainstorm any images or photographs that represent for them an important moment or experience they will never forget. Amazingly, Minh-Dang (Mindy), a grandchild of Vietnamese boat refugees, recalls seeing in her history textbook a photograph of a Vietnamese girl running through the streets covered with napalm. I tell her I recall seeing that photograph, too, how it became emblematic of an entire era, and I suggest to her to try to write a poem on viewing that photograph. Other students recall images from the Kennedy assassination they have seen. I tell my students that some images like the little Polish boy, the napalmed young girl, or JFK Jr. saluting the coffin of his assassinated father are so profound that they become part of our collective consciousness, reflecting the feelings of an entire community or nation.

Next, I distribute the writing assignment. (See Figure 2.)

After discussing the long-range assignment, I take my students to the school library to find images that affect them. They browse through photography and art books as well as magazines, newspapers, and popular literature. I have placed upon a central table collections of some of the most important photographers and photojournalists of our century: Edward Steichen, Alfred Eisenstaedt, Roman Vishniac, Henri Cartier-Bresson, Dorthea Lange, Robert Capra, Gordon Parks, and Brian Lanker, to name a few available in our high school library. My students consult photographic essays of important eras: photography of the Depression, World War II, the Holocaust, Korea, the Civil Rights Movement, and Vietnam, to name a few. Particularly popular collections are Roman Vishniac's *A Vanished World*, the Time/Life collections on each decade, *The Family of Man*, and recent Time/Life books such as *The Meaning of Life: Reflections in Words and Pictures on Why We are Here.*

Find a photograph, piece of art, monument, or sculpture that profoundly affects or inspires you. If possible, strive to have this work affect you as the "Little Polish Boy" affected Peter L. Fischl. You may need to search for some time in libraries, photography books, and newspapers, as well as in your travels to museums, monuments, and memorials. Copy or acquire a copy of the work of art or photograph to display for the class. Your final poetic responses will be due at the completion of the unit. At that time you will present the image/work and your poetic response(s) to the class.

Step One: Find a Work That Affects You Profoundly

Step Two: Write a Poetic Response to That Work
Choose a Poetic Stance:
1. Describe what you see in detail, step by step.
2. Address a subject in the work.
3. Take on the identity/persona of a subject in the work. Imagine what that subject is thinking or about to do. Or, let the subject speak.
4. Reflect upon what you see; meditate upon the moment of viewing.

Step Three: Copy or Acquire a Picture of the Work for Display

Step Four: Present Your Poem to the Class

Figure 2. Ecphrastic poetry writing assignment general directions.

        I give my students several weeks to search for a work that truly inspires and engages them "to enter into the spirit." The results of this researching and reflecting time prove to be highly productive, as students' ecphrastic responses help them to enter, define, and develop a curriculum of peace.

Student Ecphrastic Poems

The poems my students produce from the long-range, follow-up lesson affirm the power of poetry to enable poet and reader alike to "enter the terrain" of human suffering, pain, and grief, expanding the circle of empathy connecting us all. Students respond to a wide range of works: art, sculpture, monuments, and photography. I offer here two examples of ecphrastic responses: one that connects photojournalism of the past to personal, family history and heritage; the other that sees recent photojournalism through the lens of our teaching of empathy.

        Minh-Dang (Mindy) chooses to "enter that terrain" as she connects personal, family history in her poem of address to the photographic image of a fleeing, young Vietnamese girl covered with napalm:

Everything Stands Still

I close my eyes
And I hear your screams
You are running from the Devil
Who has taken your Home
Your Family
Your Clothes
And you are crying for me
For my hands and my help
To take away the hurt
And everything stands still . . .

I open my eyes
And sit in the road
As my Friends, my Family
Run past me
I see you fleeing our home
With your arms outstretched
Trying to fly from the fire
Trying to calm the burning
With the tears running down your face
And everything stands still . . .

This morning you played
You sang the songs of our home
And you tasted the fruits of our land
This morning our mother kissed you
Dressed you for the day
Combed the knots from your black hair
This morning you kissed our father
Before he went to the fields
And lost his life.

This afternoon
The screams came from the sky
Spreading tears of Hell
This afternoon our mother screamed
Somewhere where you could not reach her
And you knew you would never hear her voice again
This afternoon the gods were angry
And they stole your clothes and stung your eyes
Now you run to me.

I open my arms
Ready to embrace you
And shelter you from the pain
Hoping to smooth your hair

Clothe your burning skin
Wipe your tears away
Your screams reach into my heart
How I wish that I could help you
I wish that our hands could meet
And everything stands still . . .

Sister, this morning you kissed the sun
This afternoon it fell from the sky
Your tears haunt me
Your cries echo in time
Just when I almost touch you
When I can almost save you
Everything stands still . . .

You are my nightmare
You are my regret.

Lily chooses to "enter the terrain" as she views a recent photographic image of a skull buried in dirt in a *Time* magazine article on the war in Kosovo.

Morning Coffee, 7:42 A.M.

Today the paper said that
Thousands of bodies were found in
Landfills across Eastern Europe—

This body is half-decayed and blasted,
Hair shot back and half there, exposing
A broken-down skull, lined with cracks and
Footsteps, dirt-stained and parasitic—

I look to see what sex the thing is,
(I smoked too much last night and my lungs
feel tight and raspy, my throat is raw and tastes like
salt, and if I cough real hard I can still taste the
tobacco.) and the caption tells me it's female—

Here a sexless, bloodless body shares the page
With a family on a picnic in central park—

Final Reflections

I am not so naive to think that poetry, ecphrastic or any other kind, could possibly "solve" all the problems of violence in our society. The underlying causes of one person's inhumanity to another lie in centuries of practice, prejudice, and paradox unimaginable and unknowable. And yet, I am an English teacher, and I must do what I do best—teach the essence of my discipline. And what is that essence? It has been and always will be for me engagement—imaginatively, aesthetically, and emotionally—with "the text." That engagement, the ability to enter into the spirit and feeling of others, defines what it is to be human, and that, I believe, is the heart of any curriculum of peace.

Lily reveals such engagement when she can no longer drink her morning coffee while turning the pages reflecting horror and tragedy in the magazine before her. I can think of no other weapon more important to combat violence, prejudice, and hatred than the heightened sensitivity of our young people to the plethora of horrific images of inhumanity in the media today.

Without question, the photograph of the little Polish boy and Peter Fischl's response to it have touched the hearts and souls of my students, producing not only mature, serious, and empathetic poetry, but a transformational awareness that is both lifelong and portable.

Hopefully, through the teaching of empathy, our curriculum of peace *will* take us one step closer to the time when, in Fischl's words, "no one will have to go through what that little Polish boy went through again."

Notes

1. *The New Lexicon Webster's Dictionary of the English Language* (New York: Lexicon Publications, Inc. 1989) offers a definition of empathy particularly useful for our purposes: "The *power* to *enter* into emotional harmony with a work of art and so derive aesthetic satisfaction; the power to enter into the feeling and spirit of others" [my italics].

2. The "Little Polish Boy" poster (28"H × 18"W), including the photograph and reprinted poem beneath, is available from the *Holocaust Resources and Materials* catalogue, published by the Social Studies School Service, 10200 Jefferson Boulevard, Room J5, P.O. Box 802, Culver City, CA 902320802 (1-800-421-4246) (Fax: 1-800-944-5432) catalogue #PFL100-J8; fee $12. (Includes a French translation of the poem.) The companion resource material, *Light from the Yellow Star: A Lesson of Love from the Holocaust* by Robert O. Fisch, is also available at $9.95 in the paperback edition, Catalogue #0P136-J8.

3. The photograph of the little Polish boy was first published in *The Report of Jurgen Stroop Concerning the Uprising in the Ghetto of Warsaw and the Liquidation of the Jewish Residential Area.* It is accessible from the Simon Wiesenthal Center library, 9760 W. Pico Boulevard, Los Angeles, California 90035. This amazing document, with an introduction by Professor B. Mark, serves as a testimony in the Nazi's own words of Jewish heroism and resistance.

4. Note that the yellow star of David does *not* appear on the coat of the little Polish boy in the original photograph. Fischl takes poetic license and refers to it in the poem, as he, and all Jews, were required to wear the star.

Special Note

Teachers may secure permission free of charge from Holocaust artist Peter L. Fischl to teach his copyrighted poem, "To the Little Polish Boy Standing with His Arms Up," by writing to him at P.O. Box 656, Burbank, CA 91503-0656. Please include your name, school address, approximate date of teaching the poem, and a self-addressed, stamped envelope with your request.

Works Cited

Casagrande, June."Burbank Poet to Appear at Holocaust Center." *The Burbank Leader* 11 Feb. 1998: A10.

Fisch, Robert O. *Light from the Yellow Star: A Lesson of Love from the Holocaust.* Minneapolis: Frederick Weisman Art Museum of the University of Minnesota, 1994.

Fischl, Peter L. "To the Little Polish Boy Standing with his Arms Up." Archives of Simon Wiesenthal Center, Los Angeles, 1994.

———. *The Burbank Leader.* 11 Feb. 1998.

"Glossary of Terms," *The Betrayal of Mankind.* New Jersey Commission on Holocaust Education, 1994.

Gorrell, Nancy. "Teaching the Holocaust: *Light from the Yellow Star* Leads the Way." *English Journal* 86.8 (1997): 50–55.

Hollander, John. *The Gazer's Spirit: Poems Speaking to Silent Works of Art.* Chicago: University of Chicago Press, 1995.

Karski, Jan. "Foreword." *The Triumphant Spirit: Portraits and Stories of Holocaust Survivors . . . Their Messages of Hope and Compassion.* Ed. Nick Del Calzo. Denver: Triumphant Spirit Publishing, 1997. 10.

"Word from the Ghetto." *Newsweek* 8 March 1999: 47.

8 Peace by Piece: The Freeing Power of Language and Literacy through the Arts

Mary F. Wright and Sandra Kowalczyk

Thirty years ago we were approaching adolescence, the age of the students we teach today. Mention the year 1969, and the words peace, love, and happiness come to mind. During that time newspapers and magazines splashed pictures of "Love-Ins" or "Sit-Ins," with flower children participating in colorful nonviolent forms of protest. The television and radio media coverage flashed gruesome images of war and showed young people coming out in droves to protest US involvement. Even the music surrounding our generation was telling us "All You Need Is Love" and "Give Peace a Chance." It was clear that the tide had turned; young people were coming together for the good of humanity. As Bob Dylan sang "The Times, They Are a-Changin'," we really believed we could make a difference, and through that belief came a valid sense of spiritual togetherness.

Thirty years later, we find ourselves still carrying that message to the young people we touch today through our teaching. Although we are up against some tough times in the teaching profession, children, now more than ever, need to hear, read, think, and feel the message of peace in the world. In a time when parents are busy working out of the household, children are often watching too much violence on TV, listening to music lyrics that sometimes embrace dark satanic viewpoints, or playing unnecessarily violent video games. Our students are becoming desensitized to the message of peace.

The work teachers do has the power to make a difference in the world. Giving our students meaningful opportunities to hope, think, dream, read, and write about peace is worth striving for. We can empower our students and in return nurture our own sense of peace

---

This essay appeared in *English Journal* 89.5 (2000) on pages 55–63.

and hopefulness. Several years ago we collaborated to involve our students in a year of integrated peace studies, with the goal of staging an end-of-the-year dramatic student production titled "Peace by Piece: The Freeing Power of Language and Literacy through the Arts." Focusing on the theme of peace and tolerance issues, we chose to incorporate the word "piece" in the title, emblematic of our joint philosophy toward hands-on interdisciplinary learning. We believe that it is important to allow students the opportunity to piece together their own meaning. The arts facilitate this process beautifully, allowing students to express themselves, create, and feel the language come alive in new ways. Depending upon their artistic sensibilities, students can interpret literature and celebrate language through the arts: music, dance, drama, storytelling, and creative writing.

Over the past eight years, teaching seventh- and eighth-grade reading and language arts across the hall from one another, we have successfully collaborated on theme-based units, interdisciplinary projects, and original theatrical student productions, celebrating language and literacy through the arts. As we strive toward incorporating the teaching of peace, our ideas have been evolving for years. This retrospective, then, highlights many years of teaching the language and literature of peace and student projects that exemplify learning and growth in this area.

The following activities provide a brief overview of some ways we integrate peace and diversity issues into the middle school language arts/reading curriculum. They were created with an extended purpose in mind—to be celebrated through drama, dance, creative writing, storytelling, music, and visual arts in our dramatic student retrospective.

The Essence of Peace: Nature

Peace resides in nature. The natural world and how we relate to it affects our sense of peace. An important first step in teaching students about peace is to cultivate a sense of it within, because peace starts with individuals living in harmony with their natural surroundings. Students need to know how to seek the peace they wish to feel and share, and one way of fostering an appreciation for the concept of peace is by having students focus on the natural world. During the course of the year, the language arts students observed nature as they captured each month's essence in poetic verse. The nature poetry writing project involved students in collecting field note observations about each particular month. We asked them to collect data about weather changes—

Figure 1. Language arts students perform a dance to Vivaldi's "Winter" in celebration of the nature poetry project.

to note changes in sky patterns, wind, temperature, flora, and fauna. They then used these observations to enrich their writing.

Each new month, a classroom display board proudly published beautifully illustrated student poems. These were taken down each month and saved for a "Nature Poetry Calendar Book" to be published at the end of the school year. The student poetry reflects a true communion with nature, as their well-chosen words echo seasonal transformations, and their illustrations justly depict the autumn gold of September, the icy magic of December, and the green promise of March. Students worked on bringing the nature poetry project to life for the dramatic "Peace by Piece" retrospective. As the four seasons—autumn, winter, spring, and summer—were represented in the poetry, the students choreographed a dance to Vivaldi's "Four Seasons." While they danced on stage (see Figure 1), the colorfully illustrated poetry was scrolled onto a large video screen for the audience to read. This project heightened student awareness of the peace found in nature, providing a positive place to begin laying the groundwork for exploring peace studies in the language arts curriculum.

The Language of Peace: Peace Banners

Kicking off a year-long collaborative language arts/reading department emphasis on social issues concerning world peace, we involved our students in the making of peace banners to proudly display in our rooms and throughout the halls of the school. The banners were displayed at our dramatic retrospective, serving as a backdrop for students on stage, as well as surrounding the audience on the walls of the auditorium. This collaborative activity engaged our students in a meaningful exploration of the language of peace. Individual classes worked together to create six 36" × 90" banners proclaiming the power of "Peace by Piece: The Freeing Power of Language and Literacy through the Arts." To personalize their contributions, each student's hand was traced, designed, and colored in an interlocking chain centered across the paper banner. Picasso art prints supporting a peace theme inspired students to generate their own ideas for peace symbols to be placed on the banner. As a result, beautiful images symbolic of peace grace the top of the banners: doves, dancers around a sun, people holding hands around the earth, flowers, rainbows, peace signs, and Yin-Yang symbols. Students recorded peace quotes on the banners from notable peacemakers around the world such as Mahatma Gandhi, Martin Luther King Jr., Mother Theresa, Jane Addams, and John Lennon. Their moving words inspired students to make a personal spiritual contribution by writing their own thoughts about peace across the banners. This activity brought students together, focusing on the language of peace and tolerance, which we would continue to discuss and celebrate throughout the year.

Symbols of Peace

The celebration of cultural diversity through literature and the arts is an integral component of the reading program. Each year students are engaged in a variety of long term collaborative learning projects inspired by culturally based art forms designed to promote respect for the values of cultural identities, intercultural dialogue, and cultural cooperation. During a literature unit focusing on West African cultural traditions of oral storytelling and communication through proverbs, students were introduced to the language of adinkra (ah DIN krah) cloth, traditionally created by the Asante people in Ghana, West Africa (see Figure 2). A cloth that can be read as well as worn, adinkra communicates through handstamped symbols that also serve to enhance the beauty of the cloth. Adinkra symbols evoke specific proverbs to express ideas. For instance, a chief on a mission of peace might wear clothing printed with the Binkabi (been KAH bee) symbol related to the proverb, "Do not bite one another," standing for the ideas of harmony and unity.

Another symbol promoting unity among different groups of people abstractly depicts two crocodiles sharing the same stomach,

Figure 2. Inspired by adinkra, a hand-sewn, hand-stamped cloth traditionally made by the Asante people in Ghana, West Africa, students worked collaboratively to create a "Peace by Piece" cloth.

recalling the proverb, "Afuntun mmireku, denkyem mmireku" (ah FOON toon mir eh Koo, den CHEM mir eh KOO), "Bellies mixed up, crocodiles mixed up." Students were introduced to the meanings of additional adinkra symbols extolling many of the virtues we were interested in promoting: the wisdom of learning from the past, strength of mind, body and soul, tolerance, cooperation, love, benevolence, and goodwill.

In previous years, after examining authentic adinkra cloth, students worked together as a class to communicate their ideas visually by creating their own version of the cloth. Some years students collaboratively created cloths that drew heavily on traditional adinkra symbolism. Other years they opted to handstamp their cloth with original symbols having a personal meaning. This year students excitedly planned a themed adinkra cloth, a "Peace by Piece" cloth, on which they could design and hand-stamp symbols to promote peace and tolerance.

In the manner traditionally practiced by the Asante people, students first divided a dyed swath of cotton into four equal sized strips, hemming the edges. For several weeks, rotating small groups of students sat side by side, connecting the panels by hand sewing a traditional joining stitch in a bright repeated sequence of color. The next labor-intensive step involved dividing the cloth into a series of grids or parallel lines, using a large wooden African comb to imprint the thick black dye.

Whereas the Asante carve adinkra stamps from a calabash, a type of gourd, the students carefully carved their designs into synthetic rubber. Stamps of doves; hands interlocking; choirs of hand-holding people circling the earth; peace signs; and other symbols promoting the principles of freedom, justice, tolerance, solidarity, and the rejection of violence were pressed into black acrylic paint and imprinted onto the cloth in a strong visual design. The completed cloth served as a dramatic backdrop in the reading classroom as students delivered original essays reflecting their thoughts for peace. Symbolic of the values, attitudes, and behaviors necessary for a culture of peace, the "Peace by Piece" cloth was also proudly displayed on stage during our theatrical production.

Peace in the Freedom to Dream

In a language arts poetry unit, students learn that with dreams comes the freedom to express inner thoughts, unleash fears, and set forth hopes. There is peace in the freedom to dream. Unconstrained, the dreamer loses "self " in the moment. There are no thoughts devoted to the past or future; rather, a stream of feelings, emotions, and unconstructed thought patterns emerges and fades with each dream. Far away from the daily troubles of the student's family life or the chaotic pace of the world at large, students who are taught to believe in their dreams have discovered a way to insulate themselves from the roughness of everyday life. Within this unit of study, students read literature about dreamers of all kinds and their struggles to achieve their dreams, learning that dreams can often shape character and give meaning to who we are and how we live with others. While reading "The Dream Keeper" by Langston Hughes, students see a dream as precious, deserving to be wrapped "In a blue cloud cloth, away from the too-rough fingers of the world."

Reading poetry extolling the virtues of dreaming stimulates discussion about the power of dreaming. Both night dreams and daydreams are discussed as a significant source of releasing tension, relieving boredom, and offering harmless ways of expressing wishes, fears, and hopes. Their discussion empowers students to participate in a poetry writing workshop driven by dreams. The freedom of dreaming while wide awake gives conscious birth to "freedom of imagination." Allowing our students ways of expressing their dreams enables them to experience the sense of peace found in the freedom to dream. Through their poetry, students recognize the freedom of dreams in having no limits:

Somewhere

I'm in a little world with no limits
Ignoring everything around me
It's black
Then I see colors
You and me flying along like feathers
Stress free and together
I will live on forever

Karol's poem speaks directly of the peace found in dreams:

When I go to sleep
I dream of a place
That is filled with peace
Every face has a joyful smile
filled with love and warmth
When I am dreaming
It is as though the whole world
Is at peace

Taking the student poems to publication resulted in new artistic methods in a classroom celebrating the arts. Going beyond the usual classroom publication, the students' ideals, dreams, and beliefs were represented as powerful symbols of freedom, peace, and unity on eight black and blue felt dream flags. Students wrote and illustrated their poems on separate geometric cloth shapes, outlining their words with colorful fluorescent markers and illustration. The cloth poems were then appliqued onto the felt flags. Eighty student dream poems now boldly graced eight colorful felt dream flags.

In preparation for the Peace by Piece retrospective, students choreographed a dance with their dream flags to the music of the Beatles' song, "I'm Only Sleeping." Using a large screen video projector, the students' dream poems were simultaneously projected as they performed an interpretive dance. The poetry dream flag project reinforced the importance of believing in dreams, creating an awareness about the power of peace found within them. The performance celebrated dreams through creative writing, music, dance, art, and video technology.

The Rhythm of Peace

The impact and influence popular music has on teenagers should be recognized as a powerful teaching tool. Student analysis of lyrics and musical forms extends critical thinking skills and acts as a catalyst for both imaginative and philosophical writing. During our year of peace studies in the language arts classroom, students were asked to contribute one song for "music response" sessions. The one requirement was that their song feature lyrics embracing the theme of peace, love, harmony, or tolerance.

Each student brought in a sheet of typed song lyrics, including the title of the song and artist. The music could be chosen from any genre, including classical, rock, country, jazz, and the blues. After checking the lyrics for appropriate words or topics, we made classroom copies. Before the students presented the songs to the class, we asked them to leave their musical taste preferences behind and be open-minded to each song for its valid message about peace. The presentation procedure went as follows:

1. Student passes out typed song lyrics.
2. Student interprets the song lyrics, capturing the essence of the piece.
3. Student then reads the lyrics aloud, as the class listens.
4. We all listen to the song as we respond in our notebooks.
5. Responses are meant to capture a feeling or reaction from the listener. Students are encouraged to be honest, reflecting their thoughts and feelings through poetry, prose, or graphics with word lists. They are encouraged to try a variety of modes of expression.
6. The responses are then given to the student who brought in the song. Responses are chosen by the person who brought in the song for placement in a music response journal to be shared with other classes.

The music response journal entries reflect both cognitive and affective responses to the diversity of music shared. Modeling artistic/verbal expression, Mary's response to Silverchair's "Pure Massacre," represents the duality of living with the possibility of peace and violence every day. (See Figure 3.) Similarly, her written response to

Figure 3. Student response to Silverchair's song "Pure Massacre."

Korn's song "Shoots and Ladders" about child abuse, recognizes the struggle between peace and violence:

> Anger influencing innocence
> Rhythms repeated, depleted
> safety surrenders
> to evil and danger
> down, down under
> under darkness
> under cover
> cover up the childhood dreams
> Dreams die . . .

Celebrating peace together through music, students explored the rich and exciting relationship between words and music, while highlighting the meaning and message of the song lyrics. The act of responding to music has given students the opportunity to participate in a studio/workshop approach to learning—taking risks, generating strong opinions and outspoken views, and stimulating a positive dialogue about peace issues. The music response project dignifies music as a valid way to promote the message of peace.

The Spirit of Peace

Men, women, and children left Africa in the holds of slave ships. Under slavery people were considered property with no safeguards against force, threats, punishment, and other forms of violence. Reading students found the ex-slave narratives in the Newbery Honor Book, *To Be a Slave,* by Julius Lester, powerful tools for exploring the slave experience. Until the abolition of slavery, fleeing was the only means of escape. In black folklore the disappearance of slaves coincided with accounts of slaves flying away. The dream of freedom was the impetus behind a literature-based dance/drama created by reading students after exploring Newbery award winning author Virginia Hamilton's masterful retelling of *The People Could Fly.* The dance/drama, like the tale, began long ago in Africa, capturing the rhythm of daily life before slave ships harbored nearby. Scenes came to life as students entered and studied the story through dance. As alternating narrators unfolded the tale, a student ensemble improvised with choreographed movements to capture the essence of the undulations of the too-crowded ship at sea, the misery of laboring in the fields from sunup to sundown, and whips cracking over the slow to make them move faster. Using gesture, stance, and creative movement, students expressed the hardness of the overseer and the slaves' forlorn sense of suffering. The dream of freedom was realized when the ancient magic words were spoken. The weight of oppression lifted as the slaves, one by one, rose into the air and flew, free as a bird, wings flapping, all the way to freedom.

Combining dance and drama with literature enhanced student conceptualization as they expressed ideas, feelings, and sensory impressions symbolically in movement form. Students prepared for the performance of "The People Could Fly" while learning further about theater arts by creating costumes, props, lighting, and scenery. In a celebration of the human spirit, the dance/drama was staged as part of the "Peace by Piece" performance.

The Quest for Peace: The Holocaust

To understand the need for world peace, it is our responsibility to look back upon times when world peace was violated, shattering the lives of millions of people during times of war. Sadly, there are numerous external conflicts over many centuries throughout history, disproving any lessons learned. And still today we live in a world in which fighting has become a way of life for children born to conflicts in places such as the Middle East, Northern Ireland, or Kosovo.

One of the most unbelievable tragedies emerging during wartime was that of the Holocaust of World War II. As teachers, we consciously make our students painfully aware of these horrors of human hatred in the hope that, through their knowledge and active form of remembrance, they will come to have forgiveness and understanding, forging a belief system in the need for maintaining a personal quest for peace.

In the language arts classroom, the Holocaust study involves research and reading a variety of literature, including the novel *Night* by Elie Wiesel. It involves not only the process of acquiring and gaining knowledge, but the act and art of expressing thoughts and feelings about this horrific event. The weight of the unit rests upon students as they seek to explore their response to what they have learned through a variety of project options. Through projects we allow our students to seek multiple ways of expressing themselves, depending upon their strengths, abilities, and interests. Projects are shared by students on Holocaust Remembrance Day in a classroom observance ceremony.

Some students translated this incomprehensible world of the Holocaust into words through poetry surrounded by powerful self-generated images. To express their feelings, students inscribed their poetry on natural materials, which they physically carried with them on the day of the presentation. Symbolizing the philosophical weight of the students' words, poems were etched on barn boards strewn with a zigzag pattern of barbed wire, small blocks of granite, smooth stones, seashells, and driftwood (see Figure 4). Still others worked with origami paper, writing their poems on a carefully folded dove to hang on the classroom peace poetry tree.

Creative movement in the form of dance to peace-themed music was another mode of expression students chose (see Figure 5). Introducing music response journaling into the language arts curriculum already facilitated choreographing dances to songs speaking to prejudice, war, pain, hatred, or the need for peace. Previous discovery of meaning through music enabled students to easily pair up to choreograph a symbolic dance as a tribute to the survivors of the Holocaust. The choice of costumes and movement reflected their grave understanding of this tragic event. Integrating video technology, three boys came in over many lunch periods to create a video montage of documentary clips enhanced with haunting words and images depicting

Figure 4. Holocaust poems were written on slabs of granite, rocks, barn boards, seashells, and smooth stones.

Figure 5. Students perform a solemn dance dedicated to the survivors of the Holocaust.

the Holocaust. Students used contemporary background music of a protest song by the rock group Rage Against the Machine. In their video, hollow-eyed faces of starving concentration camp prisoners, cities obliterated by bombs, steely-eyed soldiers bearing weapons of war, and other images of a war-torn world portrayed the horrors of a ravaged region.

At the Holocaust Day of Remembrance observance, we were deeply moved by the participation and heartfelt response our students displayed. Expressing themselves through the arts, they were able to reflect, do some soul-searching, and represent their knowledge thoughtfully, while expressing their feelings honestly and artistically. It is likely that learning about the Holocaust through self-expression and the arts has made a lasting impact on these students.

The Quest for Peace: The Story of Sadako Sasaki

Students focused on the horrors of nuclear war to learn the important goal of promoting world peace by reading the story *Sadako and the Thousand Paper Cranes,* based on the life of a young girl who developed leukemia as a result of radiation from the bombing of Hiroshima. The story of Sadako inspired a worldwide children's peace movement, resulting in the erection of a statue in her honor in Peace Park, Hiroshima. This story inspired our students to learn origami, the Japanese art of paper folding, as they wrote haiku peace poetry. As part of a celebration of the children's peace movement, our students typed their poems on the wings of paper doves, which they hung suspended from the limbs of peace poetry trees, along with their folded origami cranes. We played traditional Japanese music as the students read their poetry. To further promote the message of peace, we sent their poems to a children's committee in Albuquerque, New Mexico, who were in the process of erecting a sister statue to the one in Hiroshima. The statue sits on the site of the military plant where the atomic bomb dropped on Japan was built. At that dedication ceremony, a choir from Hiroshima sang, and children performed original peace poems and songs. Our students' names were read as ones who had contributed their efforts toward world peace.

The Quest for Peace: Kosovo

Recent political events spurred our students into social action. As the television brought daily images of forlorn refugees suffering in Kosovo, our students found themselves discussing the tragic events and asking, "What can we do to help?" Peace quotes, proverbs, song lyrics, and lines of poetry were generated and used as a springboard for discussion. The quotes were typed up by students, printed on neon paper, laminated, and then cut up into strips to be worn as literary badges proclaiming an underlying belief system in peace and tolerance.

To contribute to a locally organized refugee relief fund, our students began each class period with a fund raising effort. As one musically talented student played the guitar in front of the class, cleverly substituting John Lennon's lyrics from the song, "Oh Yoko," for a war time parody titled "Kosovo," we passed a hat containing the philosophical peace quote strips for a minimum contribution of one dollar per strip. Our one hundred and forty students raised over two hundred dollars to contribute to the local Kosovo Refugee Relief Fund.

Following a school-wide campaign effort, the junior high and high school students initiated a fund raising peace rally at our city park with the goal of raising $10,000 toward the relief fund. The rally brought our school and community together in an organized effort, including activities such as a pig roast, raffle, silent auction, and dance with five local bands contributing their time and talent for the cause.

The conscious focus on the conflict in Kosovo and our fund raising efforts gave students an opportunity to play the role of humanitarians, recognizing our responsibility to act on our belief system. This project taught our students that, by working together and answering to a collective moral responsibility, we can make a positive difference, "Piece by Peace."

Final Thoughts on Peace Education

The universal and constant quest for peace is omnipresent and necessary; therefore, we cannot abandon this consciousness in the classroom. Our commitment as teachers includes relaying the principles of freedom, justice, solidarity, tolerance, peace, and understanding. We do this by creating an environment of social interaction, providing opportunities for collaborative learning, allowing our students to make interdisciplinary connections, and engaging students in meaningful language-based activities through the arts. The varied activities we have presented represent a mere sampling of the infinite possibilities for integrating peace studies within the language arts and reading curriculum. It is our hope that we have created a positive awareness of the vital role the arts can play in stimulating creativity, provoking thought, transcending disciplines, and building bridges between people and cultures in the quest for peace.

In our classrooms, students should be free to celebrate their language and literacy as readers, writers, thinkers, poets, dancers, musicians, artists, and dreamers. It is equally imperative that we as teachers see ourselves as part of a community of intellectuals, poets, writers, creative artists, philosophers, social activists, and humanitarians—each piece contributing to the whole of our collective consciousness. The culture of peace is nonlinear; we are all included within the circle of peace. As educators we should heed the words of Mahatma Gandhi, "You must be the change you wish to see in the world." Day by day, Peace by Piece, we as teachers can act as instruments of change for a better, more peaceful world.

Works Cited

Coerr, Eleanor. *Sadako and the Thousand Paper Cranes.* New York: Putnam, 1977.

Hamilton, Virginia. *The People Could Fly.* New York: Knopf, 1985.

Hughes, Langston. *The Dreamkeeper and Other Poems.* New York: Random, 1960.

Lester, Julius. *To Be a Slave.* New York: Scholastic, 1968.

Malecka, Janina. *The Multicultural Treasury.* Portland: Walch, 1993.

Wiesel, Elie. *Night.* New York: Bantam, 1960.

9 Warriors with Words: Toward a Post-Columbine Writing Curriculum

G. Lynn Nelson

Violence and authentic communication are mutually exclusive.

Rollo May

We teach now in the shadow of the tragedy at Columbine High School. Yes, there were school tragedies before, and there will, I am sadly certain, be others in the future. But the extent and images of Columbine are locked now in our collective memories, congealing our previous vague anxiety and concern into stark images of black-clad youths with guns and other children running, bleeding, dying—images frozen in our minds, not unlike scenes from Vietnam. But this was a school, a school in America, a school not so different from the one in which you and I teach and spend our days.

So what are we to do in our schools, schools no longer immune to reflecting the violence of our culture at large? Yes, we can install metal detectors and surveillance cameras and hire guards and enforce more rigid rules of school conduct. But while such actions may somewhat limit instances of overt violence, they will not prevent it, nor will they reduce the prevalence of lesser forms of violence—rudeness, name-calling, harassment, intimidation, racism, sexism. *And such actions will never treat the source of all such violence.*

There is, however, one powerful place to address the source of violence in our schools and in our culture. It is already there in our schools, waiting to help us toward peace. It is just down the hall in the English department. It is the writing class.

This essay appeared in *English Journal* 89.5 (2000) on pages 42–46.

Initially, this may seem puzzling to some, especially those steeped in the traditional teaching of "Composition" and those who believe the measure of a writing class lies in a state assessment test. But teaching writing is teaching the use of language, and our language greatly determines how we see the world and how we act in the world. Language is both the source of much violence in our society—and its potential cure.

In *The Peaceable Classroom*, Mary Rose O'Reilley poses the question, "Is it possible to teach English so that people stop killing each other?" (9). Over the years, as I have gradually shed my orthodox pedagogical training in "composition," and as I have taught writing in elementary schools and high schools and universities and prisons and churches and senior centers and spiritual retreats, I have watched innumerable writers answer that question with a demonstrable "Yes." So, I have come to believe strongly that we who teach writing can readily become forces for peace in our schools and, by extension, in our society at large.

When I talk about teaching "peace," I am talking about something far deeper than just the absence of violence. I am talking about a gentler and more harmonious way of seeing the world and being in the world that arises from our "care-full" use of worlds. I am talking about a "language of that greater yield" that Linda Hogan sees and knows so much better than I: "We want a language of that different yield. A yield rich as the harvests of earth, a yield that returns us to our own sacredness, to a self-love and respect that will carry out to others" (60).

Those words feel a world away from gun-children spraying bullets and from drive-by shootings and racism and rudeness and disrespect. A world where I want to live. A world all children deserve. A world that can begin in my writing classroom. But to become writing teachers who are, by the fundamental nature of our work, also peace-teachers, we must have personal story at the center of our curriculum.

The Power of Personal Story

I will tell you something about stories,
    [he said]
They aren't just entertainment.
    Don't be fooled.
They are all we have, you see,
  All we have to fight off
    Illness and death.
(Silko, *Ceremony* 2)

If we are to promote peace and well-being (as well as powerful literacy) in our classrooms, we must return to personal story as the primary focus of our writing curriculum. I say "personal story" as opposed to the critical essay or the five-paragraph essay, which are traditionally treated as the be-all and end-all of the act of writing. Not (to paraphrase Seinfeld) that there is anything wrong with those forms, but they will not allay our societal drift toward isolation and alienation; they will not keep us from killing each other. And I say "return" to story because, before the left-brained, reductionist, mechanistic, scientific obsession of the last 400 years or so, story was the primary use of language. Telling our stories is a deep human need, as ancient as the 20,000 year-old drawings on the walls of the caves of Lascaux—a need more denied now than ever before—as witness its aberrant forms on the *Jerry Springer Show,* in the graffiti on the wall down the street, and in the latest drive-by shooting.

And ultimately, of course, as we are finally beginning to realize, everything is story—i.e., whatever form our language takes, it is a tentative description of something, our limited perception moved into a form of language. e.e. cummings's "your little voice / over the wires came leaping" is a story about love. Genesis is a creation story. Einstein's $E = MC^2$ is a story about light. So returning to story does not exclude the critical essay or the five-paragraph essay; it just puts them in place alongside many other ways to tell a story—and allows them to be superseded at the center of our curriculum by the writing of personal story.

Why personal story? Because without that, nothing else matters. Without that, the violence will not stop. Given story, allowed story, all else becomes meaningful. Because the story and the story writer become meaningful. Because the story writer begins to find voice and identity. In an increasingly impersonal society, personal story affords self-affirmation, a modicum of esteem. In *Death of a Salesman,* Willie Loman's wife says of him after his death, "His name was never in the papers . . . he's a human being . . . So attention must be paid . . ." For many students, my writing class may be one of the few remaining places where attention is paid to them. Without that, nothing matters. Witness this segment of a poem posted on the Internet by one of the killers at Columbine High School: "He died from no acclaim / I heard his dying words / As his final breath he gave / He wanted to be taken seriously / Now he's taken to his grave" (unsigned, *Arizona Republic,* A12, 4/21/99). Our stories must be told. Attention must be paid.

Deny me my stories, as the modern, dominant culture does, and I will eventually turn to the language of violence. In our schools, as in society at large, we rush toward computers and the Internet of the

Information Age with open arms, as though toward salvation. We don't seem to understand that we are leaving our hearts, our humanity, our stories further and further behind. We don't seem to understand that our stories *will* get published, one way or another. In a society where our own voices cannot be heard over the shouting of commercials and the blare of entertainment and within a curriculum that values a heartless critical essay over personal story, our stories sit in us, waiting to be told, to be acknowledged. Untold and unacknowledged, they will eventually translate themselves into other languages—languages of abuse and addiction, of suicide and violence. In such a society and in such schools we are literally dying to tell our stories. The tragedy at Columbine High School, like all such violence, was a publishing of untold stories, unheard needs, unhealed hurts.

Consider the irony and the sadness of this sentence from the suicide note of a fifteen-year-old written shortly before he shot himself with his father's pistol: "I'm not in English class so my spelling doesn't have to be perfect" (*The New York Times* 1). I would wish for this young man, as I wish for all young people today, an English classroom and curriculum that, yes, taught him the value of correct spelling, but beyond that afforded him a place to tell his stories and heal himself so that he might not have to kill himself or others.

You may be familiar with an old classroom film (based on a short story by Jean Mizer) called "Cipher in the Snow." It begins with a junior high boy who one morning gets off the school bus, falls into the snow, and dies. An autopsy finds no physical cause for his death. The film gradually reveals that he was a shy boy who came from a broken and dysfunctional home, a boy who had no friends, was labeled "slow" at school, and who was largely ignored by his teachers. In terms of society, he was a nobody, a zero, a cipher. No attention was paid. And so, as one of his teachers observes, "He just turned his face to the wall and died."

Some of our students will do that—dying by overdose, or suicide, or addiction. Others will refuse to be zeros, refuse to have their stories unacknowledged. In one terrible moment, they will force us to acknowledge them, to see them, to pay attention to them. Violence, as Rollo May reminds us, is itself a form of communication, a form turned to when "authentic communication" (245) is denied.

Personal story leads to authentic communication, speaking from our hearts, from our wholeness. But authentic communication demands a listener. So story asks of us another change from the orthodox writing class. It asks us to value listening over grading.

Deep Listening

> *But our stories are caught in our throats. We need someone to listen to*
> *our stuttering, stammering plea to be heard. We need deep listening.*
> (O'Reilley, *Radical Presence* 26).

It has been estimated that the average person in the United States is exposed to over two thousand advertisements per day—and that the average high school graduate has watched over 20,000 hours of television. N. Scott Momaday's unflinching description of the state of language in the dominant society describes it best:

> In the white man's world, language . . . has undergone a process
> of change. The white man takes . . . words and literatures for
> granted, as indeed he must, for nothing in his world is so com-
> monplace. On every side of him there are words by the millions.
> . . . He has diluted and multiplied the word, and words have
> begun to close in upon him. He is sated and insensitive; his
> regard for language—for the Word itself—as an instrument of
> creation has diminished nearly to the point of no return. It may
> be that he will perish by the word. (95)

In a society filled with "words by the millions"—the I-It words of advertising and information and entertainment—we learn not to listen. We grow deaf as well as blind, sinking further into isolation and alienation. Perishing "by the word."

Only the human heart, telling its stories, brings language back to life and taps into the power of the Word "as an instrument of creation." That changes everything—sends the blood of life pumping through our words. Personal story changes language/writing from a mere subject in school into a tool for survival and peace. But the "telling is not all"—there must be another there to listen.

In Sherman Alexie's *Reservation Blues*, Thomas Builds-the-Fire tells stories, trying to survive:

> Thomas thought back to all those stories he had told. He had
> whispered his stories into the ears of drunks passed out behind
> the Trading Post. He had written his stories down on paper and
> mailed them to congressmen and game show hosts. He had
> climbed up trees and told his stories to bird eggs. He had always
> shared his stories with a passive audience . . . (212)

But Thomas needs more than just his stories if he is to survive, if he is not to sink into alcoholism or suicide. He needs someone to listen.

In his treatise on the transformational power of story, *If You Meet the Buddha on the Road, Kill Him*, psychotherapist Sheldon Kopp observes that we must each work at telling our stories if we are to reclaim personal identity. He describes this psychotherapeutic pilgrimage as "an adventure in narration." Story is a "second look at personal history" that can transform a person from one who is "trapped in his past" to one who is "freed by it." But, he notes, the telling is not all. "Along the way, on his pilgrimage, each [person] must have a chance to tell his tale. And, as each [person] tells his tale, there must be another there to listen" (21). To Listen. Not: To Grade. Not: To Psychoanalyze. Not: To Solve. Just: To Listen.

"Deep listening" is Mary Rose O'Reilley's term. We work on it daily in my classroom. Because not only have the I-It words of a consumer culture made us blind, but such words have also made us deaf. We hear, but we do not listen—because most of the words in our world are meaningless I-It words that require no active listening. A curriculum that values story promotes active listening. When we sit in the circle and read our stories, a silence falls upon us, the silence of deep listening. "When this attentive silence opens to me, I gather the courage to speak, to be heard, to hear myself " (O'Reilley 26). Such listening grows out of respect for this process, out of caring for these words, for this human heart that is speaking to us. As one of my Navajo students once observed, "It becomes sacred, like ceremony."

And again, Mary Rose O'Reilley observes:

> One can, I think, listen someone into existence, encourage a stronger self to emerge or a new talent to flourish. Good teachers listen this way, as do terrific grandfathers and similar heroes of the spirit. The critical hearer, by contrast, crushes our spirits . . . (21)

As a composition teacher, I was trained to listen/read critically—and, of course, when I ask my students to write critically and impersonally, there is not much else to do but get out my red pen and go to work. But when we are allowed to write our stories and when someone actually listens to us, powerful language begins to emerge. Voice emerges. Sense of self grows. Maybe that is all we need (could it be so simple?)— all we need to become powerfully literate and to heal ourselves.

So my curriculum for all my writing classes and workshops, from elementary school through graduate school, now looks like this:

> Tell me a story—a small story, a true story (or as true as you can tell it)—a story from your heart, a story from your life. Tell me of a time when you were hurt—or afraid—or tell me of a time when you lost something—your keys, your heart, your mind, your mother or father, your way in the world—or tell me about

a small joy you had today. Tell me a story—and your telling it will change you—and your telling it to me will change me—and such stories will move us both a little closer to the light. Tell me a story—and then tell me another—and I will tell you mine—and we will sit in a circle and listen carefully to each other. And then we will write thank-you notes to each other for gifts given in these stories. And then we will do it again, anew. And we will continue doing this—until everything begins to become properly precious, until we stop killing each other and destroying the Earth—until we care for it all so much that we ache—until we and the world are changed . . .

A few weeks ago at the start of the semester I asked the students in my Native American first year composition class to design a personal logo for their portfolios. They were then to write about their logo in their journals and bring to our circle a personal story arising from their logos. Here is Kyle's story:

Broken Arrows, Broken Hearts: I Will Fight No More

When I was twenty years old, I found myself away from Dinetah,
Away from my mother, away from my home.
I found myself filled with rage, violence, and anger.
It led me to the back of a police car, caged like an animal.

While the handcuffs cut into my wrists, my heart bled, and I
    thought back to when I was eight years old:

I played Cowboys and Indians.
Always the Heroic Cowboy,
I was never Geronimo,
never dreamed of Crazy Horse . . .

While my father was fighting his own war against himself,
40 miles away in the arms of another lover,
I chased my brother, shooting silver bullets out of my forefinger.
When I was out of rounds, he fell and lay on the earth and bled.

As he lay in the dirt, I asked, "Why didn't the Indians fight back?"
Colen smiled, formed two fists, one behind the other,
drew back the bowstring and shot me with a magic arrow.
The cowboy died young.

At the precinct, Officer Carson took off the cuffs without noticing
    that I was bleeding. I formed two fists and shot him with Colen's
    magic arrow. An Indian warrior was born. Officer Carson
    laughed and told me those days were over; then he left to round
    up more Indians.

In the holding cell, I realized I was fighting a war with Geronimo,
    Crazy Horse, and my father.

No, I was behind Basha's in Pinon, Arizona, drinking Kool-Aid
   flavored hairspray.
Or was I in the hospital in Fort Defiance, treating an old Navajo
   man because his grandchild beat him up for ten dollars. Ten
   dollars.
Or I could have been burying my friend Rodney Johnson who
   went AWOL—or was it MIA— and then DOA.
An Indian murdered Rodney. The same killer stole the lives of
   Chris and Fernando. Indians fighting Indians.
Senseless violence. Broken Arrows. Broken Hearts.

Earlier that night, I had waged a war with my brother.
I formed a fist and hammered at his face with clumsy rage.
For many nights before, I dreamed I was fist-fighting my way
   through life.
Some of my opponents were my own people, my brothers and
   sisters.
We all fought for our lives. Communal efforts didn't exist in these
   cages. There were only bloody mouths and bruised hearts,
   clenched fists and clenched teeth.
Then my brother grabbed my shoulders and shook me from
   my dream to exorcise the demon that possessed my body.
   My soul.

I felt like taking my baptismal vows all over again. I was reborn.
Heroic Cowboy turned Young Indian Warrior:
This savage wanted to end this war.
I wanted to be a doctor,
Travel back in time,
And cure Christopher Columbus of the disease that ate his soul.
Exorcise the demon.
I wanted to cook frybread and eat fried potatoes with corn stew
   like Grandpa.
I wanted to kiss my mother on the cheek as she held me close.
I wanted to hug my brother and say,
"I love you."
But most of all, I wanted to fight no more. We all have bled enough
   while fighting with Broken Arrows, Broken Hearts.

For the logo on his portfolio, Kyle had drawn a bow, stretched
taut—but in place of the arrow was a pencil. . . .

To tell our stories and to have someone hear them is a form of
power. Story is gentle power. Story leads away from violence and
toward caring. That is what Linda Hogan is talking about when she
refers to a "language of that different yield"—a yield that first returns
us "to our own sacredness" and from there to a "self-love and respect
that will carry out to others." That is what we need in our schools, in
our world. Peaceful warriors. Warriors with words.

Works Cited

Alexie, Sherman. *Reservation Blues.* New York: Warner Books, 1995.

Hogan, Linda. *Dwellings: A Spiritual History of the Living World.* New York: W. W. Norton & Company, 1995.

"In a Little City Safe from Violence . . ." *New York Times* 147 (1998): 1.

Kopp, Sheldon B. *If You Meet the Buddha on the Road, Kill Him.* New York: Bantam Books, 1973.

May, Rollo. *Power and Innocence: A Search for the Sources of Violence.* New York: W. W. Norton, 1972.

Momaday, N. Scott. *House Made of Dawn.* New York: Harper and Row, 1966.

O'Reilley, Mary Rose. *The Peaceable Classroom.* Portsmouth, NH: Boynton/Cook, 1993.

———. *Radical Presence: Teaching as Contemplative Practice.* Portsmouth, NH: Boynton/Cook, 1998.

Silko, Leslie Marmon. *Ceremony.* New York: Viking Press, 1977.

III Peace and Our Schools

If the Standards Police had observed my class for the first forty minutes that day, I would probably have been arrested. But had they stayed for the second half of that day's class, they would have witnessed a discussion on the nature of art and consciousness the memory of which still sends shivers down my spine.

Marion Wrye, "The Silent Classroom"

10 A Place for Every Student

Sara Dalmas Jonsberg

"At the high school, I was lost all the time." Ruth looked at me earnestly, her reason for leaving school permanently after only two weeks in the ninth grade so clear and so real to her. The memory brought tears to her eyes. She wanted me to understand how she had felt, how isolated she had been, how alone. Of course she left school; why stay in so alien a place, where no one seemed to even notice her or care about her welfare? Great echoing halls. Crowds of young people traveling in clusters, seeming so sure of themselves, sure of where they were going. But she was always lost. And afraid.

How could I not approve of her decision to leave that school? How not applaud the decision she was making now: to earn her GED at an alternative school for pregnant and parenting teens? This was a place where she would not be lost in the crowd or lost in the halls. Here she would succeed, not just because the school was small and the curriculum personalized, but because all-school meetings provided a place for sharing concerns and because the absolute rule of life was mutual respect—among students and between students and teachers. In this school, students helped make decisions about what to study and how to govern the community; they had a sense of being in control of their lives which, happily, often extended to their worlds beyond school. Their little school was a safe and rewarding place to be, a place to grow and become someone new and strong.

My dissertation research focused on a cluster of young women who had left the traditional school before graduation. Though they were "teen mothers" when I met them through their alternative school, most did not leave the high school because they were pregnant. Rather, their reasons for leaving were all variations on Ruth's succinct explanation: "At the high school, I was lost all the time." Again and again, there was that sense of isolation, the look in their eyes that admitted without wanting to speak the words, "I was alone and afraid."

This essay appeared in *English Journal* 89.5 (2000) on pages 27–31.

Dylan Klebold and Eric Harris, the young men of Columbine High School who massacred their peers and themselves last year, must surely have been no less alone and afraid. Their "solution" to their terror was hideous beyond words and violent in a way that the women I wrote about would never have imagined. But the course of action Harris and Klebold chose and the young women's decision to drop out are equally self-destructive; both will have far-reaching—though admittedly far different—consequences. Both stories might have come out differently, I believe, if school were a different kind of place.

No, I don't believe that how we do school is the key to repairing all of our nation's social ills. But, yes, I do believe that we can invent or construct a very different environment from the one that too often prevails within the tall walls and echoing halls. I don't think the visible curriculum matters very much. We could teach peace with any text, even one that seemed to celebrate violence—for we could read against it, as Scholes points out, read critically, questioningly, testing and debunking the premises on which it was built, and come ultimately to a conclusion that favored peace. But truly, more importantly, it is the hidden curriculum such as Giroux discusses that we must attend to if we mean to foster peace in our schools. In other words, as I reiterate to my students in the English methods class, WHAT we teach doesn't matter half so much as HOW we teach it. WHO we are, what values we model, has far more effect on our students than the words they may read or hear.

Two basic premises underlie our traditional way of doing school: competition and conformity. Speaking first of competition, an inherently violent tool for motivation, we have always relied on grades to inspire our students. Do well, get an A; do well, go to the head of the class; do well, and you will be privileged above your peers. Doing well in school is about winning, about beating out the others. By means of a system that relies on tests of individual mastery, we discourage collaboration and mutual support; we encourage separation, solitude, dog-eat-dog, and may the best, or most aggressive, student win. Such a strategy is, at base, a fierce and potentially abusive device for pushing students forward: Those who succeed do so at the expense of others. Couldn't all students in the class earn A's? Why do grades matter anyway? Isn't the important thing a student's sense of self as learning and growing, gathering skills and abilities that will be useful in future attempts to answer questions that matter?

The violence we teachers purvey begins when we ignore or fail to take into account what a student already knows on entering our classrooms. We all know that new learning must build on old, but we too often forget to take the time to assess what is known. Too often we fail to take time, period, time to get to know our students, find out who they are, what they are interested in, what joy and what anguish travels with them in class and out. The violence begins when we are so controlled by a curriculum or by the relentless, bell-ringing, forty-minute schedule that we do not listen to the learner. We do not take the time, as Randy Bomer advises us, to help our students make meaning of their lives, of the swirl of events around them, of the confusions and complexities of the fast-paced, often overwhelming world in which they find themselves.

Requiring conformity has its element of violence as well. It is too easy to join in the chorus of defining what is "normal" in a way that will be hurtful to those not included in our definition. School has traditionally expected all to move at the same pace, age-segregated, ability-segregated, marching in clusters to single drummers. Our reliance on testing is proof of our desire for conformity: We expect that all will have absorbed the same body of information, reached the same level of understanding, by a given date, and we punish those who for some reason have fallen behind. Grading that final exam on *King Lear* or *Hamlet,* we do not stop to consider why some may fail: because they came in knowing less about the subject at hand, with less experience of particular kinds of texts; because they came from a cultural background whose basic assumptions do not match our dominant ones; because they were distracted by some family tragedy or by a personal dilemma. We punish with bad grades and detentions, with removal of privilege and increased isolation, any lack of conformity in the learning process.

I agree with the British theorist Valerie Walkerdine, who has argued that school as we know it "pathologizes"—treats as abnormal—all who are not of the dominant class, that is, women, people of color, the poor. I would add to her list gay students, language minority students, students with any kind of disability, probably also "computer geeks," nascent artists dressed in black, awkward too-tall daydreamers, all students who are for any reason disconnected or in any way special. We emphasize, build a syllabus and activities around a median, a pattern of performance, and then we wonder why our students punish each other just as we do, for failing to be "normal." Why do we too often close our ears to students being cruel to one another? In one recent story which, unlike the Columbine tragedy, drew no national attention, teachers knew, so the papers said, that the student who later fatally stabbed his tormentor was continually being taunted with homophobic epithets. Not one teacher took any action. "Oh, kids are just like that," we too easily say, turning aside because we are afraid of confrontation.

"Oh, cliques are just part of high school," we too easily shrug, wondering ourselves about the lonely and brooding youngster with quadruple ear-piercings. Chris Mercogliano, in an article published on the Internet, "The Teachings of Tragedy," argues that cliques are "a stress response, a symptom." Teenagers make up cliques, he says, because "their schools are hostile, high-pressure environments, places of overcrowded captivity, competition, judgment." Cliques signify a search for security, a sense of belonging; they are a way of overcoming the isolation of being "lost all the time."

Teachers could make sure that there are better ways. So Bomer argues. So I argue with the prospective English teachers in my methods class. Bomer talks about building a sense of "us" in the classroom that includes every single student, no matter how "odd," no matter how "different," no matter how apparently or secretly confused or in distress. How students feel in a classroom seems to me to be much more important than what they "get" there. They'll get plenty if there is safety and trust and respect for their specialness, their uniqueness. We have only so much control anyway over what they will get; they get what they attend to, what seems to matter, what is worthwhile to them, no matter how much we may badger and fuss or threaten with tests and grades.

The curriculum can help: We can read texts that will open our students' minds to all the ways of being that exist in a welcoming world. I do most profoundly wish we could throw out the canon altogether and give teachers the license—by trusting their wisdom and professional judgment—to choose whatever texts seem best for any given group of students. Or let them follow Nancie Atwell's workshop approach to reading: Anything goes, more or less, as long as students are learning and growing and then sharing what has made them bigger and wiser. Learning to respect a wide array of reading tastes would echo and reinforce the mutual and interactive attentiveness of that classroom dedicated to building an "us" that truly includes and indeed celebrates every single student.

In most semesters of my Methods in Teaching English class I invite students to read a poem by Adrienne Rich entitled "Frame." I have two objectives in this exercise, one related to content, one to process; both are relevant to my argument here. I read this poem as a dramatic and passionate persuasian to engagement with oppression both systemic and situational. Over the two-page text, the poet seems to observe a brutality unfold as on a cinema screen. As the story ends, her role as witness is called into question. A sudden change of verb tense in the last five words—"I say I am there"—declares that witness is tireless and ongoing, an act of constant presence. It is a universal obligation to defend the rights, the private spaces, of others. Especially I believe—and I would argue that Rich is also speaking from this perspective—it is an obligation of the privileged in our culture to defend the rights of the less privileged, the "pathologized"—for whites to speak up about racism, men about sexism, straights about homophobia, football players about respect for "geeks," and so on. Maybe, as Rich says elsewhere, such defense of others is "an unnatural act" ("Anger"), but the climate of our future may be transformed if such unnatural acts become commonplace. I do not, of course, say all this to the students; I merely hope that their reading of Rich's text will, to some extent, match mine—that they will draw more or less the same message from the poem.

My second goal in reading "Frame" relates to process: I want the students to experience sharply and anew the fact of varied readings. This poem seems to work particularly well in this regard, though any text that is both accessible and ambiguous in the way that "Frame" is would work equally well. It may happen as we talk together that my reading of the "moral," sketched above, is almost lost in the energy of our classroom differences. But those very differences underscore the message of mutual respect in an immediate and personal way. Students hear and see the poem, freewrite their first response, then talk together in groups about how and what they read. Finally, we exchange reading experiences as a whole group.

Always the students are astonished at the variations in how they see the action and where they focus their attention: Some see two women in the poem (as I do), some see only one; some become engaged with the shifting of typeface from standard to italics, trying to define the poet's reasons, as if understanding this detail will reveal all meaning; some engage the metaphor of "frame" and outline its multiple meanings in the text; some become furious with the apparent inaction of the observer in the poem ("why doesn't she DO something?"); others are puzzled by how the writer can know what the victim is thinking. Some see that the story may be remembered or even invented from a scrap of newspaper account and so are initially frustrated with their more literal-minded peers. Some students indeed may back away in a kind of anxious fear, made hesitant perhaps by personal recollections.

No matter what their own perspectives on the poem, the methods class students come to see—considering such an interchange now more as teachers hearing all than as students defending turf—that we read from where we are. Our ways of seeing are individually shaped by all the events in our lives to date, a different sequence of events for every reader. So we could read text after text to highlight over and over the fact of differences and to celebrate over and over the fun of variety they provide. Even in a classroom where everyone looks more or less alike—de facto segregation being still too much our way of life—differences are present: in the way students think and experience text, in the depth and variety of their feelings, in the array of stories they carry with them that create the pattern of their lives so far.

Respect is born of understanding first the source of a reader's unique vision—seeing that there are reasons behind a particular reading of a text, reasons of experience, gender, religion, cultural, and/or linguistic background. With that introspective understanding comes an awareness that others will read differently, out of their experiences and genders and religious training and so on. In our classrooms, we must read the differences, write the differences, hear and speak the multiplicity. Let every voice be heard. Let there be a place at the discussion table, at the listening table, for every student.

With columnist Ellen Goodman, I grieve at our armed camp answers to violence in the schools—metal detectors, bar-coded ID cards, guards at every entrance and exit. These are surface and simple-minded defenses against something that is profound and complex. One Web site providing a review of the events at Columbine offers a chance for Websurfers to vote for their chosen "cause" for the killings—as if it were so easy to find a single reason. "Who's to blame for the recent spate of school shootings?" the poll inquires and gives five choices: parents, drugs, television violence, permissive gun laws, or the perpetrators. Where in that list are isolation, alienation, disconnection, loneliness, desperation, the complications and terror of living in a fast-paced, materialistic, blood-lustily competitive modern world? And why does our gaze always linger on the victims, refusing compassion or empathy for the perpetrators? So it was in the stabbing tragedy I referred to earlier: Media mourning was only for the boy who was killed. But what, I kept wondering, of that other young life destroyed? Can't we hear his heartache too? Couldn't we have done something to change this story?

From our seats behind big desks in English classrooms around the country, we can't fix the world. But we can step out from behind those desks, as Nancie Atwell advises us, to sit down with our students and talk: We can take the time, as Randy Bomer suggests, to work on "becoming 'us' by investigating . . . the lives of the people in this place" (19) and so "cultivate an awareness of and respect of each other as members of this community" (24). Here in this classroom is at least one spot on the globe where all members are welcome in the fullness of their being, all members are safe from every kind of abuse. *Teaching as a Subversive Activity* was the tantalizing title of Neil Postman and Charles Weingartner's 1960s challenge to more engaging ways of being and doing in the classroom; what could be more deliciously subversive in a violent society—or more healing—than a hidden curriculum of peace?

Works Cited

APBNews.com Poll. www.apbnews.com/resourcecenter/in-depth/columbine.

Atwell, Nancie. *In the Middle: New Understandings about Writing, Reading, and Learning.* 2nd ed. Portsmouth, NH: Heinemann/Boynton Cook, 1998.

Bomer, Randy. *Time for Meaning: Crafting Literate Lives in Middle and High School.* Portsmouth, NH: Heinemann, 1995.

Giroux, Henry. *The Hidden Curriculum and Moral Education: Deception or Discovery?* Berkeley, CA: McCutchan Publishing Company, 1983.

Goodman, Ellen. "Our Schools Needn't Be Quarantined." Newark [NJ] *Star-Ledger,* 31 August 1999: 13.

Mercogliano, Chris. "The Teachings of Tragedy." AERO-The Alternative Education Resources Organization, May 1999. www.edrev.org/archives/tragedy.htm.

Postman, Neil, and Charles Weingartner. *Teaching as a Subversive Activity.* New York: Dell, 1969.

Rich, Adrienne. "The Phenomenology of Anger." *Diving Into the Wreck: Poems 1971–1972.* New York: W. W. Norton, 1973.

———. "Frame." *A Wild Patience Has Taken Me This Far: Poems 1978–1981.* New York: W. W. Norton, 1981.

Scholes, Robert. *Textual Power: Literary Theory and the Teaching of English.* New Haven: Yale UP, 1985.

Walkerdine, Valerie. "On the Regulation of Speaking and Silence: Subjectivity, Class and Gender in Contemporary Schooling." *Schoolgirl Fictions.* London: Verso, 1990.

11 Get Real: Violence in Popular Culture *and* in English Class

Marsha Lee Holmes

Violence has literally invaded school grounds. Since December of 1997, teenagers have injured or killed each other, their teachers, and/or themselves at schools whose towns now reverberate in Americans' daily vocabulary: Paducah, Jonesboro, Springfield, Littleton, Conyers. Early in the fall of 1999, nearer my home in Cullowhee, I listened to a close acquaintance in her second year of teaching tell me about her high school's first drill for mass destruction. During the drill, one of her students claimed, "I'm going to bring a gun to school, and you're the first person I'm going to kill." When she reported the incident, her principal responded, "He probably wasn't serious." Despite the complacency of his comment, she sensed an urgency to do something to decrease the chances of another violent act by a teenager. She couldn't pretend that her life or her students' lives were separate from the classroom anymore. She was experiencing, as Michael Blitz and C. Mark Hurlbert describe it, the concrete reality of her profession: "The teaching of writing is connected to living. Not living in the abstract, but *living*— and *dying*" (1). She wanted to know, How can teachers use occasions or potential occasions of violence as opportunities for peacemaking?

While acts of violence by and against teenagers blur the boundaries between world and school, many educational leaders work hard and fast to reinforce the divisions. Administrators and politicians barricade schools from violence—fencing, gating, frisking, detecting, or otherwise blocking its intrusion. They ban potentially destructive sights and sounds of teenage life—book bags, logos, music, caps, and other popular paraphernalia. They appoint task forces to identify, study, and implement multiple ways to prevent "the real world" from destroying school. Curricula, however, remain largely unchanged: Lesson plans are carried out, essays are written, research papers are done,

---

This essay appeared in *English Journal* 89.5 (2000) on pages 104–110.

standardized tests are taken, state curricular objectives are measured, national averages are compared. Rather than open classroom doors to the world's violence *in order to examine, interpret, and reduce it*, teachers shut them tight, consciously or unconsciously. No wonder. Opening the doors exposes them and their students to emotionally, physically, and spiritually charged violence. At a time of murderous outbursts on school grounds, however, a society can least afford to academically barricade "the real world" from, as students often think of it, "not-real" school. Rather than follow the lead of administrators, politicians, and parents, who fortify the divisions between world and school, teachers need to bridge the two so that students can learn ways to turn from violence toward peacemaking. Teachers need to focus critical inquiry in their classrooms on the subject of violence—in particular, the violence in popular culture.

In my English classroom, the study of violence in popular culture compels critical inquiry. It has worked in first and second semester college composition courses at two universities with distinctly dissimilar student populations, both academically and socioeconomically, and it has suited English departments with relatively strict and relaxed guidelines. At both schools, these first-year students were usually a day or a summer beyond high school, and their interests in entertainment had developed largely during middle and high school years. Like all subject matter, this topic requires taking into account the level of students' social and intellectual maturity. Teachers can design appropriate assignments by involving students in making choices among the genres and examples to be studied. Focusing on entertainment that already receives the most widespread current play in students' lives also can guide lesson plans. Assignments can range from one unit to an entire semester in which the study of violence in popular culture is linked to studies of violence already common in curricula. For instance, students can report on a current violent event or a kind of violence and then review a related fictional representation—a report on a local rape case followed by an analysis of Tori Amos's song "Me and a Gun," or a report on women who stay with abusive partners followed by a review of the movie *Sleeping with the Enemy*.

Teachers also need to articulate lesson plans with the level of administrators' support in mind by explaining the need for this critical inquiry in terms of the school's most pressing administrative or political concerns. A study of violence in popular culture, for instance, serves the principal's desire for students to recognize the harm in today's music; it responds to the gubernatorial task force's call for new ways to combat violence in schools. If a student or situation presents special resistance to the topic, the study can shift to examples of peacemaking in popular culture. I have never been instructed by superiors to abandon this topic of inquiry, although several colleagues have admitted admiration for its poignancy and popularity among students. Occasionally a student has responded with initial, adamant dislike for violence and therefore its study. Talking individually with him or her uncovered an especially keen peacemaking spirit to which I offered kinship. The students appreciated the option to modify the assignment if an overt study of violence proved too troubling, and all but one eased into the inquiry's original design. With sensitive and sensible planning, then, violence in popular culture is a highly versatile topic for students in middle school language arts and high school English classes.

Although other kinds of violence (in war; in gender, racial, or familial relationships; in literature) have provided meaningful study in my classes, violence in popular culture has invigorated the minds and touched the hearts of my students and me with writing, reading, and discussion that we will remember. Its potency arises for two reasons. First, it invites students and teacher to investigate other issues of particular consequence to them—for instance, looking at violence in films can lead to insights about violence in male-female relationships; violence in music can open up dialogue about interracial violence. Secondly, and more crucial to its success, violence in popular culture represents a subject about which *most* students *most* likely bring *most* first-hand knowledge and experience. In other words, it "Begin[s] with where they are," as one of Ann Berthoff's teaching maxims puts it so well (9). Popular culture saturates contemporary times, and students especially stand in its drench. It means something to them and does something for them, even though they do not fully recognize what it means or does. Nor do I. So, I *want* them to study— to analyze and interpret—popular songs, movies, magazines, music and game videos, advertisements, cartoons, Web sites, and whatever else they come up with in order to learn more *through their own words* about violence and thus themselves, others, and the world. I want to learn more, too, about violence, myself, others—especially my students—and my reality.

This investigative approach to subject matter fits Paulo Freire's description of a "problem-posing education" in which students study "generative themes" that shape their "epoch" (*Oppressed* 76–78, 82–85). Freire would call violence a "generative theme" of late twentieth century America because it significantly affects all of us, whether we are conscious of it or not. In this kind of education, learning occurs when world and school are purposefully united rather than divided. "Knowledge emerges only through invention and re-invention," Freire writes, "through the restless, impatient, continuing, hopeful inquiry [that] human beings pursue in the world, with the world, and with each other" (*Oppressed* 53). Furthermore, teachers and students unite because the teacher takes a nonviolent stance of learning alongside, rather than teaching over, students. As Freire formulates it, "Authentic education is not carried on by 'A' *for* 'B' or for 'A' *about* 'B,' but rather by 'A' *with* 'B' . . ." (*Oppressed* 74). My students' ownership of this generative theme attests to Freire's claim.

Regardless of total number of days or weeks dedicated to this inquiry, I sequence activities in three major phases that work especially well because they put students squarely in the act of researching that which they know or *think* they know. The examples and quotes with which I illustrate the sequence are recalled from classes within the last four years. (Because artifacts in popular culture go in and out of favor quickly, they may seem dated to some readers.)

Exploration and Discovery

If logistics or preference has prevented students' involvement in choosing the topic, I do not begin by announcing it, defining violence, and declaring popular culture violent. Rather, I begin by explaining students' invisible influence on my decision-making—me imagining who my students would be, what they would be interested in, what their world is like, what knowledge and experience they would bring to the class, how they could do their best work in it, why they would (or wouldn't) be willing to do their best. Many students begin taking ownership of the topic quickly because its familiarity makes it seem "interesting" or at least "not boring."

Popular culture, I explain, is equated with entertainment. I disallow violence in sports because it is such a large subtheme in and of itself. I focus the inquiry on entertainment's representations of or about violence, rather than the violence itself on playing fields. I also give permission early on for the use of words or mention of acts that do not have common currency in school. It's necessary to say "fuck" *if* we are quoting a lyric that uses that word; it's logical to discuss attitudes toward sexual intercourse if that's what the song is about. I set a tone of responsibility and maturity with which to approach the language and situations of violence. The tone needs my continual reassertion, depending on the group's level of maturity. I also encourage self-governance, asking them to decide, for instance, when it will be okay to use profanity in these discussions and whether there are any topics they want to make off limits.

After establishing this rationale and approach, I lead into exploration and discovery by posing a few questions and then listening to
what they want to know. Often I make notes on the chalkboard (or
electronic overhead or computer screen, depending on location),
recording being my frequent task. "So, what kinds of things make up
popular culture—entertainment—for you?" I might ask. (I can introduce the word "genre" if it seems good timing.) "What are some examples of violence in those kinds of entertainment? What makes these
examples violent?" If I ask opening questions with genuine, intellectual curiosity, we are launched into exploration. If discussion seems
uncommonly slow, I encourage students to get the expedition underway by asking, "What questions do *you* have about violence in popular
culture?" Larger questions are raised sooner rather than later, usually
by them rather than me—questions such as, What *is* violence? What
isn't violent? Is violence *really* a problem?

Nearly immediately, students start responding. One student's
comment instigates another to pose a question. A student might claim,
"It's not violent unless it's physical." Another student queries, "What
about mental abuse?" And from someone else comes a rejoinder, "Yeah,
like girls who are treated like crap by their boyfriends." And another:
"Yeah, or like Julia Roberts in *Sleeping with the Enemy*. She gets it physically *and* mentally." They move back and forth between comments
about violence and examples of it, testing both the general and the particular. Is the movie *Pulp Fiction* funny, or violent, or both? What's
wrong—or right—about laughing at violence? What about the way rap
songs talk about women? Are rappers just in it for the money? What
about the way Tori Amos sings about being raped? If a woman wants to
pose for *Playboy*, what's wrong with that? Is violence ever justified—
like the revenge in *An Eye for an Eye* or *A Time to Kill?*

Throughout this first phase, mutual exploration proceeds from
one class meeting to the next, as I summarize what students have discovered and indicated they want to know next. For instance, after the
inevitable discussion of whether nature or nurture creates violent people, students continue the discussion by bringing in lyrics to a song
that supports their view. In the concrete comparisons of the examples,
they teach themselves a "both-and" answer to the nature-nurture
question. I provide group activities to assist exploration and advance
discovery. For instance, they compile lists of violent acts by genre
(e.g., video games, television soap operas) or by characteristic (e.g.,
men against women or vice-versa; violence with or without weapons).
They look across the lists for similarities or differences. It's a wonderful moment of discovery when a group reports, "There's something

going on here with power in every kind of violence." Or when somebody speculates, "Maybe physical violence isn't always the worst kind." Sometimes we dig deeper into one question they've raised. For instance, we look at violence that might serve a nonviolent purpose, prompted by students who bring in the political lyrics of Pearl Jam or Bruce Springsteen. Or we work extensively with one or two examples—the cartoon images in *The Maxx,* for instance, confiscated by a student from her thirteen-year-old brother's stash. One of the most dramatic results of exploration and discovery occurred during a semester when one small group became captivated by a genre that I hadn't even considered: symbols. To begin their class presentation on contemporary popular symbols, they flung a large, worn Confederate flag over the tables around which we gathered. And then they sat silently for several weighty seconds as we contemplated the symbol's meaning—first relative to our own experience, and then, as the seconds ticked on, relative to the experience of others who may be of a different racial or ethnic group. (I'm so glad that I didn't follow my initial impulse to say "no" to including symbols in our studies; little did I know what they would find.)

In Freirian terms, students and teacher in this phase work between posing problems and identifying examples from their "coded existential situation" (*Oppressed* 86). The goal is for learners to broaden their concept of what violence is and their awareness of its presence in popular culture. They are being introduced to, as Freire puts it, "a critical form of thinking about their world" (*Oppressed* 85). As students discover the luxurious position of choosing among rather than conjuring up interesting things about which to write and read, they also become more informed writers who will compose from a newly educated stance.

Investigation and Interpretation

Studying violence provokes the desire and need to focus on a tangible piece of this enormous, abstract theme and its uncountable concrete examples. Otherwise, learners remain overwhelmed. The turn from the first to second phase in this lesson sequence, from "exploration and discovery" to "investigation and interpretation," begins to occur somewhere in this search for focus. Students tend to begin this phase in one of three ways: They are drawn to a particular example of violence ("I want to study *Cosmopolitan.*"); they are interested in a general kind of violence ("I want to study *Violence against Women.*"); they want to prove a point ("I want to prove that the violence in *Higher Learning* is necessary."). Rather than generate potential thesis statements, I help students pose research questions. Questions, more so than statements, propel them into investigations that can turn up unexpected and richer findings because they won't seek evidence only to support what they already think. As they interpret these findings, they will arrive at a thesis, I promise them. For example, instead of hypothesizing, "*Cosmopolitan* portrays negative images of women," a student asks, "What images of women does *Cosmopolitan* portray?" Instead of "Violence in popular culture encourages males to abuse females," a student queries, "What attitudes toward women do the lyrics of N.W.A. portray?" Rather than "The violence in *Higher Learning* is really nonviolent," an open-ended question asks, "What happens as a result of the violent acts portrayed in the movie *Higher Learning*?"

Focused interests (in other words, manageable topics) naturally lead to questions about how to investigate and interpret: Where do I start? What if I don't find out anything? What if I don't know what to do with what I find out? I remind students that they are researchers now, charting new territory. (And I'm reminded of Shirley Brice Heath's elementary-aged farming researchers whose laboratories included both field and classroom.) I describe the adventurous nature of *primary* research, and I provide tools with which to investigate. For instance, Kenneth Burke's pentad prompts them to identify and relate the who, what, when, where, how, and why of the violence they study. (And I don't even have to say "Burke's pentad" or use his Agent, Act, Agency, Scene, and Purpose lexicon, if that makes the tools less handy.) Secondary research can be incorporated, too, as long as it does not squelch the essential emphasis on students making meaning (as Berthoff philosophizes it) through primary study. No more shifting of words they found in some dusty old book or on a fly-by-night Web site. I explain research as a recursive activity between what researchers observe and what they interpret those observations to mean. I give them the pair of questions—What do I see? What do I make of it?—so that as researchers they move back and forth between data and conclusion as often as necessary (or as often as time allows). Collaboration naturally arises, as students are eager to discuss initial findings: "Do you know what Dr. Dre and Snoop Doggy Dog actually say about women in their song 'Women Ain't Shit'?" As questions about violence become more complex, they want insight and inspiration from fellow investigators: "Why do I hate all the violence in the movie *Goodfellas*, and my boyfriend keeps telling me it's a great movie?"

In this second phase, then, the goal is to move learners from identifying a text, to conducting hands-on research, to interpreting findings.

Students take charge of their own learning, as well as the education of their colleagues and teacher. Hyphenating the nouns *teacher* and *student*, Freire explains the collaborative principle of this active learning. The teacher-student is not "the authority of knowledge" but a person who possesses "his or her own professional authority" (*Oppressed* 54). Student-teachers are "neither utter ignoramuses nor perfect sages [neither developmentally nor academically gifted]; they are only people who are attempting, together, to learn more than they now know" (*Oppressed* 71). As a result, students shape opinion and assumption into interpretations that consider other points of view, provide detailed and relevant evidence, and speak with a voice of authority and insight—characteristics of quality writing and effective peacemaking.

Analysis and Implication

I explain to students that, in this final phase of analysis and implication, they make the intellectual step that most distinguishes the quality and importance of research. Not only have they observed and interpreted, they now look to the future to see what difference their conclusions can make for what we do about violence. "So what?" they need to ask of the results of their studies. So what that, for instance, the premeditated violence, including murder, in *Higher Learning* shows how little white and black teenagers know about each other? So what that *Cosmopolitan* equates beauty with young women who are sickly thin and have extraordinarily large (exposed, augmented) breasts? Near the "end" of their studies, students are at the "beginning" again, imagining change. I provide a pragmatic thinker's prompt: "What difference would it make if . . . ?" What difference would it make if teenage moviegoers paid closer attention to the lessons about violence that movies teach, such as in *Higher Learning*? What difference would it make if *Cosmo* published covers with photos of women who look, say, like the women in this class? A second "So?" question directly links implications to communication: "So who needs to know?" Who needs to know about this research? What do you want them to do, think, or feel after reading your study? How can you present yourself and your findings with authority and credibility to them? Students sense that it's time to write because they now have something worth writing and, therefore, worth reading. As their teacher-reader, I am eager to read what they have to say. Furthermore, reading each other's finished pieces seems natural and necessary.

This final phase is crucial for another reason. Some students express hopelessness as the pervasiveness of violence becomes more real to them: "It seems like there's violence everywhere I turn now; there's no way one person can make a difference." Others cling to cynicism or determinism: "You can't change it; that's the way the world is; it's human nature." They need guidance through disparity toward hope, and this third phase provides opportunity for proposing peaceful solutions to violent problems. Possible solution: Teachers and students watch movies together so that they both understand them more fully. Possible solution: Young women identify role models other than the ones presented in popular magazines marketed to them.

Concluding studies of violence in popular culture with this move toward peace ensures that critical inquiry is active, not passive. Freire calls it "praxis: reflection and action upon the world in order to transform it" (*Oppressed* 33). Without both, school seems "not real" because it does not explicitly connect real learning *about* the real world *with* real readers, or at least real intended readers. Students need to experience their words making a difference *in* their world *to* their fellow inhabitants. Communication, then, the unrestrainable act of sharing thought, makes the final phase in this sequence dynamic.

Bringing violence into the content of English class unites world and school. As a result, school provides a realistic place in which to write and thus occasions genuine communication; students write with developing maturity, and thus their words reshape their world. Because students and teachers are free *and* responsible to be real, they can give each other hope for peacemaking. Hope is why I teach the topic of violence in popular culture. I am heartened each time an image is re-viewed, a word re-heard, a thought re-cast— when one student urges another, "It's important for you to understand that . . ." or a student asserts, "No, Dr. Holmes, that's not the way it is . . ." or a student suggests, "What about from the other person's point of view?" and another replies, "I never thought about it that way before." Here are some more words from these educational moments that, each time recollected, keep me going:

> "I can't watch a movie in the same way I used to any more! I'm driving my friends crazy, too."

> "I didn't realize that those were the words to that song. I won't dance to it any more."

> "I didn't realize that there was so much violence everywhere."

> "What'd you do when you found your little cousin cruising porn on the Net?"

> "What you've got to understand is that there's a big difference in the words 'nigga' and 'nigger'!"

"I've definitely decided that I want to do something with my life to help eliminate some of this violence."

"I took the rebel flag off my bedroom wall after I thought about how offensive some people had said it was."

My students and I have deepened ownership in school work; escalated language's importance in daily living; discovered each other as people who have dreams, fears, and shortcomings; mixed intellectual, emotional, and spiritual responses to the text at hand; stood face-to-face with evidence of racism and sexism in late twentieth century America, even when some of us wanted to deny its existence; discussed topics that included profanity, pornography, and brutality; laughed, cried, fumed, and blushed together.

Students and teachers of English have yearned chronically for something worth writing and reading about. Students want to write and read about what they're interested in. Teachers want them to be interested in what they assign for writing and reading. Occasionally preferences coincide, but more often not. In the search for a mutually satisfactory balance of interest, intellect, and importance, teachers worry about just how much worse students' writing and reading will become. Students wonder how much more boring teachers' assignments can be. The search will prove endless unless teachers open the doors of school in order to query the world.

"Hope as an ontological need," Freire asserts, "demands an anchoring in practice . . . Just to hope is to hope in vain" (*Hope* 9). He warns teachers about hopeless journeys: "One of the tasks of a progressive educator . . . is to unveil opportunities for hope, no matter what the obstacles may be. After all, without hope there is little we can do" (9). For Freire and thousands of other teachers around the globe, obstacles to unveiling hope include acts of physical, psychological, and spiritual violence. Hanging, beating, and exile fortunately are not common attacks on American teachers, although events in Kentucky, Arkansas, Oregon, Colorado, Georgia, and perhaps next in North Carolina indicate a teacher's work is increasingly life-threatening. My nearby teaching acquaintance told me about the mass destruction drill after reading a draft of this essay. In discussing the feasibility of such a study in her high school classroom, she voiced concerns about students' immaturity and administrators' lack of insight and support. When I asked her which obstacle was the most obstructive and difficult to overcome, she immediately replied, "administrators." For many teachers, lack of legislative insight and administrative support present the greatest challenges to peacemaking pedagogy. What motivates them to move forward given these conditions? I suspect the same emotions that compelled Freire, who wrote *The Pedagogy of Hope* "in rage and love, without which there is no hope" (*Hope* 10). Rage against a violent world; rage against decisions that thwart real learning; love for whatever and whoever keep them walking back into the classroom and evolving teaching methods every day, every year with unflinching persistence. Like Blitz and Hurlbert, these teachers recognize that "What is at stake in teaching is the people in the room" (2). They, too, cannot "imagine why anyone would choose teaching as a profession unless he or she had a notion that educating people is somehow involved in making better neighborhoods, better communities, a better world" (2).

How can teachers use occasions or potential occasions of violence as opportunities for peacemaking? Each teacher with each group of students within each classroom within each school, system, and state needs to reflect on and discuss with fellow educators appropriate ways to study violence as a way of making peace. In her book, *The Peaceable Classroom*, Mary Rose O'Reilley revisits a provocative question posed by one of her graduate professors: "Is it possible to teach English so that people stop killing each other?" (9). Like O'Reilley, who cannot ignore the possibility of "Yes," I approach an English class as a peacemaking opportunity. My students know that I see our collaborative endeavors as important because, in addition to inquiries like the one I've sketched here, I tell them so through course policies and requirements, as well as personal demeanor. Sometimes I quake at the violence they bring to our studies, but I tremble more to think that I might remain oblivious to these influences on their lives and that they might remain ill-prepared to reckon with them.

Works Cited

Berthoff, Ann E. *The Making of Meaning: Metaphors, Models, and Maxims for Writing Teachers.* Upper Montclair, NJ: Boynton/Cook, 1981.

Blitz, Michael, and C. Mark Hurlbert. *Letters for the Living: Teaching Writing in a Violent Age.* Urbana: NCTE, 1998.

Burke, Kenneth. *A Grammar of Motives.* Berkeley: University of California Press, 1945.

Freire, Paulo. *Pedagogy of Hope: Reliving Pedagogy of the Oppressed.* New York: Continuum, 1996.

———. *Pedagogy of the Oppressed.* Revised ed. New York: Continuum, 1997.

Heath, Shirley Brice. *Ways with Words: Language, Life and Work in Communities and Classrooms.* Cambridge UP, 1983.

O'Reilley, Mary Rose. *The Peaceable Classroom.* Portsmouth, NH: Boynton/Cook, 1993.

12 "Who You Dissin', Dude?" At-Risk Students Learn Assertive Communication Skills

Barbara R. Cangelosi

It's 6:00 p.m. on a May evening; I'm pumping gas at the self-service island while a man in his thirties fills his truck's tank. We make eye contact and smile innocuously. I finish, pay inside, and continue on my way four miles north to the mall. I get out of my car there and see this same man pull up alongside me, blocking my way to the mall entrance. Through his open truck window he says, "I just had to follow you to ask you your name," to which I respond, while briskly walking around him toward the relative safety of the crowded mall, "No, you don't," smiling stringently as I take in his face, truck type, and license and calculate the number of steps left to get inside—all along wondering whether or not his hidden hand is on a gun. I'm a forty-seven-year-old mother to three grown daughters. I think, "What would one of them have done had it happened to them?" Elise, thirty, would have torn him a new orifice (or two) while lambasting his gross impertinence and crudeness, unless he had looked like Brad Pitt, which terrifies me much more. Emmy, twenty, would have blanched and hyperventilated her way into the mall, seething at his rudeness and vulgarity—an old man like that behaving as if he were even in the running with a twenty year old! Jess, eighteen, would have turned beet red and stammered in the parking lot while she spelled her name for him, wanting desperately to get away but feeling trapped by her own awkwardness and discomfort.

I'm furious at the guy. Should I have lectured him at length about the inappropriateness of his acts and then called the police?

This essay appeared in *English Journal* 89.5 (2000) on pages 111–118.

Instead, I'd shined him on (as we used to say in the 70s). I effectively took the wind out of his sails, unruffledly shrugged off his advances, and left him, I believe, unoffended, unangered, but also unanswered. I took control of the situation without costing him a loss of respect, without venting a preachy put-down or further antagonizing a possibly dangerous situation.

On the campus of the alternative high school for at-risk students where I teach English, I've often observed students taunting one another—leaving some feeling victimized with threatened egos and diminished psyches. I've successfully (sometimes) hovered and smiled the group into an ending or remission of conflict. In my English classroom, students' safety from such unpleasant encounters is of paramount concern, and I demand strict adherence to appropriate verbal exchanges dealing with the business of the class curriculum at hand. I believe students welcome this strictness as a respite from personal hostilities. We focus on content rather than last weekend's drug bust or love fest. But am I helping these students prepare for the bumps and jostles of their real worlds—like the creepy, scary surprises encountered in mall parking lots? How quickly might my recent scenario have escalated had I not responded in a nonthreatening, face-saving way for him?

Since teens, especially at-risk students, often communicate inappropriately, assertive communication needs to supplant the typical passive-aggressive cycle. They want to be treated with respect but don't necessarily show respect to authority because they don't know how to do it without losing face. My years of experience teaching these students tells me that, to them, showing respect to authority is often confused with "kissing up," fawning favor. The fear of embarrassment and the loss of peer approval is immense. Consequently, the discomfort with their awkwardness and their desire to be one of the pack who is not to be singled out for any reason work against rational, calm interactions. That is not to say that most teens don't deal appropriately despite all these same factors, but my experience with at-risk students tells me they need instruction in assertive communication.

So I'm perceptive. I identify this need in the students. But there's a glitch: I also observe that there's immediate and immense gratification in students' aggressive behavior—whether it's verbal or physical. It's very cathartic to deck that kid who's irritating, or shove her into the wall, or cuss him out if he's a problem; these kids are impulsive. It's the "act now, think later" syndrome. When they do think about it later, it's almost always as a victim: "I couldn't help it!" "She made me so mad!" "It's his fault!" Deflect responsibility; deny choice.

I begin to reflect on all these observations and this knowledge as I assess the students' needs and decide to use this power/control issue as it relates to respect as a guideline for a unit of instruction. I decide to use the drawbacks or negative side effects as the "hook" to engage the students and get them to buy into assertive communication. The draw-backs and negative side effects include jail time, lawsuits, escalation of violence in retaliations, and increased likelihood of injury to them-selves. I "sell" assertive communication to them as the mode of choice because it gives them power and control over a situation without the negative consequences. Punching somebody out is very satisfying at the moment, but the cost is too high—don't put yourself in a situation where it "costs" you. Assertive communication enables you to get what you need and take control without the problems of aggressive communication. Passive communication is ineffective also because the message does not get across due to fear and/or intimidation by others. It is characterized by whining, blaming, and labeling others. Assertive communication, on the other hand, is characterized by open, direct, honest communication without sounding intimidating or being intimi-dated by others. It empowers students appropriately to address issues of manipulation by others and stick to their opinions in the face of opposition. So, to teach my students assertive communication as a means of empowerment, a way of taking control and staying in charge of situations, I developed a four-week unit.

Organizing the Content and Implementing the Curriculum

I introduce the unit with a personal values inventory (see Figure 1) that I devised in anticipation of the unit's content: general communication information, the *Time* magazine article the students will be reading on emotional intelligence (EQ), the video they will watch about barriers and builders in communication, issues of personal responsibility, and issues of power and control. The inventory is a list of fifteen statements to which students respond by circling SA (strongly agree), AS (agree somewhat), DS (disagree somewhat), or SD (strongly disagree). After they silently respond individually, I call upon the class to walk with their inventories to the corner of the classroom that has the sign match-ing their answer for statement #1 (i.e., either "SA," "AS," "DS," or "SD"). I direct individuals to explain the reasoning behind their choic-es and, before continuing on to the next statement, ask individuals in an opposite corner to paraphrase the previous response and then give their points of view. The inventory now becomes a listening exercise, and listening is a key to respect in communication.

1. I feel important in school.	SD	SA	DS	AS
2. My parents (siblings/girlfriend/boyfriend) can make me so mad that I hit them.	SD	SA	DS	AS
3. If I saw a homeless person on the street corner begging for food, I would ignore him.	SD	SA	DS	AS
4. If I'm at work and my boss screams at me for arriving late again, I would scream back at the boss in my own defense.	SD	SA	DS	AS
5. If an underage drunk driver kills a pedestrian, the driver's parents should be held legally responsible and should be successfully sued by the deceased's surviving family for a reasonable amount of money.	SD	SA	DS	AS

Figure 1. Five items from personal values inventory.

I introduce them to the concept of control theory through William Glasser's book, *The Quality School,* in which he states:

> . . . control theory contends that all human beings are born with five basic needs built into their genetic structure: survival, love, power, fun and freedom. All of our lives we must attempt to live in a way that will best satisfy one or more of these needs. Control theory is a descriptive term because we try to control our own behavior so that we choose to do the most need-satisfying thing we can do at the time. (43–44)

Exposing the students to control as an issue in the outside world (e.g., in psychology) stresses its importance and relevance to them. Most of them work jobs, and many have been through counseling, therapy, and/or drug rehab. But they are not as adept as they should be at reading social situations. Since communication is overwhelmingly nonverbal (H. A. Smith 466), students need to get better at reading between the lines, inferring from words, tone, and body language what really is being communicated; thus, the students engage in a series of lessons and activities to build these skills.

To illustrate the significance of nonverbal cuing in effective communication, a series of activities demonstrate how difficult it is to be precise and accurate when certain aspects of communication are removed or thwarted. Examples include a peanut butter sandwich demonstration and an action-out-of-context transparency activity. In the former, one student goes to the front of the room, facing away from the class and blindfolded. Unbeknownst to this person, I place a loaf of bread, a jar of peanut butter, and a knife on a desktop in the rear of the room. I then direct the student to describe to me how to make a peanut butter sandwich, while signaling the rest of the class to silence. The student begins, "Well, I don't know—you get a piece of bread—" So I rip into the plastic bag of bread and tear off a two-inch piece "—and put some peanut butter on it." So I stab the knife through the plastic peanut butter jar and smear a gob on the two-inch piece of bread. "Then you get another piece of bread and put it on top of the other one, and you've got a sandwich." I tear off another two-inch piece of bread, stack it over the other one, and invite the student to remove the blindfold and eat the delectable sandwich as I stand nearby sticky-fisted. Everybody hoots—mostly because I am such a mess! Then we discuss the lessons of this demonstration: Be careful with the assumptions you make in communication, be precise in your language use, and seek feedback to correct inaccurate information (e.g., if the student were able to see me tear off the two-inch piece of bread, the directions probably would be corrected by saying precisely, "one whole slice of bread").

The action-out-of-context series consists of ten to twelve overhead transparencies onto which have been traced individual photos, with only the body outlines of figures in the photograph and all background context removed (Figure 2).

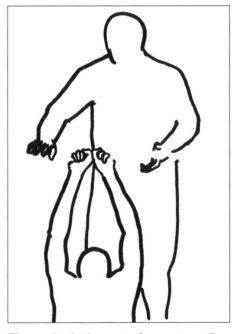

Figure 2. Action-out-of-context outline.

Figure 3. Action-out-of-context photo. Seated: Casey Cangelosi; standing; Kasey Mitchell. Photo by Donna Karchner.

The outlines are purposely kept gender-neutral, focusing on the body language. Students view each transparency and silently write down three logical guesses for each, reflecting what they think the person(s) could be doing given that body language: positions of heads, arms, legs, and torsos. No facial expressions are shown and clothing is not detailed. I ask students to consider whether their answers would vary based on the gender of the person in the drawings. After they view all transparencies, students share their responses and the reasoning behind them. The class is treated to a wide variety of answers. Then I display the actual photos, emphasizing that there are no right or wrong answers. (Figure 3 is the photo corresponding to Figure 2.)

It is their use of logical application that is key. This activity reveals that meaning is shaped by our interpretation and past experiences. Assertive communication requires that students learn to be cautious in making assumptions about others, to seek feedback that they're getting the message across, to be precise in their language use, and to acknowledge that we are individuals with different experiences that shape our interpretation of the world around us.

Building on the success of the students' respectful interactions in the earlier activities, I ask them to read Gibbs's article "The EQ Factor" aloud together and complete a comprehensive study guide to help them organize its content. The phrase "emotional intelligence" was coined by psychologists Peter Salovey and John Mayer to describe qualities like understanding one's own feelings, empathy for the feelings of others, and "the regulation of emotion in a way that enhances living" (Gibbs 62). Gibbs quotes Daniel Goleman from his best-selling book, *Emotional Intelligence*. "When it comes to predicting people's success, brainpower as measured by IQ and standardized achievement tests may actually matter less than the qualities of mind once thought of as 'character'" (Gibbs 62). The article cautions:

> . . . EQ is not the opposite of IQ . . . [but may be used to explain] how one's ability to handle stress, for instance, affects the ability to concentrate and put intelligence to use . . . Perhaps the most visible emotional skills, the ones we recognize most readily, are the "people skills" like empathy, graciousness, and the ability to read a social situation. Researchers believe that about 90% of emotional communication is nonverbal. (63–65)

Randy, one of my students, wrote:

> The aspects of EQ [are something] I had thought about a lot this year. It was nice to know that someone wrote a book about it. I think that these aspects of life make life. It is when people become people and not just emotionally sensitive animals. It would be a nice society if everyone used the process of looking at their emotions and used them to better their own existence instead of letting their emotions control it. If you use assertiveness, it makes you have a better day.

To provide students with actual conversational tools for assertive communication, the class views H. Stephen Glenn's video "Empowering Others" in which communication barriers and builders are introduced and discussed. According to Glenn, people need to supplant the barriers they use in communications with the following builders instead:

1. assuming	→	1. checking it out
2. rescuing	→	2. exploring
3. directing	→	3. encouraging
4. expecting	→	4. celebrating
5. adultism	→	5. respecting

Students apply these techniques to original samples they write. (See Rinh's example in Figure 4.)

Material from the book *Yes, I Can Say No* by Manuel J. Smith is presented as a model for assertiveness strategies to implement in the

Barriers	Builders
1. ASSUMING	1. CHECKING IT OUT
Mom: You broke the window; I can't believe you broke the window! Do you even have a brain in your head? How could you do that?	Mom: I noticed that the window is broken. Do you know what happened?
2. RESCUING	2. EXPLORING
Teacher: You idiot! I can't believe you dropped the books all over the floor! Get out of here, so I can clean it up. How could you have done that?	Teacher: I see the way you were carrying the books didn't work. Can you think of a better way to carry them?
3. DIRECTING	3. ENCOURAGING
Mom: Clean up your clothes, mop the floor, pick up the garbage, do the dishes . . .	Mom: I'm expecting company a little later on. Do you think you could help me with tidying up?
4. EXPECTING	4. CELEBRATING
Mom: Why didn't you vacuum out the car and wash it like I told you to? You are so incompetent.	Mom: Thank you very much for cleaning all of the garbage out of the car. That was very nice of you.
5. ADULTISM	5. RESPECTING
Boss: Why haven't you been producing as much as you're supposed to? Damn it! Why is that so hard for you?	Boss: I've noticed that your productivity has been slipping. Is there a reason for that?

Figure 4. Barriers and builders: Student sample.

face of peer pressure and/or social criticism. Students learn techniques such as fogging, negative assertion, negative inquiry, workable compromise, positive assertion, broken record, and self-disclosure and apply them to sample dialogues between two fictional characters from *Ordinary People* and *I Know Why the Caged Bird Sings*, which the students rewrite in assertive style via Smith's strategies. The seven strategies studied are as follows:

1. Fogging: repeating and/or agreeing with a criticism (e.g., "You are stupid." "I sure could be smarter.")

2. Negative assertion: admitting a mistake (e.g., "Why are you so late?" "I know I'm late.")

3. Negative inquiry: questioning a criticism to exhaust the tormentor (e.g., "You are stupid." "What is it about me that is stupid?")

4. Self-disclosure: revealing your own personal feelings (e.g., "You're late again!" "I'm sorry; my car wouldn't start.")

5. Positive assertion: agreeing with a criticism using phrases like "Yes," "You're right," "You've got my number all right!" (e.g., "You are ugly." "You're right. I am ugly.")

6. Workable compromise: coming up with a middle ground proposal to resolve a problem or conflict (e.g., "You're late again! What's wrong with you? Can't you just get to work on time?" "What if I call you next time when I know I'm going to be late?")

7. Broken record: repeating your opinion in the face of opposition or manipulation (e.g., "I want to borrow your sweater. I have let you borrow my clothes before." "You have let me borrow your clothes before, but I'm not lending you my sweater.")

Following is a student sample of a revised excerpted conversation from *Ordinary People:*

Coach: Jarrett, you gotta be kidding me. I don't get it. I excuse you from practice twice a week so you can see some shrink. I work with you every damn night *at your convenience;* now what the hell more am I supposed to be doing for you?

Conrad: Nothing. I don't appreciate your derogatory use of the word shrink. I'm seeing a psychiatrist. (SELF-DISCLOSURE)

Coach: A bright kid like you with everything going for him. I don't get it. Why do you want to keep messing up your life?

Conrad: You're right, I have messed up before. What is it about my life you think I keep messing up now? (POSITIVE ASSERTION, NEGATIVE ASSERTION, NEGATIVE INQUIRY)

Coach: Well, you're quitting the team, you stupid jerk!

Conrad: I am a stupid jerk, but I don't think it'll mess up my life if I stop swimming. (FOGGING)

Coach: Okay, this is it. You're a big kid now and actions have consequences. You're messing up big time, but I'm not taking you back. You remember that.

Conrad: I'll remember, but I don't think it'll mess up my life if I stop swimming. (BROKEN RECORD)

Coach: You quit the swim team and you're seeing a shrink . . . I call that messing up your life.

Conrad: I'll tell you what'll straighten out this mess: I quit the swim team and *you* start seeing a psychiatrist for your complete lack of understanding and compassion! (WORKABLE COMPROMISE)

The students' final writing assignment for this unit requires them to create at least thirty lines of original dialogue using assertive communication in the workplace scenario. Students can incorporate any of H. Stephen Glenn's barriers and builders techniques. Their original assertiveness in the workplace scenes are performed in front of the whole class. For example, one student, Trina, wrote "Employee Learns How to Deal with Angry Bosses." (The employer and manager are two different people here.):

Employer: Work faster, you good-for-nothing employee! You're working too slow.

Employee: Yes, I know I'm working a little slow today. (NEGATIVE ASSERTION)

Employer: Well, speed it up or you'll be finding yourself on the unemployment line!

Employee: I understand; I will snap out of my laziness. (SELF-DISCLOSURE)

Employer: Well, that makes me feel lots better, let me tell you.

Employee: I'm sure you have better things to do than to stand here and tell me to hurry up. I will speed up my pace. (NEGATIVE ASSERTION, FOGGING)

Employer: Stop feeding me B.S. You are the worst and slowest worker I've ever hired.

Employee: I'm sorry you feel that way, but what is it that makes you look at me so low? (SELF-DISCLOSURE, NEGATIVE INQUIRY)

Employer: Because you are a lazy employee.

Employee: I've changed; I just don't know why I'm being so slow today.

Employer: Just speed up your pace.

Employee: Yes, sir.

Manager: I told you to get to work.

Employee: You're right I should have listened to you. (FOGGING)

Manager: What can I do to make you work so I don't get in trouble?

Employee: You can try to get me a raise so I can work and it will be worth my while. (WORKABLE COMPROMISE)

Manager: No way! You don't deserve a raise!

Employee: If you get me a raise, I will work harder. (BROKEN RECORD, WORKABLE COMPROMISE)

Manager: I will do anything else, but you're not getting the raise.

Employee: I'm telling you, get me the raise and I will become a fast worker and you won't get in trouble. (BROKEN RECORD, WORKABLE COMPROMISE)

Manager: No way, now drop it.

Co-Worker: I heard that the manager came down hard on you.

Employee: Yes, I feel really miserable right now. (SELF-DISCLOSURE)

Co-Worker: I really need a favor from you, and that is I need someone to work for me on Saturday.

Employee: Don't look at me, I'm busy that night.

Co-Worker: Please . . . I will forever be in your debt.

Employee: No, I can't.

Co-Worker: Fine!

Employee: Why don't you try someone else, and I'll work for you some other time. (WORKABLE COMPROMISE)

Co-Worker: Well, OK, thanks for your help.

Employee: Anytime.

On the unit test students have access to all their notes and resources. Afterwards, they reflect on the unit in an evaluation questionnaire. Trina's written comment typifies the reflections of a significant segment of the class: "I feel that my attitude has changed. I feel that I don't lose my temper as fast and using these strategies keeps me calm. But it makes the other person upset because I'm not fighting back." Kevin stated, "I believe it has helped me out a little. Most of these things I already knew about except EQ. I am taking a lesson in anger management because I am aggressive most of the time or passive some of the time. I am not really assertive but have both of the others. I think if I were to become assertive it would help me out a lot." Jeff stated, "Now I often find myself using fogging, negative inquiry, and the others in conversations. I find myself talking to my mother in a more respecting way."

Conclusions

Feedback from students throughout the unit, on the tests, and in their written evaluations of the unit was very positive and enthusiastic. Overall, they viewed the content as helpful and necessary; several students remarked how cool it was that we were learning about this sort of personally useful and practical communication that everyone needs daily to cope with others. Approaching the unit from the personal safety zone of the initial SA/AS/DS/SD inventory was productive because it opened the students to a tone of respect for their individual differences and presented a model for listening to those differences appropriately. Glasser's control theory provided an appropriate vehicle for the students' embracing assertiveness because of his basic needs component, which gave them a handle on the psychology behind the motivations for their choices and presented the notion that we are all responsible for our own decisions—nobody makes us do or say anything we haven't decided to do or say.

The idea of control as a means of gaining respect from others being the basis of assertiveness caused students to pause and think about how they themselves communicate and interact at home, at school, and in their social circles. Prior experiences in which they were manipulated by others' aggressive or passive communications hooked students into the unit. The EQ article enlightened students to the concept of emotional intelligence and addressed the very real need that exists in the work world for employees with people skills. Activities like the action-out-of-context transparencies reinforced the need for assertive communication skills and precision in language. The barriers and builders presented by H. Stephen Glenn's video, *Empowering Others,* and the assertive response models from Manuel J. Smith's book, *Yes, I Can Say No,* equipped the class with strategies for putting assertiveness into practice. Students worked assiduously on their writing assignments, shared examples and ideas with each other, and frequently checked with me for accuracy in their original scripts.

I plan to incorporate support material such as CD-ROMs on this or related topics for use as enrichment and reinforcement of the unit objectives. The number of assertiveness strategy models would be expanded to include mirroring and other techniques Smith used in his book. In subsequent school terms, we will explore the theme of anger management in two young adult novels, *Iceman* by Chris Lynch and *Ironman* by Chris Crutcher, for which the previous implementation of assertive communication strategies lays a solid foundation. We will examine sample scenarios from the novels for communication styles and analyze them according to the assertiveness standards already studied.

Collaborating with a vocational teacher at the mainstream high school, I'm investigating the idea of the at-risk students peer-teaching this same unit to a Teen Living and Life Skills class there. Both groups of students seem eager and enthusiastic about this cooperative project. You really know you've learned something if you can teach it to someone else.

Works Cited

Empowering Others. Videotape. Narr. H. Stephen Glenn. Sunrise Productions, 1990. 82 min.

Gibbs, Nancy. "The EQ Factor." *Time* 146 October 1995: 60–68.

Glasser, William. *The Quality School.* New York: Harper Perennial, 1992.

Simon, Sidney, Leland Howe, and Howard Kirschenbaum. *Values Clarification.* New York: Hart Publishing, 1978.

Smith, H. A. "Nonverbal Communication." *The International Encyclopedia of Teaching and Teacher Education.* Ed. Michael J. Dunkin. Oxford: Pergamon Press, 1987. 466–76.

Smith, Manuel J. *Yes, I Can Say No.* New York: Arbor House, 1986.

13 The Teaching of Anti-Violence Strategies within the English Curriculum

Rosemarie Coghlan

Curriculum of Peace? Oh, no, I bristled. What effect would these three words have on the English III reading list? Were English teachers again going to have to confront more efforts to censor reading materials in their classrooms? I had weathered attacks on Salinger and Morrison. But would I now be accused of promoting violence if I taught Golding's *Lord of the Flies*?

Still, the words "curriculum of peace" made me pause. Did my students who daily have to ward off the violence that invades their homes through their newspapers, television shows, music, and movies, if not in actual violent acts, really need to envision Macduff triumphantly carrying Macbeth's head onto the stage at the end of *Macbeth?* Perhaps we could just as well read a different Shakespearean play? But which one is violence-free? And would my students be less prepared for college if they never met Conrad's Kurtz? Of course not. I might as well delete *Beowulf* from the British Lit curriculum as well. It is, after all, *sooo* hard to interest the females in the class in the troubles caused by a carnivorous monster. Of course, that meant Dickens's *A Tale of Two Cities* would have to go . . . and Chaucer's "The Pardoner's Tale" . . . and Bolt's *A Man for All Seasons* . . . and Bronte's *Wuthering Heights.* But what was left? And aren't the verbal comments of Austen's Wickham in *Pride and Prejudice* just as violent? Could we spend the entire year discussing "Tintern Abbey"? Perhaps the better question is, "Should we?"

As I began to assume my defensive mode in preparation for attack, I recalled the recent research on violence in America's schools: "About 21 percent of all public high schools and 19 percent of all public middle schools reported at least one serious violent crime to the police

---

This essay appeared in *English Journal* 89.5 (2000) on pages 84–89.

or other law enforcement representatives" during the 1996–1997 school year (U.S. Department of Education 10). And recent news events have taught my fellow colleagues in suburban middle class schools that "no school is immune to the potential of extreme violence" (Wolfe 51). The need to do something is apparent and urgent.

But school administrators have been addressing this concern for years. However, to date, most of the response by school administrators to violence in their schools has been reactive. Student discipline codes have been rewritten to convey a philosophy of intolerance for violent behavior, and students have been quickly suspended, and even expelled, for threats of violence. School budgets, already stretched to the seams for technology expenses, have reallocated precious funds for security guards and metal detectors. While these interventions are necessary, "such measures skim the surface of violence prevention and may instill a false sense of security" (Halford 1).

"Experts" outside of the schools have also attempted to confront this deadly issue. Federal agencies have produced written guides for school administrators. Titles such as *Early Warning, Timely Response: A Guide to Safe Schools; Preventing Youth Hate Crimes: A Manual for Communities;* and *Creating Safe and Drug-Free Schools: An Action Guide* are readily available over the Internet. Educational publishing houses have also produced "Peace Curricula" with titles such as *First Step to Success, The Anger Coping Program, Positive Adolescent Choices Training (PACT),* and *Promoting Alternative Thinking Strategies* (*PATHS*).

Research on these programs, which aim to teach social skills, is scant, yet early studies indicate some progress on violence prevention when such programs are implemented conscientiously (Walker 3). However, these various guidelines and programs frequently fail because teachers do not have the time or training to implement their directives, often complaining about the inability to fit "the program into an already overcrowded teaching schedule" (Elias, et al. 17).

Even if teachers did implement these programs, Eric Schaps points to another concern: He insists that "the dimensions of social, intellectual, and ethical development are interconnected in children. [Schools] can't do surgical strikes on intellectual growth" (qtd. in Halford 3). Violence prevention strategies will only work "when they are congruent with teaching and learning overall" (Halford 3). In other words, violence prevention programs cannot be conducted in isolation, as entities in themselves. To be effective, they must be fully integrated into the student's program of study.

Gradually, then, the phrase "curriculum of peace" assumed a new meaning for me. I sighed in relief as I realized that these words would not mean that my students would never meet Macbeth or Kurtz. Our students, unfortunately, do live in a violent world, if not one exactly similar to those of these literary characters. We, as English teachers, need to teach our students how to live in it, and, more importantly, how to work to improve it. The English classroom provides a fitting place to integrate anti-violence teaching into the academic curriculum. It readily offers opportunities to teach conflict resolution strategies, instill respect for cultural diversity, provide an atmosphere for cooperative learning while acknowledging controversy, and heighten personalization, empathy, and respect—all factors that, violence prevention programs indicate, contribute to the reduction of violence.

First, teaching conflict resolution skills is one way the school, and especially the English teacher, can be proactive in stemming the rising violence in society. Programs such as *First Steps* aim to teach students how to resolve differences peacefully. Aleta Meyer and Wendy Northup have conducted a research study on the effect of role-playing, which is the core of a violence prevention program entitled *Responding in Peaceful and Positive Ways* (RIPP). In a 1995–96 study, these researchers found that RIPP participants "reported significantly fewer violence-related injuries . . . [developed] more positive changes in self esteem, and . . . use[d] resources such as peer mediation at a higher rate than did non-participants" (33). Dean Walker states that, although research information about the effectiveness of these programs is "limited . . . data are accumulating that show peer conflict-resolution programs reduce discipline referrals; improve the school climate; and increase self-esteem, confidence, and responsibility in the students who go through training" (3). David Johnson insists that conditions in society and in the schools have made such training mandatory, for "without conflict resolution, most students have two strategies: coercion or withdrawal" (qtd. in Halford 2).

Barbara Stanford, a former high school teacher who served as project director for a statewide program in interdisciplinary humanities and conflict management, would agree with Halford and Walker and has pointed to the benefits of integrating conflict resolution teaching, such as that which is the basis of RIPP, with the English curriculum. In an essay entitled "Conflict and the Story of Our Lives: Teaching English for Violence Prevention," she details how a short story unit can provide particularly effective anti-violence education. She begins by having her students identify the conflicts in the short stories. The students are then taught to determine the style used by the characters in the short stories to deal with the conflict—that is, whether the character's response is aggressive, submissive, or assertive. To help her students understand the differences in these styles, she asks them to role-play responses to a scene of conflict, illustrating each of the three types of responses. After the students realize that there are options in responding to conflict, they suggest ways in which the characters might have responded more appropriately. She also has her students identify the places in the short stories where the main characters made poor choices leading to a situation of conflict. Because "real life" does not always have happy endings, she stresses the importance of including a "range of literature in which conflicts are resolved effectively and those in which they are not" (42). Literature, she believes, provides a way for students to view the world and imagine the possibilities beyond the world of violence they see too often in their neighborhoods and on television. Stanford's suggestions can readily be applied to characters in longer works of literature, as well, such as Heathcliff in *Wuthering Heights* and Macduff in *Macbeth*.

Having students formulate "peace contracts" is another way to teach conflict resolution strategies. This activity works very well with literature that centers on the perennial clash between good and evil such as *Beowulf*. Students are divided into teams, each representing a "force" in the literature, such as Beowulf, Grendel, and Hrothgar. Each team is directed to compose a list of the assigned character's needs. After this list is formulated, students form new groups in which each character is represented. Representatives present their needs to the entire group, which is then charged with the task of composing a "peace agreement" that acknowledges the desires/needs of each individual force while working to bring peace to the entire community. While the results are often hilarious—such as requiring Hrothgar to find an alternative food source for Grendel—the students learn that a "win-win" situation can be achieved if all work together, show respect for each other, and compromise where possible. This activity also gives students a rudimentary glimpse into the real-life challenges of adopting international peace accords and resolving local labor union disputes.

Teaching tolerance and respect for cultural, sexual, and racial differences is another way in which the school, and particularly English teachers, can be proactive in preventing violence in both the schools and society. Wendy Schwartz asserts that our society teaches children that "intolerance is an acceptable reaction to diversity" (1). Such intolerance often results in conflict, anger, and violence. Indeed, students are exposed to manifestations of hatred among "different" groups on a daily basis. They see pictures of the effects of the ethnic war in Albania, they watch television coverage of a Neo-Nazi shooting pedestrians on Chicago streets, they hear racial slurs and disparaging remarks about jocks in school hallways. The resulting exposure to violence only further "desensitizes them [the students] to their own pain and that of others" (Berreth and Berman 25). The school can work to counter these societal lessons. Joan Halford states that "curricular materials and instructional processes that present, affirm, and encourage respect for student diversity also contribute to peaceable schools . . . Multicultural education, then, reinforces violence prevention" (4).

The English teacher can expose students to the literature of different cultures and races. Through discussions, students can be led to appreciate the humanity that the peoples of different nationalities, religions, classes, cultures, and even sexes and socioeconomic groups, share. Once the common human bond is recognized, empathy for those who are "different" will develop. This is exactly what Conrad's Marlow learns as he journeys down the river in *Heart of Darkness.*

Besides examples found in the traditional canon of American and British literature, appropriate multicultural literature is readily available for students of all ages. Major literature textbooks published in the last decade include such works, and major paperback publishers print literature by multicultural authors. In fact, teacher resource companies such as *Teacher's Discovery* sell publications such as *12 Multicultural Novels*, a work containing teaching strategies for novels written by writers such as Sandra Cisneros and Helen Kim, and *Multicultural Education: Resource Guide,* which includes curriculum guidelines and lists of software and other audio-visual materials. The United Nations also provides materials to teachers, including *U.N. Study Kits* and online lesson plans; in addition, the UN conducts workshops for teachers, suggesting ways to use these materials. By exposing students to such multicultural literature, the English teacher is fostering tolerance and empathy and, thus, nonviolence in the students.

Of course, the English teacher can foster respect for diversity by more direct contacts. Kathy Checkley relates the suggestion of Theodore Eisenman, a communication specialist for the Peace Corps World Wise Schools program. Eisenman encourages teachers to use Peace Corps volunteers. An English teacher might invite the Peace Corps worker to visit classes. "In sharing what they learn about their host countries, volunteers help students see 'what life is like for an average citizen in another part of the world,' states Eisenman" (qtd. in Checkley, par. 14).

In addition to inviting speakers to their classrooms, English teachers can encourage direct communication with students from other countries. Checkley tells of teacher Mary Ann Huntley, who worked with a Peace Corps volunteer. Huntley states, "The volunteer helps lift the curtain on another way of life" (qtd. in Checkley, par. 15). Through a pen pal arrangement facilitated by the volunteer, Huntley's students not only got a direct, personal look at life in post-communist Bulgaria, but also learned to "realize how different circumstances make for differences in culture . . . [and to] learn that 'just because our culture is different, it doesn't mean it's better' " (qtd. in Checkley, par. 18).

Cooperative learning has been recognized as another tool for preventing violence. Robert Sylwester, author of *A Celebration of Neurons,* claims that, on the basis of recent scientific findings, "It's difficult to think of linguistic, musical, and interpersonal intelligence out of the context of social and cooperative activity, and other forms of intelligence are likewise principally social in normal practice" (qtd. in Elias et al. 16). Bolstered further by the research Dan Goleman presented in Emotional Intelligence, and by Howard Gardner's theory of multiple intelligences, Elias et al. reinforce the need for cooperative settings, concluding that "to succeed in school, family, friendships, the workplace, community life, and democratic participation, students need a full complement of skills—social, emotional, and academic" (16). Pete DeSisto, Director of the Cooperative Discipline Institute, sees the implication of such claims for preventing violence. He insists that cooperative learning aids in the students' "making and maintaining friendships across racial, ethnic, social, and economic lines" (1). As a result, conflicts among these groups may be reduced. In fact, insists David Hamburg, the president of the Carnegie Corporation,

> reversing the trend of violence among the young depends on teaching children how to share, work cooperatively with others, and to help others. The more children and adolescents work in cooperative learning groups, the greater will be their psychological health, self-esteem, social competencies, and resilience in the face of adversity and stress (qtd. in Johnson & Johnson 65).

Furthermore, claims Halford, "Engaging, student-centered curriculums also reduce alienation, especially for students with special needs" (4). The implication, of course, is that a sense of belonging enhances the building of community in the classroom and/or school, where conflicts can be resolved constructively. David W. Johnson, a professor of educational psychology, and Roger T. Johnson, a professor of curriculum and instruction at the University of Minnesota, both of whom have written extensively about cooperative learning and its role in creating peacemakers, point out the danger of not striving to build such communities: "Anything that allows students to fail, remain apart from classmates, and be socially inept and have low self-esteem, increases the probability that students will use destructive conflict strategies" (65).

The English classroom is readily adapted to methods using cooperative learning. This does not mean that the English teacher must avoid topics that have conflicts. In fact, by encouraging "academic controversy," teachers can help students find ways of handling opposing views. Johnson and Johnson offer this strategy, which can be used in literature classes and as pre-writing activity for writing lessons. They suggest that teachers assign students to cooperative learning groups, within which students are paired and assigned pro and con positions on an issue. Each pair is directed to prepare a presentation (consisting of a thesis, support, and conclusion) in which the pair tries to persuade the other side. During a discussion period, the opposition can attempt to refute the others' arguments. The procedure is then reversed. After both sides have presented and defended their positions, each side is asked to state the most convincing point the other side has offered, thus coming to an awareness of the other side's perspective (66). Topics such as Is *The Adventures of Huckleberry Finn* a racist novel? or Is Hester Prynne a good mother? can be discussed in this fashion. After discussion, students could be directed to write a persuasive essay in which they argue a point of view that includes recognition of the opposing view's arguments. "Developing sensitivity to what we read and see, heightening our awareness of the feelings and experience of other people is at the heart of both anti-violence training and good English teaching" (Carey-Webb 37).

In addition to utilizing certain strategies within the traditional English curriculum, the English classroom, by its nature, offers yet another way in which English teachers can be proactive in fostering violence prevention. "Language can be a catalyst for violence or for peace" (Wolfe 52). Foul language is, indeed, a force that results in violence. Notes an elementary school principal, "Most physical violence in my school . . . begins with foul language" (qtd. in Lickona 16). Denny Wolfe, in an article entitled "Three Approaches to Coping with School Violence," states that, "since language is our own business, in our own classrooms we can work to help students speak to one another with civil tongues" and thus build "learning environments where students feel secure" (52). Teaching the power of language can help students understand the effects of their own words on others. The written words students receive from English teachers can also foster a setting to promote violence reduction. R. Baird Schuman cautions English teachers to avoid the use of "insult, negativity, [and] sarcasm" when grading students' papers (28). Instead, words of encouragement, communicating a respect for the human being, however poor a student, can be used to build a connection, rather than create a gap, between teacher and student. Reducing a student's sense of alienation lowers the potential for violence. Dean Walker notes that, when students feel connected to the school, violence has decreased (2). Halford agrees: "Personalization . . . can create contexts to counter violence . . . When students feel a strong connection to their school, they are less likely to engage in violent behaviors or tolerate them among peers" (2).

Anti-violence education within the framework of the English curriculum—even when the works studied contain violence—can be effective. Examining the nature of conflict within works of literature helps students to learn productive strategies of conflict resolution applicable in their own lives. Reading and analyzing multicultural literature heightens empathy for those who are perceived to be different, thus reducing attitudes of intolerance that often lead to violent actions. Using cooperative learning in English classes to explore controversy helps students listen to opposing views and come to a realization that differences can coexist peacefully. The English teacher can be most effective when using these methods in a respectful, student-centered environment that stresses the power and the potential of verbal and written language.

This method of violence prevention teaching *does not* take time from the academic curriculum, a complaint waged against the use of "peace curricula." Furthermore, not only does such integration enhance the English program—by teaching plot structure, characterization, point of view, tone, close textual reading, enhanced listening, and analytical/persuasive writing skills—but also studies on the use of academic controversy and on cooperative learning have shown that they "result in increased student achievement, critical thinking, [and] intrinsic motivation to learn" (Johnson and Johnson 66). In addition, Elias et al. state that "social and emotional learning is strongly related to several of our national educational goals and standards" (17).

Certainly, such integration takes planning on the part of the English teacher, and "there is no reason to expect . . . that the process [of teaching to manage conflict] will be quick or easy" (Johnson and Johnson 67), for America is a violent land. But what has typically been done to prevent violence in the past has had no or very little effect. Teachers, especially English teachers, have the opportunity to address this national nightmare, not by changing the content of the English curriculum, but by integrating proven violence prevention strategies into it. They need to help students learn nonviolent ways of handling conflict so that school shootings will cease to be "routine" (Cloud 34), and school administrators can go back to worrying about more important things than the cost of metal detectors.

Works Cited

Berreth, Diane, and Sheldon Berman. "The Moral Dimensions of Schools." *Educational Leadership* 54 (May 1997): 24–27.

Carey-Webb, Allen. "Youth Violence and the Language Arts: A Topic for the Classroom." *English Journal* 84 (September 1995): 29–37.

Checkley, Kathy. "Teaching for Peace." *ASCD: Curriculum Update.* Summer 1998. [Online] Available: www. ascd.org/otb/benefit.htm/

Clearinghouse on Educational Management. ERIC Reproduction Service No. 379786. [Online]. Available: www.shinesite.org/home-mstr.htm/

Cloud, John. "Just a Routine School Shooting." *Time* 31 (May 1999): 34–38.

DeSisto, Pete. "Interventions for Violent Adolescents." 4 June 1997 [Online]. Available: www.uncg.edu/edu/ericcass/violence/docs/interven/htm/.

Elias, Maurice, et al. "How to Launch a Social and Emotional Learning Program." *Educational Leadership* 54 (May 1997): 15–19.

Eric Reproduction Service NO. 377255. [Online]. Available: www.shinesite.org/home-mstr.htm/.

Halford, Joan Montgomery. "Preventing School Violence: Policies for Safety, Caring, and Achievement." *ASCD: INFOBRIEF,* Autumn 1996.

Johnson, David W., and Roger T. Johnson. "Why Violence Prevention Programs Don't Work—and What Does." *Educational Leadership* 52 (February 1995): 63–67.

Lickona, Thomas. *Educating for Character: How Our Schools Can Teach Respect and Responsibility.* New York: Bantam, 1991.

Meyer, Aleta, and Wendy Northup. "What Is Violence Prevention, Anyway?" *Educational Leadership* 54 (May 1997): 31–33.

Schuman, R. Baird. "Big Guns, Thwarted Dreams: School Violence and the English Teacher." *English Journal* 84.5 (1995): 23–28.

Schwartz, Wendy. "Anti-Bias and Conflict Resolution Curricula: Theory and Practice." *ERIC/CUE Digest No. 97.* May 1994. New York: ERIC Clearinghouse on Urban Education.

Stanford, Barbara. "Conflict and the Story of Our Lives: Teaching English for Violence Prevention." *English Journal* 84.5 (1995): 38–42.

U.S. Department of Education. *Annual Report on School Safety.* Washington, DC, 1998.

Walker, Dean. "School Violence Prevention." *ERIC DIGEST No. 94.* March 1995. Eugene, Oregon: ERIC.

Wolfe, Denny. "Three Approaches to Coping with School Violence." *English Journal* 84.5 (1995): 51–54.

14 The Ada Valley Simulation: Exploring the Nature of Conflict

Daniel Mindich

We have given you an opportunity, and you should be thankful for it. You came here to work in our factories, you have made a good living for yourselves, started many businesses, but the valley is too crowded, and it is time to stop the number of Hos coming into the valley. If you make a big stink of this, we'll kick all of you out of the valley," states Paul, a usually shy student, now one of the leaders of the Kakungan people for the purposes of this role play.

"I don't see how you Kakungans can stop people who want to make a better life for themselves. Our brothers and sisters, fathers and mothers are suffering in Ho-hum because of a civil war out of their control. How can you tell them they can't come here?" asks Lexi, a girl from the affluent hill section of this California town.

"You are not listening. The valley is too crowded. We can't just let everybody in," complains Tran, a Vietnamese refugee who weeks before had written about hiding from the Vietcong coast guard while fleeing Vietnam. For the moment he is a Kakungan settler whose family has a potato farm.

"So why don't you go back to Kakunga where you came from? We have as much right to this area as you do. Who made you in charge? My family has lived here for almost fifty years. We don't have to take this from you," says another member of the Ho immigrant group.

"You guys are trying to change history. This is already done. You can't make us move back because, for one, Kakunga is a desert now, and two, we have been here for a long time and we are not moving. And anyway we are not even trying to kick you out. We are just saying that you can't bring anymore of your people into the valley. I mean, it is not just us. Think about the Wanyamans," responds Paul.

This essay appeared in *English Journal* 89.5 (2000) on pages 128–133.

"Yeah, both of you guys are arguing over this place like you own it. This land was ours. We grazed on the land peacefully until you Kakungans came in here and started messing things up," says Walter, an angry nomadic Wanyaman.

Such is life in Ada Valley, a simulated society that I created eight years ago. Early on in my teaching I realized that, while students were quick to say that prejudice and aggression are wrong, rarely did they think through the forces that cause people to come into conflict. In response to this gap between reality and sentiment, I developed Ada Valley. Ada's society is made up of three ethnic groups: an indigenous group, well-established settlers, and a new immigrant population. Each has its own interests and demands. The situation in Ada forces people to think about how the different basic needs of ethnic, socioeconomic, or demographic groups can cause tension, and to say who is at fault is often very difficult if not irrelevant.

While I had used role plays and other means of getting the students to personalize the complexity of typical conflict situations, the depth of the students' thinking was limited by their quick decisions as to who was supposed to be right and who was supposed to be wrong. For instance, students playing the roles of white jurors during the trial scene from *To Kill a Mockingbird* were hesitant to create realistic personas ("crawl into the skin" of the citizens of Maycomb, as Atticus Finch would say). Few had the empathy to see the dynamics of the jurors' motivations beyond the fact that they were racist for convicting a clearly innocent African American man. Were the jurors scared of the repercussions of finding Tom innocent? Were the poor whites trying to exert power over the only group they could control? Were whites so indoctrinated that they could not see the truth, even though it seems obvious today? In a familiar historical context, it was easy to say that one person or group's behavior was wrong without looking at the factors that contributed to that action.

I designed Ada Valley to be a place that intrigued students and about which there would be no preconceived notions. I wanted to create a place where no groups are clearly good or bad and where no one would be afraid to use names that would smack of racism or politically incorrect thinking. In fact, throughout the whole simulation (until the debriefing), there is no referring to "real life" groups. Even the actual date of what is happening is left nebulous to avoid historical comparisons, and technology is controlled to keep groups from solving their problems with easy solutions (i.e., bombing the enemy out of existence). In addition, most of the surrounding land is either uninhabitable or taken by other groups, making it difficult to relocate large numbers of people. Geographically, the fertile valley surrounded by mountains could be anywhere in the world. The unit supplies enough detail to help the participants make a real connection but leaves large sections of the narrative unscripted; the students are compelled by the history of the people and the valley as well as their own interpretations of the state of the valley.

The crux of the socio-political strife in Ada is that the three main groups of people—the indigenous people, the settlers, and the immigrants—have distinctly different lifestyles that put them in conflict. Some of these differences pose real barriers to coexistence, and some are perceived problems.

The indigenous people of Ada are the Wanyamans, who have lived in the valley for as long as anyone can remember, raising their domesticated bears and living as nomads. When the settlers first arrived, the Wanyamans never thought there would be a problem. In fact, the Wanyamans welcomed the newcomers as allies against menacing neighbors.

The settlers, the Kakungans, came *en masse* a few hundred years ago following a famine and the ensuing desertification of their homeland, and they have slowly taken over more and more of the valley and a greater percentage of the population (56 percent as compared to the Wanyamans' 20 percent). They, too, live simply, but their lifestyle is more sedentary, and their farms have claimed much of the land in the valley. They have also discovered a way of manufacturing fish oil that brings in money from exporting. While they have achieved a certain comfort level, they do not aspire to make lots of money, only to live comfortably. (Their mottoes are "A happy family is a busy family" and "Money should never come between sisters.")

Once they started to industrialize, the Kakungans needed workers for their factories besides themselves. Neighbors from the country of Ho-hum, which has been experiencing civil war for fifty years, began filling the need for those jobs. As the Ho people saw the opportunity to make a new life in a more peaceful country and the war at home got worse, more and more Hos started coming in to Ada. Currently, they make up the remaining 24 percent of the valley's population.

At first, the Kakungans looked down on the Ho people. The Kakungans assumed that, because the Hos were taking low-level jobs, they were able to do only low-level work. The Hos, however, have shown a keen business sense and have excelled in trade. They have the highest per capita wealth and have bought one of the fish fuel refineries. This economic competition has made the Kakungans feel a little threatened. The Ho people's culture has also created some tension.

Their flamboyant traditions of late night singing and dancing and wearing bright clothes are in stark contrast to the more somber Kakungan ways. Seeing the increasing population of the valley and perhaps threatened by the growing success of the Hos, the Kakungans cut off immigration into the valley, making the first political maneuver in the valley's previously anarchistic history.

The Wanyamans, meanwhile, are realizing too late that what they thought was an endlessly abundant universe is now closing in on them, and they are no longer able to live in their traditional way. In the middle of this political situation, a Ho student is killed, and that event brings the groups together to have a "town meeting," not to discuss the murder itself but to bring out the issues that face the valley as a whole.

There are many questions for the residents of the valley to ponder. Are the Wanyaman people due a certain amount of land to maintain their traditional ways? Do they even want to maintain that lifestyle? How should overcrowding in Ada be handled? Is it fair to limit Hos from coming into the valley when they face misery and hardship at home? Do the Kakungans have the right to make decisions for the valley? How should decisions be made? How do people get what they want or keep what they have?

Initially, students are not equipped to make these decisions. The first few days are spent helping the students become familiar with the historical, cultural, and economic background of the situation in the valley. I provide the students with a detailed objective description of life in Ada, and they fill out matrixes that organize that information. There are further readings that show differing political views and interpretations of what is going on. We talk about the way history is written and how that can affect the way groups are treated.

After the second or third day, the students divide into their groups. The number of students in each group corresponds to the valley's demographic breakdown. The ensuing few days focus on helping the students to see themselves as group members. They create a national identity through poster making and song/anthem writing. Later on they can question their groups' decisions, but at first, I want them to value the strengths of their cultures. The students now have enough information to begin to internalize the situation.

The next step involves quick role plays that address how individuals would react to everyday conflicts in Ada. Students begin to realize that there is no single "group response" for any situation. For instance, when two Wanyamans go to a Kakungan employment agency, one Wanyaman may look forward to working in the Kakungans' factories, while another might resent being forced to give up his traditional ways. A Kakungan might be eager to assimilate the Wanyamans into her economic system or she might look down on her nomadic neighbors. Through these practice skits, the students begin formulating their own opinions about their culture and its future, leading to the creation of their own Ada personalities.

Prior to the town meeting, each student is responsible for creating a character who represents a large group of like-minded constituents. It is amazing to me that, even though the students are allowed to choose their own roles, there is always a broad range of personalities. That is to say that there are not eight chiefs of the Hos or seven Wanyaman rebels. The interesting, always changing, mixture of views both supports and questions the ways of each particular group. There are Kakungan potato farmers who hate the loud, ebullient Hos, and there are curious Kakungan factory workers intrigued by the expressiveness of Ho music and culture. There are Wanyamans fiercely devoted to keeping up their way of life and others who, deciding that they don't care for herding their milk-bearing bears, have moved to the big cities to start tour companies to cash in on their traditional cousins.

It is only after this series of steps that the class is ready to take on the issues of the town meeting with a sense of informed investment. With the characters chosen, the groups meet separately to discuss majority and minority positions. All students write out opening speeches, and one person is elected to speak for the group. After each culture has given its opening statement, the floor is open for dissent, minority opinion, and debate. I act as the facilitator of the meeting, sometimes letting the participants talk freely back and forth, sometimes controlling the flow of discussion by setting up the order of speakers, and sometimes calling on the less talkative members to voice their opinions. It is important that all voices in the society are heard, yet it is also a good lesson to see that sometimes the most talkative people make decisions that might not be popular with the rest.

Each time I wonder if the students will try to end things too quickly and easily, but the beauty of the situation is that there is no simple way to say, "Can't we all just get along?" An example that typifies the difficulty of reaching an easy solution began when a girl in the powerful Kakungan settler group was making very aggressive comments, and another girl in the immigrant Ho group said to her, "Hey why are you acting so crazy?"

"Well, it will be too easy if I act nice," she responded.

"Don't worry about it being too easy," I said. "Just play the part of the role you have created, and you will see how things play out."

"OK," the Kakungan girl continued, "if you Hos promise to not bring anymore people into the area, we will let you live here as you have for the last few decades."

"Ha-ha, you guys are ho's," laughed another Kakungan. The added American pop culture meaning of the Hos name makes for a great cause of tension and a realistic example of how elements of culture that seem ordinary at home can cause difficulties in a new land.

"Shut up, we are proud to be from Ho-Hum even if you want to make fun of our name, and why do you care if we come in here? We don't take up much space. We just live in towns, working in your factories and running our businesses. It's your farms that have really displaced the Wanyamans," responded another student, and the conflict had begun.

"Yeah, well you don't have the power to say either way so take it or leave it."

"Now you think that you have the right to tell us what we can and can't do. Who gave you that right anyway?"

Soon enough, the students were enveloped in the issues. Once caught in the quagmire of questions, one of the central elements of Ada Valley is how these issues can be resolved. Will students have the patience to work through them nonviolently and cooperatively, or will frustration lead to harsh, aggressive, and possibly violent settlements?

In another example, Jojo Wanyaman (his character name) was sitting with his sheet (the traditional clothing of the Wanyaman people) draped over his head in the middle of the room, holding a silent protest for peace. Jojo had been largely ignored in the commotion that centered around Poncho, also a Wanyaman, who was calling for the removal of all non-Wanyamans from the Ada Valley. Poncho had not been this articulate all year. He had been a straight "F" student and handed in hardly any assignments. He relished the opportunity to control the actions of his more academically successful classmates. In fact, the night before, he spent what must have been hours drawing up battle plans, explaining how his undermanned Wanyaman army was going to carry out his bold threats. "I will not rest until you are all out of my valley. You can try to kill me off, but I represent many thousands of Wanyamans who follow my beliefs. We invited you into the valley, and you abused the privilege, and now it is time for you to go, or be killed," he said proudly.

"What's wrong with you, Poncho? We're trying to negotiate this, and you are just fooling around," said a frustrated Kakungan. The ones arguing were mostly high achieving students who believed that everyone should just let bygones be bygones and live peacefully in the valley, which for these Kakungans conveniently meant stopping Ho immigration and not returning much land to the Wanyamans. "That's not fair. We don't want to go to war," some pleaded, but others were saying, "If that's what he [Poncho] wants, then that's what he'll get."

In the end, through forceful, stubborn negotiation, Poncho got almost half of the valley returned to the Wanyamans. He never did use violence, but his threat of using it left many Kakungans hurt and uncomfortable. It could be argued whether his intentions were violent or whether he used the threat to avoid actual conflict. Either way, the students saw that he got what he wanted.

There is no specific end to the meeting, no desired outcome. After periods of bedlam, fascinating problem solving, and painfully boring talking in circles, the meeting ends when there is no further room for discussion—generally after three to four hours of class time. The situations that bring the talks to a close are a call to war, a peaceful cooperative resolution, or a grudgingly accepted compromise. Whatever the final settlement, the facilitator ensures that the participants know the ramifications of their decisions. War cannot actually be played out. The groups can only accept that many people would die as a result of their breakdown in negotiations. Any attempt at declaring peace must be similarly questioned by the facilitator. For instance, many times students will propose moving groups to different areas. While this solution is theoretically possible, it is important that all the people involved understand that it is not just a matter of one person or a few people moving but that thousands of people like them would have to make that same decision. Would so many people choose to move off of the farms they have lived on for centuries in order to return land to the Wanyamans? Probably not. But perhaps with the threat of guerrilla attacks as voiced earlier by Poncho, that resistance to relocation could change. The range of what the individual participants and their group dynamic create is fascinating.

It is that uncertainty of outcome that continues to make the activity interesting to me after years of doing it with many classes. The Hos and the Wanyamans might join together to get revenge on the Kakungans. A large group of Kakungans could "convert" to the more fun-loving Ho ways, putting pressure on traditional Kakungans and Wanyamans to loosen immigration restrictions. Or, as was the case in the previous example, a small minority of Wanyamans might stand up against an overwhelming majority and broker a land redistribution. Interestingly, only twice in some twenty times has a truly cooperative, peaceful solution been found in which the participants accepted the fact that everyone would have to make significant, realistic sacrifices

and that new ways of looking at the valley's resources would be needed in order for the different communities to coexist happily. The students understood that certain government systems (which I will
discuss in detail later) would have to be put into place to maintain this
delicate balance.

The tendency towards hostility is troubling. The frustrating complexity of Ada's issues often leads to flaring tempers and fighting.
Though the students laugh when I tell them that they shouldn't carry
their anger out of the classroom, invariably I have to mediate overheat-
ed debates of students as they leave class. A student's comparison of the
Hos to Japanese Americans once nearly caused a brawl. Often people
like Jojo, asking for the patience to work things out peacefully, are
drowned out by the people looking to solve things quickly by force.
Students feeling powerless—because their "leaders" are not listening to
them—stand back silently while decisions they don't support are made
for them. As disturbing as these moments can be, they are true to life.

The most important step in dealing with the harsh realities that
this process brings out is the debriefing, where we discuss what happened in the meeting on a number of different levels. First, we analyze
the specific behaviors of the people in the class. Generally, people are
shocked at how angry they got in the course of the discussions, how
frustrating it is when people don't listen to each other, or how certain
people dominated the talks. To notice some of the negative patterns in
our negotiation techniques, we look at Roger Fisher and William Ury's
book on conflict resolution, *Getting to Yes*. We then begin to make connections to the outside world. While there are no exact crossovers,
there are many places that are reminiscent of the Ada Valley. Interestingly, while many people notice how similar Ada is to America, few
students can imagine the United States giving up the same amount of
land to the Native Americans as the Wanyamans were willing to fight
for in Ada. As crazy as partitioning up the valley may seem, the students recognize that the people of the former Yugoslavia are doing just
that right now. The connections are not limited to global politics. Students notice parallel behaviors and reactions in their dealings with
parents, student relationships, athletics, and many other day-to-day
moments. Stepping away from the experience, analyzing their behavior, and relating it to other similar predicaments allows the students to
appreciate the lessons learned in Ada Valley.

Similar to what was done in the few cases that ended with a nonviolent cooperative solution, I have all the groups eventually discuss
what needs to happen in order for there to be peaceful coexistence in
Ada, even if the meeting participants were far from going in that direc-

tion. Students are put in ministries (immigration, government, culture, environment, etc.) to think through the different areas where conflict arises and to set up systems to ensure sustainable harmony. How would governments work to protect the interests of the majority and the rights of the minority? What is a fair level of immigration given the suffering in Ho-hum, and are the urban Hos the real issue in the Wanyamans' loss of grazing land? What issues in the cultures are truly hard to resolve (e.g., the Wanyaman tradition of grazing over large areas of land and the large number of Kakungan farmers), and which are just matters of taste (e.g., the Hos' wearing of bright colors).

Beyond the obviously strong social studies overlap, the Ada Valley simulation covers specific English standards. Throughout the unit, the students practice reading and interpretive skills, using details to create well-developed characters and finding a sense of empathy to support the public speaking and reflective pieces they do as their characters. In the first part of the final project, the students choose one of those informal pieces to polish and submit (e.g., a free write describing their character's life or an opening speech in the voice of their character). The second and most important section is an essay in which they analyze the issues in Ada Valley and/or the behaviors exhibited in the meeting. The final task is to create an artistic interpretation that does not merely depict the situation (e.g., a map or a drawing of a mango) but demonstrates their insights into what they have learned. In these various forms, the project asks the students to use details from the readings in order to synthesize original analytical thought. The unit is often the lead-in for the reading of Chinua Achebe's *Things Fall Apart,* and throughout the rest of the year the work we do on Ada Valley becomes a point of reference for looking at character development, analytical writing, and the ways groups interact.

Students remember the work on Ada for years to come. Participants from simulations years ago still e-mail me about Ada Valley, and when I see former students, they often bring up their roles with startling detail. Ada Valley has provided some of the most intense, exciting teaching moments I have had.

The reason for Ada's success is that it allows students to empathize with characters involved in common conflicts. The lessons learned can be applied to the way people get along in the cafeteria at school, dating, the diplomacy between nations, the perspective of an isolated student, or the escalation of gang violence. The simulation reminds students to think before judging or voicing an opinion and exposes them to the difficulty of the art of negotiation. They realize that having individuals and groups work/live together is much more than just being nice; it takes work and requires compromise. They also experience who speaks for a group, how decisions get made, how frustration can accompany working out a complex issue, and how willingness to sacrifice is at the core of all successful negotiations between parties with clashing interests. Those are powerful lessons.

Learning the hard truths of group dynamics is not a negative lesson. It is important for all people to understand that getting along in this complicated world is just that, complicated. To assume anything else is a setup for failure. Just saying violence is bad or having students make posters about the results of violence does not get them to see the reality of what causes it. We are a society that likes to solve things easily. We see this kind of thinking when relatively safe schools buy metal detectors rather than work on the issues that breed these problems. Only when we better understand the difficulty of negotiation and the human propensity for anger and violence will we start constructively dealing with those issues, and participating in "Ada Valley" is a step in that direction.

For more information on the Ada Valley visit our Web site at: www.AdaValley.org.

15 A Thousand Cranes: A Curriculum of Peace

Linda W. Rees

As teachers, we hope to teach our students those ideals inherent in our academic disciplines. We set goals, make plans, perform research, and choose literary selections to transmit our love for literature to our students, who also bring their dreams, hopes, frustrations, and shortcomings to our classrooms. We inhabit a world, a time and place in which we come together. Sometimes we reach their minds, their hearts, their souls; more often, they reach ours. I met one such student in August, 1996, and what she has taught me about understanding, forgiveness, and peace has haunted me ever since.

My friend, Nikki, the French teacher, introduced Marii Oishi as a new tenth-grade student from Japan during registration, a few days before classes began at Saint Stephen's Episcopal School, a college preparatory school in Bradenton, a small community on Florida's Gulf Coast. A cozy, open atmosphere prevails at this small school, and we have taken pride in our sense of family. Like any family, we have our dysfunctional moments. Kids aren't perfect, and neither are their adult mentors, but we try. Our school attracts the children of the well-off families living along the river or on the gulf islands, as well as scholarship kids; about one-third arrive from neighboring Sarasota, while the athletes from the nearby Bollettieri Tennis and Sports Academy make up the rest. The Academy kids attend classes until 12:30 and train in tennis, golf, soccer, and baseball. They come from all over the United States and the world; many are talented athletes, and I have always enjoyed the diversity of languages and cultures they have brought to the school. I first thought that Marii was an Academy student, but, instead, she had studied English at the Yazigi Language Study Center on the Academy campus and then decided to spend the rest of her high school years in a US school—ours. Hoping to draw out the soft-spoken young woman and gauge her proficiency in English, I chatted with her, finally asking where in Japan was home. "Hiroshima," she replied, making my attempts at good-natured conversation suddenly feel hollow and silly.

This essay appeared in *English Journal* 89.5 (2000) on pages 95–99.

What does one say when confronted with a place where such horror occurred? Nikki's blue eyes clouded over, and I murmured something articulate like a flat, "Oh." Marii nodded solemnly, and we whisked her off to register after I told her I looked forward to seeing her in my tenth-grade English class.

During the early weeks of that year, I had a few problems of my own. Due to a healthy growth spurt in enrollment, I was out of a classroom. For a while, I carted my papers, dictionaries, and stacks of books to an empty classroom each period of the day, feeling very put out. I'm as territorial about my space as a wolf, so I complained a lot and was finally rewarded with my own space, a corner of the library created by arranging the fiction stacks in an L-shaped alcove by the back wall. It was far from perfect, but I got a big bulletin board, a dry erase board, a computer, and best of all, tables and chairs, which foster discussions better than rows of desks.

I also got a location at the heart of the school; the library is the open center of the Upper School with classrooms opening off its perimeter. The school was originally constructed in the early 1970s, when the "open" classroom was the great educational experiment, one that didn't work all that well, especially as the school continued to grow. Our board of trustees does not particularly subscribe to the "field of dreams" theory of school construction: If you build it, they will come. Rather, having witnessed the downfall of other independent schools, our board prudently waits until the school population justifies expansion. Over the years, the open spaces were gradually enclosed with some permanent and semi-permanent walls, so my arrangement, while slightly more bizarre than usual, was hardly unprecedented. Plans were in the works for an annex, and negotiations to purchase an abutting shopping center were underway, so I decided to make the best of my current situation.

Computers were lined up in a row outside one of my classroom's fiction stacks, and tables and chairs placed throughout the library accommodated the study halls that year. A sizable crowd occupied those computers and tables every period of the day. Another distraction was my view through the other fiction stack and up the ramp to the school's main door. My new digs were a nosy person's delight; I had a barely impeded view of all who passed near the library. It also worked the other way; not much that happened in my classroom was missed by those just beyond my fiction stacks. My classroom was an open book.

It was in this space, then, that Marii experienced her first American classroom. It must have seemed strange, indeed, for one coming from the orderly Japanese system. She joined an eclectic group that third period. Along with the ten or so home-growns, the class included Tarou, a Japanese-American student who had traveled back and forth between the two countries; Eric, a Swedish exchange student; and Jeannie, a Parisian-born Korean girl, fluent in English, French, and Korean, and also a talented golfer. Others had just moved to Florida and were homesick for their old school, weather, and friends. While everyone spoke English well, reading and writing proficiency varied widely. We were working in three or four levels of vocabulary texts but reading the same selections: *Oedipus, Beowulf,* and *Things Fall Apart.* I knew that I had my work cut out for me.

Surprisingly, everyone clicked. They were a cheerful bunch who enjoyed the give and take of class discussion. They wrote a lot and usually enjoyed going around the room sharing their writing with the class, at least until it was Marii's turn. She said her English was awful and her writing was stupid. I coaxed her and tried to joke her into reading; the other kids joined in, one boy remarking that they had all read their stupid writing; at least *she* had an excuse. So laughing, but still reluctant, she shyly read her work. Everyone applauded when she finished. I felt so proud of those kids and their kind support of this new girl. Marii definitely relaxed after that and soon became an enthusiastic class member. She even contributed this poem, written during class, to our literary magazine, *Aerie:*

Sunday Afternoon

Sunday afternoon, I escape to the beach
On the gleaming white sand, alone I stand.
Waves singing. Endless wave song.
Ocean
Where does it start and where does it end?
While I was contemplating the ocean,
I remember my family.
Over this expanse, there is my family
My friends, my teachers.
    Over this ocean,
there are people that I love.
I remember them in the sounds of the waves.
Sunday afternoon, I escape to the beach.

All was well, or so I thought in the spring as I watched the class work on a vocabulary lesson. Marii and Eric were working together; Jeannie was helping them out, and since Marii had studied in Korea, both were eager to speak Korean, while Tarou jumped in periodically to contribute more Japanese. Everyone was working somewhat noisily in small groups, with the multilingual merriment the loudest.

"Doesn't this drive you nuts?" asked Jim, who seemed to be developing a crush on both Marii and Jeannie. I just laughed with him and thought about how much progress kids can make in a year.

Marii continued to become more comfortable with the informality and friendliness of our group. Before class, she passed around Japanese teen magazines, shared Japanese candy and gum, and wrote out everyone's name in Japanese. We were all growing as learners, I thought, particularly when she demonstrated her skill with origami, which Japanese children begin to learn in kindergarten. We marveled at the intricacy of the shapes, while she downplayed its complexity, saying it was easy. She had made an origami display as a project for geometry class. The projects were then displayed in the library; many were marvelous studies in shape and design, and hers was received with great praise.

I was about to conclude that her first year, though difficult for her, was quite a success, when she arrived in class one day subdued and obviously upset. As class time passed, her agitation increased. When I quietly approached her and asked if something was wrong, she shook her head and tried to smile, but her eyes were full of tears. Then, her reserve broke, and she was shaking with sobs while she chokingly tried to explain that a boy in her geometry class had crushed her origami project and muttered racially charged insults. He was only a freshman, but he was a star athlete and big, with a habit of not-so-subtle harassment disguised as jokes. Obviously, Marii's emotional distress attracted class attention; everyone was simultaneously outraged and protective. The kids at the computers were engrossed in our drama, and I was making plans to report the incident. Meanwhile, in a small gesture of comfort, Jim handed Marii a piece of gum. She looked at me for approval, as I am notorious for enforcing the no-gum rule, but in light of the present situation, I just smiled and nodded. Suddenly, hands reached into every purse and backpack and produced more and more sticks of gum, all passed to Marii, who looked down at her growing pile in amazement. We all burst into laughter. The tense mood was broken, and we resumed our class activities. As they worked quietly, I noticed that Marii had flattened the silver gum wrapper and was folding it into ever smaller shapes. She produced a minuscule silver origami crane, probably not more than one-quarter inch in height or width. Silently, she placed it in front of Jim, the boy who had given her the first piece of gum.

Over the next year, I saw Marii less often, as she was not in my English class, but she would come by to visit every so often to talk about her progress in English. Junior year is a hard one, and Marii was a perfectionist frustrated by a perceived lack of progress. She appeared happy, though; she had many friends, although that ugly incident a year ago almost made her want to return to Japan. The boy had apologized to her, though, and she decided to stay.

During her senior year, she was in my fifth period study hall, so I saw her every day again. I was back in my regular classroom, and those crazy quarters in the library were like a dimly receding nightmare. Oddly enough, those kids who shared that space with me loved to reminisce about how much fun it had been to be at the hub of all activity, proving to me yet again that teens seem to thrive on some form of organizational chaos. Marii often spoke of that sophomore English class with great fondness, of how comfortable she had felt with everyone in the class at a time when she was less comfortable with the language.

Early in her senior year, Marii's turn came to deliver her Chapel speech, a senior year requirement. While some few seniors actually looked forward to having their say, most approached the task, understandably, with trepidation. As I took my place in Chapel that morning, I smiled to remember how reluctant she had been in tenth grade to read her writing in front of her small class; how would she do, I wondered, at a podium with a microphone in front of the entire school? The student chaplain introduced her; she walked to the podium and began to deliver her speech in a calm, strong, clear voice.

Marii spoke about growing up in Hiroshima, where peace education was a significant part of the curriculum, only this education focused on the evil effects of the bomb. When she was fourteen, ever curious about language and culture, Marii decided to enroll in an international school in Korea, where she learned what the Japanese had done to the Koreans. "It was a big shock," she said, and when a Korean classmate said, "You Japanese people killed my grandfather," all she could answer was that she was sorry. "My grandparents did not go to the war, but it was their generation who occupied Korea, made them give up their own Korean language, and taught them Japanese." One winter day, as she was sitting in a McDonald's restaurant with her Japanese friends, they noticed a young employee staring at them. She wrote on the window she was cleaning, "All Japanese go home." Marii reflected, "What deep and sad words. She was just about our age." Some time later, Marii's Korean host sister warned her not to speak Japanese when she was out in public. Frightened to even go outside, Marii wondered, "What can I do to let these people know that not all Japanese people are cold? What can I do when I grow up?" Imagine her surprise when, as she was preparing to leave Korea to study in the United States, a classmate told her something she would never forget:

> I always hated Japanese people. I never knew any of them, but what I learned from school made me think that all Japanese people are mean, bad, and hateful, but when I met you and became friends with you, I realized that I was wrong. I am so glad that we became friends. If people in the world had an experience like I had, or we had, the world will change.

Her host sisters told her that she was "their real sister over the distance." Marii's "big project or dream" was decided then. She told us:

> I don't know what I can do in the future, but one thing I know is the people I love, and the country I love. . . . Can you hate or fight against the people or country you love? . . . If you really love someone, don't you wish to learn their culture and respect that culture?
>
> In front of God, everybody is equal. My parents have kept telling me this since I was little, and in the Bible, it says that our real nationality is in heaven. In front of God, we all have the same nationality. Not thinking only about your country or your family. If our generation starts to think this way and love other countries, I think the world will start to change . . . this is my dream . . . The dream is to make it come true and it will come true. This is something I learned in the USA.

I listened, enthralled, as did everyone in that audience. When she finished, a brief hush allowed us to release our held breath, followed by prolonged and thunderous applause. I felt that I had gained insight into a rare heart; she had turned those potentially ugly incidents into a plea for tolerance and understanding. She never mentioned the ugliness at her US school, but I felt its sting, and I appreciated again her transformation of the ugly into the beautiful, her seeing the ugliness in all of its dimensions, not dwelling on the hurts inflicted in the past but transforming suffering into a positive force for peace.

Later that year, a small group of students approached Nikki, the Hungarian-born French teacher, to sponsor an International Club at school. I thought it was a nobly disguised ploy to get Nikki to cook for them, as she is a fabulous and enthusiastic cook, but I was wrong. Under Marii's leadership, their first project was to send over one thousand origami cranes to the shrine of Sadako Sasaki in Hiroshima Peace Memorial Park. The story goes that, after the bombing, a young girl, Sadako, ill in the hospital with radiation sickness, decided to make a thousand origami cranes, a traditional symbol of good luck, in the hope of rejoining her classmates at school. She died, but her classmates completed her project, and today a statue, covered with many paper cranes, stands in the park.

Fifth period study hall became crane time, as everyone wanted to learn how to make those engaging birds out of the special brightly-colored origami paper. We diligently folded and creased the blue, yellow, red, green, orange, pink, and purple paper every day we could (whenever test preparation allowed!). I was particularly intrigued when the boy who had crushed her project in tenth grade sat down beside her and asked her to show him how to make one. He frowned in concentration, folding carefully and patiently until he produced a perfect crane.

In so many ways, events had come full circle, a superbly satisfying completion. How seldom does an episode conclude so soundly? How can we teach peace? Sometimes it is taught to us, if we are lucky enough to have an authentic Peace-Maker in our midst.

16 The Value of Voice: Promoting Peace through Teaching and Writing

Colleen A. Ruggieri

It is the still, small voice that the soul heeds, not the deafening blasts of doom.
William Dean Howells

May I have your attention, please? I'd like to share some information regarding graffiti that appeared in our school. I am telling you what was written on the bathroom wall so that everyone will know the facts. That way, there will be no questions and rumors about what is going on. . . .

As my high school principal delivered these words on the public address system late last school year, students in my classroom listened attentively. Usually, they would "half listen" when PA announcements came on, but as my school, along with hundreds of others, had suffered the aftermath of the Littleton, Colorado, incident in the form of copycat threats, students were riding an emotional roller-coaster. At the high school, an unknown author wrote messages on the bathroom walls that gave a date and a threat that "jocks" would be the targets of some sort of violence. The "day of doom" passed peacefully (with an absence list a mile long), while the person responsible for the writings was never discovered. Meanwhile, one of the junior high schools in our district was receiving phone calls in which an individual was making equally sinister threats. After several evacuations and weeks of investigations, the teenage culprit who made those calls, and single-handedly caused the chaos and fear that led to thousands of dollars in security costs, was taken into custody at the juvenile justice center.

Though tragic shooting sprees and their aftermath have gained national attention fairly recently, I first began thinking deeply about

This essay appeared in *English Journal* 89.5 (2000) on pages 47–54.

shocking outbursts of violence seven years ago, after a student in my classroom smashed the fingers of a student next to him with the chunky heel of his cowboy boot. While working at a nearby restaurant one evening, this angry young man, furious for being disciplined for what he had done, proceeded to tell an audience of students of his intentions to murder me, chop my body parts into pieces, and mail them to each of my family members. After hearing a report of this from some of the students who were there that night, for the first time in my career I felt sick about being a teacher.

Through reflection, it is easy to realize that American teens are screaming—and killing—in an effort to be heard by society. In nearly all of the cases involving teen violence during the last two years, there were warnings. From outright threats to revealing conversations with peers, it certainly seemed as if the assailants wanted someone to listen to them before the tragedies occurred. As school systems across the country race to offer professional development opportunities for dealing with unexpected violence and teachers collaborate to create a curriculum to "teach tolerance," educators must realize that there is already a tool at their disposal. By using personal writing as a vehicle and allowing students to discover the power of their voices, English teachers have the unique opportunity to encourage expression that can create peace within their students' hearts and minds.

While English teachers strive to teach voice from a variety of perspectives and may believe that they already include personal writing experiences in their curriculum, the fact is that, despite the promotion and general acceptance of the validity of personal writing, voice is still more often addressed in grammar lessons defining active and passive voice for the purpose of writing "third person" expository essays, or in connection with determining an author's choice in voice during the study of literature. Students learn to identify types of voices used by other authors, but when the time comes for them to write their own material, they often use removed perspectives that demonstrate no personal connection to their work. Furthermore, many teachers believe that they already know enough about personal writing experiences and that the extraneous homework assignments and "smaller" writing assignments that allow students to make personal connections are sufficient, noting that "they don't want to know" some of their students' more personal ideas. In *The Peaceable Classroom*, Mary Rose O'Reilley theorizes that teachers fear turning their classrooms into "therapy sessions." However, she noted that there is a strong need to further develop personal writing experiences that allow students to work through their issues and use the individual voice: ". . . good teaching is, in the classical sense, therapy: good teaching involves reweaving the spirit" (47). Unfortunately, some teachers still do not accept this approach to teaching, and while students appreciate the modes of communication, very few come to see writing as a personal experience. In *Writing with Passion*, Tom Romano also reflects on helping students see the value of more personal writing:

> What matters most in our classrooms, despite what test design-ers might advocate, is the quality of subjective experiences stu-dents achieve with reading and writing . . . It is crucial that students involve themselves in acts of reading and writing that evolve into optimal psychological experiences. (195)

Helping students appreciate this may be even more difficult for high school teachers because many students have been conditioned *not* to write from a personal perspective, editing away their own voices and being told that this is a "lower level," less analytical approach to their work.

Realizing, then, that if I ever wanted to allow students to resolve conflicts and use writing as a meaningful form of expression that could achieve this goal, I took a close look at my own teaching style. While I liked to believe that I allowed students to articulate their voices in their assignments and papers, due to time constraints and the desire to get through units, I caught myself slipping into the mode of the stereotypi-cal high school teacher: imparting knowledge through lecturing, neglecting to welcome students to voice their deepest thoughts through writing, and giving mechanical writing assignments that stu-dents prepared using strictly third person perspective. Though I assigned numerous, rigorous essays and personal journals, in the end I was giving writing assignments that did not lead to intimate writing experiences. A five page expository paper analyzing a short story, for example, might serve many solid purposes in good writing instruc-tion. In thinking about how much this type of paper really *mattered* to my students, though, I knew that I would have to step back and become a different type of teacher.

Support for changing my role came from a variety of sources, ranging from Howard Gardner's *Frames of Mind* to validation from Lantieri and Patti, who note in *Waging Peace in Our Schools* that teach-ers who effectively cultivate good will in their students find a way to regularly serve as facilitators for learning. This involves being able to change from lecture-based teaching to allowing students to feel a sense of power in their learning, as opposed to maintaining a controlling presence in the classroom (119). In removing myself from the center of the learning process, I realized that there could be a much greater sense of ownership and authority in my students' work.

Another revelation that occurred while planning my assignments was that, if I wanted to be a good enough writing teacher to make a difference in my students' lives, I had to take the time to know my students well. Though many teachers believe that they are there to teach content only, the truth is that high school teachers spend the better part of the day with the teenagers enrolled in their classes; therefore, they are in a position to make a substantial difference in their students' lives. In the latest edition of *In the Middle,* Nancie Atwell notes that, if teachers are to ever empower their students and help them grow into independent writers, teachers must realize their varied roles. She says, " . . . I have come to see how a good teacher takes parentlike responsibility for his or her students in terms of what they know about, what they can do, what they can accomplish" (20). This is often difficult in high schools where homerooms have been eliminated, bells ring every fifty minutes, and guidance counselors stretch themselves to reach large numbers of students. An important realization for me was that just knowing students' names and superficial information about them was simply not enough to establish a trust necessary in helping them through their conflicts. The real truth, then, was leading them to discover their voices in and beyond their reading and writing by using three new approaches: allotting more time for creative writing, teaching a research paper from a personal perspective, and extending student appreciation of voice and conflict beyond the literature studied in class.

Implementing More Creative Writing Exercises

My first major step in cultivating student voice involved the inclusion of more creative writing experiences into the curriculum. For years, I had thought about incorporating a creative writing circle or writing workshop into my classes, but I was always worried that it simply took too much time from the rest of the traditional literary canon. In fact, students and teachers I knew often viewed such endeavors as "middle school activities," and I had even heard other educators refer to creative writing as "fluff." But creative writing allows for individual expression in a more nonthreatening way than traditional writing assignments, making it an asset for cultivating peace and offering a forum for students' ideas. Furthermore, as James Moffett points out, "The processes of writing cannot be realistically perceived and taught so long as we try to work from the outside in . . . the heart of writing beats deep within a subjective inner life . . ." (92). O'Reilley offers further support when she notes that personal writing "allows each of us to try our unique experience against the univocal cultural story Western man has made up about the nature of reality" (86). Realizing that creative writing could allow students to express their deepest thoughts from a personal perspective—as opposed to an external regurgitation that could readily occur in a third person expository paper—my decision to add a weekly writing circle to my tenth grade English class ended up being one of the best choices I have ever made.

To organize and begin a writing circle, my students either purchased presentation folders with clear protective sheets that could be expanded as they wrote, or they used sketchbooks—white art paper in a spiral notebook—from local office supply or craft stores. Besides serving as an organizational tool, the sketchbooks brought a whole new facet to the writing. My students had a great sense of ownership of their books, guarding them much more carefully than they would have had their writings been placed in a three ring binder with the rest of their classroom materials.

The writing circle met one day a week and featured a writing activity that students began in class, showed me during a short conference, and finished independently for inclusion in their sketchbooks by the following week. When students put their writing into their books, they were to add creative illustrations using any format they desired. Students used pictures, computer generated clip art, markers, and crayons to enhance the pages and make them more artistic. Each week, before beginning new activities, volunteers would share their work orally with classmates eager to hear pieces of writing finished in the past week. At the end of some student readings, there were often moments of silence to ponder what had just been said. After every reading, the class applauded to show the writers support for the work they had shared with the rest of the group.

In order to give students opportunities to truly explore their inner feelings and find a voice through creative writing, I offered freewriting opportunities, as well as specific prompts to lead students to self-discovery, resolution, and reflection. During each activity, there was always an allowance for personal, freewriting approaches and creative styles. Some students regularly wrote poetry, while others chose to write fictional pieces. Students could also compose pieces in which they were not the narrators, allowing them to create and even adopt personas in their writing. This choice in genre and style allowed many students to learn to experiment with their writing and take risks in writing about ideas they might have otherwise avoided. As I chose not to initially grade these assignments (students received final grades for completed sketchbooks, but their early, creative attempts were not marked with corrections and graded individually), students worried far less about the power of the grade they would receive and more about voicing their ideas on paper. Approaching writing in this fashion truly helped my students to write in a natural voice and express ideas that might have been deadened during the editing process in a traditional writing experience (O'Reilley 44). In many cases, creative writing offered opportunities for students to vent their frustrations and come to terms with their darkest moments through their writing. Prompts such as "Write about an embarrassing moment in your life and how you have or have not come to terms with it," or "Write a satire that reveals your feelings about something that you might not feel comfortable addressing directly" helped students think about ideas and situations that bothered them. In two other freewriting experiences, students surfed the Internet and studied pictures. In one prompt, they were asked to find a picture that mirrored their feelings that day and use it as a starting point for freewriting their way into a poem or story. In the other prompt I asked students to find a picture that led them to think about a cathartic experience in their lives that they could capture in their writing.

The following poem, generated from an unprompted creative freewriting activity, clearly allowed one student to express the emotions he felt when sometimes feeling left out of his social circle:

Fifth Wheel
Always with people, but always alone;
In the midst of conversation, but speechless;
The one to whom promises are made, but never kept;
They say they'll call, but the phone stays silent.

Sometimes not even informed, then hears stories later;
Asked about things that were not attended;
Feels accepted, but only when others say so;
Knows love, just doesn't see it as much as wanted.

Wants love, but has trouble finding it;
Heart is openly and willingly put at risk, usually to be broken;
Goes home depressed, but can't show it;
Is afraid that others will run if they discover true thoughts.

Is scared that love will never come;
Is scared of betrayal, of being left out;
Feels let down by the world, unimportant;
Doesn't fit in, is unnecessary.

While the author of this narrative regularly appeared to be a happy, popular, academic achiever, his writing allows both him and the reader to discover something at the root of his conscience. Behind the smile and the appearance of being perfectly well adjusted, this student was like many teens in today's world, sometimes experiencing a sense of isolation that may lead to loneliness and unhappiness. In voicing his perspective through writing, this student found an outlet for his emotions. This same sort of emotional release was evidenced in nearly all of the student writing throughout the year. While some of the quiet students who may have seemed to be outside the loop of student popularity sometimes wrote about their fears of not being accepted by their peers, it was often the students who seemed to be outgoing and established in their social circles who came forward with their own insecurities when they were writing. This was true in the case of another popular, artistic student who developed her voice and expressed potential feelings for loneliness and a sense of inadequacy, as exemplified in her poem:

Would That I Were

Would that I were
A better artist,
Your visage would embrace my canvas constantly,
And images of you would keep my loneliness company.
Would that I were
A better musician,
I'd sing you serenades under a darkening, watery sky
And intertwine memories in the diluted harmony.
Would that I were
A better poet,
I'd write you epics and sonnets, odes and troubled lyrics,
And forge my remembrances of you into existence.
Would that I were
A better wisher,
I would will you here, and you'd appear,
Startled but hopefully contented, surprised yet happy.
Would that I were
A better dreamer,
I'd place your form in all my minds and meanderings,
And recreate all our potential possibilities in dream form.
Would that I were
A stronger person,
I would stay awake, watching you sleep longer,
Observing your gentle breathing and beautifully tranquil countenance.
Would that I were
Just a little more of everything,
I would be more "okay" with our current situation,
The distance would be easier and perhaps I'd miss you less.

From the surface, I would never have known that either of these students had ever experienced such feelings of loss and conflict. Allowing them to freewrite provided a forum for them to express feelings they may have otherwise left unexamined.

While many students were able to express personal concerns through reflections in their creative writings, other students captured their personal thoughts and voiced their anger about social issues that bothered them. For example, during another creative writing activity, I gave each member of the class two pictures that I had cut from magazines. Students used these pictures to write about a place that could provide them with a sense of serenity, a "peaceful place." Again, the format for the writing was open—students could choose options such as writing poetry, developing memoirs, or creating fictional narrative pieces. One student chose to write a short story about discovering the meanings of hope and peace after she was inspired by a magazine picture she was given that contained a butterfly. In her story, a young woman had an encounter with a holocaust victim who shared her thoughts about the horrible experience. In creating resolution for the protagonist in her story, the student writing the piece also experienced a sense of enlightenment:

> Later that evening, I walked back to the garden. Suddenly, history reports and baseball practices didn't seem important like they had been yesterday. When I reached the two lawn chairs, I saw two butterflies resting quietly inside my overturned glass of lemonade. I knew that these butterflies represented the faith, peace, and acceptance that fluttered softly in all human hearts. Anca had been right. She knew that no matter the suffering and pain, *hope* is soaring everywhere.

After sharing her story, which she titled "Healing Wings: A Celebration of the Triumphant Spirit," with the class, this student, completely on her own initiative, went on to submit it to and win a local writing contest sponsored by the Jewish community. A few months after she had submitted the piece, when she announced to the class that she had won (a surprise to all of us), the students responded with uproarious applause. As a teacher, it was a learning experience for me, in that I saw the additional effects of allowing students to find their voices through the writing circle. Through no other activity had the class grown together as a writing community; through no other activity had students expressed their emotions so strongly through writing. In addition, students' work indicated that the power to resolve internal and external conflicts through writing had already led them to seek out unsolicited writing opportunities to make a difference and to take their resolutions to the outside world.

Incorporating a Personal Research Paper

While students may discover their voices, explore their inner thoughts, and examine conflict resolutions through creative writing, great success in these areas can also be found through the writing of a full length research paper approached, like the writing circle activities, from an intrapersonal perspective. Attending a writing project workshop and reading Ken Macrorie's *The I-Search Paper* convinced me that this paper would provide students with a greater chance to see how writing could offer the opportunity for them to intimately reflect on their lives and the conflicts within them, and that I should join the ranks of other teachers already using this approach to the research paper.

In the preface of his "how to" book, Macrorie stated that, unlike traditional papers, which often achieve the undesirable effects of encouraging students to plagiarize and write assignments that are meaningless, the I-Search paper furthers "thought and reflection, that builds and sees." Written in the first person as if telling a story, this paper allows students to choose meaningful topics. After thinking about something that concerns them, students write a thesis in the form of a question. They then write about what they already know about the subject, what they want to know, what they find out through their search, and what they have learned as a result of completing the paper. In breaking the paper into such steps, students see the value of their writing during the entire process of completing the composition.

In order to use this paper as a source of conflict resolution and exploration, I took the cue from another experienced teacher's technique: First, I asked students to list five things on an index card that really mattered to them, that they deemed necessary for a happy life. Next, I had them list concerns or questions they had involving each item on the list. Finally, I had students turn the items and the concerns into questions. Many students' lists included items such as "family," "friends," and "good health." Other students listed hobbies and special interests, such as "playing the flute" or "the environment." The questions evolved into a wide range of queries from Why do families fall apart? to How important is having love in a person's life? to How much impact will a person's behavior in high school have on the rest of his or her life? These topics were very different from the usual compositions (such as literary elements of a novel, etc.) that I was accustomed to having my students write, and in beginning the I-Search students seemed much more excited about getting started with their papers than they had in the past.

Since reflection on and resolution to such deep questions does not evolve overnight, I decided to give my students two months to devote themselves to this paper. They worked independently to gather materials and write their papers during this time, and each Wednesday was designated for teacher and peer conferencing and working on the papers. Students kept a journal of their weekly progress, allowing them to record their progress, vent frustrations they had encountered, or enjoy the success they had experienced in their work. Throughout the process students were required to seek out "expert" individuals to interview who might be able to provide them with answers to their questions. I also had students seek out conflicting views on the answers to their questions, both in print sources and in their interviews, to provide further evidence that not all conflicting ideas or problems are approached or solved in the same ways.

From social workers to clergy to lawyers to psychologists, students sought out individuals who might help them resolve issues such as why their parents divorced, whether or not an individual could truly make a difference in the world, and whether or not adolescent friendships are strong enough to endure the passage of time. From the beginning, students took ownership of their work, again realizing that this was their opportunity to think about something that they really needed to know, something that bothered them—and then use English class and writing as a vehicle for discovery.

In addition to promoting student reflection and searching for the resolution of a problem, the I-Search had positive external results as well. When my students first began their papers, I could see their anxiety in taking on such a great assignment; therefore, I set aside time each Wednesday for class discussion about the papers. After doing this, I observed a great sense of camaraderie and collaboration developing among class members during the writing process, especially in providing resources and help in dealing with problems that arose. It became common for students to pass along articles they had come across that they thought would be beneficial to another writer. When students expressed difficulty in finding a good person to interview, hands in my room shot up instantly, with suggestions and phone numbers of family members and friends who could be of service to other students in the class. Students who did not typically communicate with each other began talking, learning that each individual in the class had something to offer to the group. In addition, class members came to realize that all of their peers had unique problems and concerns, and they worked together to help find the answers. From having the choice to learn the answer to a problem they had been experiencing, to being able to write their papers in their own voices, numerous students reinforced and reiterated what they had discovered in this writing process. The following commentaries from anonymous student surveys were quite typical of the general student response:

> Through the I-Search paper I learned that I can have a happy life after all. I have been angry, and I have taken out my feelings on just about everyone since my parents' divorce. I wanted to die, and I wanted other people to hurt like I did. . . . Now I have a better understanding of myself and my parents. . . .
>
>   I feel as if I had a say in what I learned, and in this paper I was allowed to voice my own views on a subject that mattered in my life. No other paper could do that.

While this paper was time consuming, as a teacher I saw the great difference in student development and quality of writing that resulted from this form of research paper. When the papers were shared with the class, nearly all of the students said that they truly felt better about the problem-turned-thesis they had investigated. Furthermore, students also learned the value of collaboration as they helped each other find sources and finish their papers. From writing thank-you notes to those they had interviewed, to finalizing their papers for submission, students learned that their writing took them far beyond what a basic prompt for an expository paper could have offered and led them to unmatchable self-discovery and resolution.

Extending Student Voice beyond the Literature

Yet another way for educators to provide students with a voice and pathway toward peace through writing is by providing enrichment experiences such as the multigenre project in conjunction with the study of literature. In this type of project, students study literary themes and conflicts in assigned readings and then search for the same ideas or themes in literary works from a variety of genres—fiction, poetry, nonfiction, etc. My curriculum features the reading of longer selections such as *A Separate Peace, Julius Caesar,* and *Fahrenheit 451.* From looking at themes of jealousy, war, friendship, and coming of age in these works, my students came to understand that literature is a mirror of the world and that there is a universality of conflict. While not all teachers use these particular works, most curricula offer novels, Shakespearean tragedies, stories, and poetry that can readily serve as appropriate works for multigenre style projects.

During the study of *A Separate Peace* I used traditional study guides, class discussion, quizzes, and tests to assess student progress during this unit, but what made the greatest impact on my students was the assignment of the multigenre project. All of my students chose a theme of conflict from the book that captured their interest, then searched for other examples of that conflict and possible resolutions in other works of fiction, poetry, and nonfiction. In addition, I required them to write an original short story, poem, and nonfiction piece of their own on the topic they had selected. When they had completed their search and had written their own materials, they placed all of the writing in their sketchbooks or on trifold presentation boards. We then spent a day of class time, armed with Post-it notes, reading the projects and writing comments, which we attached to the boards and pages of the sketchbooks. When writing their Post-it notes, the class wrote about connections they had made with the material, provided specific details about what they liked about the projects, or commented on the structure and style used by individual students in their writing.

The results of this project were positive in quite a few ways. First, the project gave students the opportunity to discover for themselves that themes of conflict really *are* universal. It often seems as if students think that what they read in English class is isolated from what goes on in the real world. Second, completing these projects allowed students to explore their own feelings and voice their opinions about conflicting subjects in the form of writing. One student, who typically offered apologies to the class when it came time to share his attempts at poetry, wrote the following poem based on his feelings about war:

The Cause Advance

The conflict rains, across the plains
As the fighting moves back and forth.
Advance, retreat, the men all run
Towards the death we all shall meet.

The drums roll, hear them roar
Like a parade, see the columns advance.
Left, right; left, right, the order is:
"March off and join the fight!"

Simply boys, with guns no more than toys
this cause advance. It is they on whom
Our chances last.
Boyhood and innocence stained,
By countries want for gain.

The trumpets call us all to attention,
Their valor and sacrifice are known,
But yet should not go without mention.

A tear, a sigh; as we wave good-bye
To love and peace stained,
By countries want for gain.

When other class members read this poem, they were impressed by the student's attempt to capture his feelings toward war. In reading his Post-it notes, he was reassured that he had "found his voice" by another student, and that he had presented a strong case for why wars exist. Through the class readings of published work, as well as these student writings, the multigenre project provided the forum for student exploration, understanding, and reflection of a wide range of conflicts existing in their own worlds, as well as in the world at large.

Reflections

As one teacher, I am not arrogant enough to think that I can save the world and make every student who enters my room a happy person. However, if teachers are to make a difference in the world through the teaching of English, they must take the time to help their students realize the importance of reflecting, collaborating, and finding their voices. In *Reshaping High School English,* Bruce Pirie notes that much of the work done in mainstream English classes is designed for the purpose of "studying works written by others" (64). While studying these works is part of an English teacher's purpose, I have found that fostering individual opportunities for growth through creative writing, personal research papers, and enriched writing opportunities—other than merely using study guides, expository papers, and pen and paper tests—has transformed my classroom. While high school teachers may see students for only an hour a day, great things can be done in that hour, for what goes on in our classrooms for just a brief period of time can extend our students' thoughts beyond the classroom walls. It is the English teacher who can help today's youth realize that the true power of peace may indeed flourish through the power of the pen.

Works Cited

Atwell, Nancie. *In the Middle.* 2nd ed. Portsmouth, NH: Boynton/Cook, 1998.

Gardner, Howard. *Frames of Mind.* New York: Basic Books, 1987.

Lantieri, Linda, and Janet Patti. *Waging Peace in Our Schools.* Boston: Beacon Press, 1996.

Macrorie, Ken. *The I-Search Paper.* Portsmouth, NH: Boynton/Cook, 1988.

Moffett, James. *Coming on Center.* Portsmouth, NH: Boynton/Cook, 1981.

O'Reilley, Mary Rose. *The Peaceable Classroom.* Portsmouth, NH: Boynton/Cook, 1993.

Pirie, Bruce. *Reshaping High School English.* Urbana: NCTE, 1997.

Romano, Tom. *Writing with Passion.* Portsmouth, NH: Boynton/Cook, 1995.

17 Giving Peace a Chance: Gandhi and King in the English Classroom

David Gill

We weren't sure when it started, the violence. Unlike other schools you read about in the news, we didn't have shootings, we didn't have metal detectors, and we didn't have security guards of any type patrolling the campus. But over the past few years, the number and severity of fights had increased steadily. More alarming was that the school culture's tolerance for violence had changed. At one time, teachers could deal with student-on-student violence fairly easily. Now, however, many teachers trying to break up fights are often attacked themselves. When did the slide start? Some of us asked ourselves this question in the faculty lounge after an especially violent fight had disrupted our annual academic awards assembly. The fight had broken out in the auditorium, and, like a fire, it took on a life of its own. Dozens, perhaps, of our students had joined the original fight, turning it into a near-riot that swept out of the auditorium and down the hallway. Before any of the faculty could regain control, some students had vandalized classrooms and continued the fight, which ended when someone threw a computer monitor down a crowded hallway. That shocked enough people that the fight was squelched and order was restored.

We didn't make the news. The next day, students barely talked about the melee. Why? we asked one another. How could they witness and participate in such an act then behave the next day as if nothing had happened? Not only were our students eager to participate in senseless violence, they were so inured to those acts that nothing seemed to faze them. This was something new, we said. Sure, fights had happened a generation, a decade, earlier, but now it was

---

This essay appeared in *English Journal* 89.5 (2000) on pages 74–77.

more than fights. It was the senselessness of it. Our students con-doned violence and even stepped back to enjoy the show, many times physically preventing adults from stopping it. By the end of that lounge conversation, I had one goal: My students would have the opportunity to see how violence and its counterpart, nonviolence, could affect their lives.

The Research

Before I could teach my classes about violence and nonviolence, how-ever, I had to learn about the nature of violence in our schools. I found two articles especially helpful. John Rich in "Predicting and Control-ling School Violence" wrote about ways to predict school violence and, more importantly, how to control it. Another article, "Teenagers Talk about Life," by Susan Kuhn made me realize that our students were not unusual in their reactions to violence. The adolescents interviewed by Kuhn demonstrated many of the same attitudes about violence, drugs, and school that my own students had shown. Most of these atti-tudes were negative, and, unfortunately, too many of the students in the article expressed a disenfranchised, emotionally detached attitude about their world.

I began looking for documentation of attempts at teaching non-violence in schools. If students in other parts of the country had simi-lar attitudes about violence, perhaps other teachers in other communities had tried something that worked. I found a curriculum guide, *Fighting Fair,* that used the life and works of Martin Luther King Jr. to teach adolescents about the philosophical background behind nonviolence. The authors of the curriculum hoped to build a supportive classroom environment on mutual respect and trust. Their teaching methods used role-playing and multimedia to make King and his followers seem more real and, subsequently, more relevant. Another program I found, *Free at Last: A History of the Civil Rights Movement and Those who Died in the Struggle,* offered examples of real people, famous and not famous, who gave their lives for a higher cause. A third teaching guide, *Into Adolescence: Stopping Violence,* explored the role of violence in our society and culminated in a lesson that compared the social protest models of Gandhi and King in order to illustrate conflict resolution. Though I decided not to use the mate-rials in the teaching guides (finding them aimed at an audience too young for my students), I used some of their ideas as a theoretical basis to develop a unit I could use in my classroom.

The Teaching

For models of nonviolence, I chose two twentieth century figures, Gandhi and Martin Luther King Jr. Both men are well-known historical figures, and their methods of nonviolent protest are well documented. King held a special status among my students, many of whom had grandparents and parents who participated in peace marches during the sixties. Beyond that, both men had published essays about their philosophies, and generations of writers had documented their lives and careers.

I wanted more than writings, however. I knew that these two figures had to be real to my students, or else their words and their methods would be abstract, no more relevant than any other essays they read in English class. King, because of his recent and immediate influence, would be fairly easy to personify. There were posters of him and film clips of his famous speeches. Gandhi, though, would be difficult.

The Dummy

To prepare for the unit, I gathered my materials: a copy of the Attenborough film *Gandhi* (chosen over other materials because of its relatively high interest level); copies of King's "Letter from Birmingham Jail"; and various film clips of King's speeches, especially the "I Have a Dream" speech delivered in 1963 in Washington, DC. I also collected a bed sheet; a wire coat hanger; brown, black, and white felt; a small piece of foam rubber; and a nylon knee-high stocking. At home, I stuffed the foam rubber into the stocking and cut out the felt to make eyebrows, eyes, and pupils. I then nailed two-by-fours together to make a stand about four feet high, and atop it I affixed another coat hanger bent inwards to form a claw shape.

The First Lesson

Though I taught the unit in four classes, I kept notes in only one. This is how things happened. Class began. I put the wooden frame in the front of the class. Murmurs followed, but no one asked any direct questions. I pulled the sheet out and draped it over the "shoulders" of the frame. I didn't respond to the few questions that students asked. Their curiosity was getting the better of them, and I didn't want to interrupt the cognitive percolating they were doing. Next, I wedged the foam-rubber-stocking head into the coat-hanger claw.

"It's a Roman," a female student called out.

I continued building the dummy. I used straight-pins to attach the eyes and eyebrows then bent a wire hanger into the shape of glasses and put them on the dummy's face. I stepped back and waited.

"Hey, that's what-his-name," Travis said.

"Yeah, that dead guy."

"I know him," said another student. "They made a movie about him 'cause he inspired MLK or something like that."

"What's his name?" I said.

"The Mahoot-man," Travis said.

"Mahatma," I said. "That's part of it. What's the rest?"

No answers. I said nothing and hoped they were thinking, trying to access a memory and not waiting for someone else to bail them out.

"Gundy," said Travis after a moment.

"That's Gandhi, dummy," said Michelle and laughed at her intentional play on words.

"That's right, Gandhi," I said. "What can you folks tell me about Gandhi?"

The answers came, though not fast and furious. I handed the chalk to Michelle, who wrote down the class responses on the board, making a cluster from the central word, "Gandhi." Collectively, they knew quite a bit about the life and works of the man called Mahatma. He had worked, according to them, to make somebody leave his people alone, and his methods had inspired King's work. To fill in the misconceptions and gaps in their knowledge, I put a prepared overhead on the projector and did a mini-lesson biography on the highlights of Gandhi's life and accomplishments. In order to strengthen the connection between King and Gandhi, I used another overhead that graphically compared the philosophies of nonviolence that Gandhi and King shared.

I passed copies of "Letter from Birmingham Jail" out to the class. Using a technique called "reading rounds" (one student begins reading a passage and can continue as long as she or he wants. Other students can join in at any time, either reading in unison—the net effect of which is a choral reading—or stepping in when there is a pause in the reading), we worked our way through the essay. Sometimes we were in sync, and sometimes we bordered on cacophony. Afterwards, we discussed King's ideas in a Socratic seminar, a technique drawn from Adler's *The Paideia Proposal* text. At first, there were few responses to my questions, but when I asked students to talk about their own lives, they began to open up.

"My granddaddy knew Dr. King," a male student said.

"My uncle did a sit-in at the drugstore downtown," Michelle said.

"Which one?" I asked.

"It's not there anymore. They tore it down. My uncle was glad."

"Why?" I asked.

"Because he got beat up for doing it."

"Doing what?" Travis asked. "Just sitting? Man, I would have knocked somebody in the head."

"You couldn't," a female student said.

When Travis wanted to know why not, several students in the group began to answer him. They explained how nonviolent protest worked, and we began to use King's text as a way of explaining to Travis and others how difficult nonviolent action is to undertake.

The next class, after the Socratic seminar, we began the task of watching the film, *Gandhi.* Robert Scholes, in "An Overview of Pacesetter English," talks about "reading" film as a text, and I wanted my students to be critical "readers" as well as viewers of the film. To do this, I adapted the reading log technique to viewing film, asking students to keep a running record of how they were perceiving the film's events. My interest was not in getting students to look critically at how the film was made, but to pay attention to the interaction among the various characters. How was Gandhi perceived early in his career? When he arrived in India? How long did his efforts take? All of these critical questions were posted on a bulletin board, and I reiterated them before beginning the film.

Throughout the "reading," I stopped the film at intervals and asked students to interpret the events. We focused on the critical questions, and I encouraged students to think about Gandhi's actions in terms of King's later actions in the American civil rights movement. What were the similarities? Were both men successful? What were some of the common and unique problems they both faced? Students wrote responses to these direct questions in the viewing logs, which were used later to compile their ideas for the final project.

Another method of assessing whether or not students were engaged in the unit was to read their journals. We began each class with a fifteen-minute writing time, and though I had previously given students a topic or quotation to respond to, in this unit I allowed them to choose their own topics. Initially, there were very few references to nonviolence, Gandhi, and King in their writings. During the next few days, however, more students began to allude to and directly address some of the other ideas discussed in class. All in all, 90 percent of students in the class had something to say about the topics during the course of the unit.

Culminating Project

It was all well and good that my students now knew about Gandhi and King. They knew what nonviolence was, and they knew it had been used to aid society. But would they, if asked, see any possible applications in their own lives? As a culminating assignment, I asked students to use their logs, notes, and journals to write a Bill of Rights for Students. Students wrote ten rights they personally believed were necessary for survival in their school and home. When they finished, they presented them to classmates in small groups and to the entire class. We posted the Bills around the room and left them there for the remainder of the year to remind us of what we thought was important (see boxed figure).

---

1. The right to be safe.
2. The right to learn without being disrupted.
3. The right to feel important.
4. The right to not be afraid.
5. The right to ask for help at home and school.
6. The right to walk home and around the neighborhood without fear.
7. The right to be proud of our school.
8. The right to have a quiet classroom.
9. The right to care about each other.
10. The right to live.

What I Learned

I never intended to turn my students into activists for nonviolence, and I had no illusion that studying about two famous twentieth century figures would directly impact their lives. Would they be less likely to fight after the unit? I doubted it. Would they be less likely to encourage and join in a fight? I didn't think so. Would their blasé attitude about violence change? Would they begin to see how destructive a culture of violence was for them, even if they had never lifted a hand once, cheered a fight on, or prevented a teacher from breaking it up? I hoped so. Because that's really what I was after—an awareness that there are alternatives, that violence is the easy way out and nonviolence is the road not taken by many because it is more difficult. I think they saw that. I cannot say that there were fewer fights the rest of that year or that my students were less likely to engage in violence-enabling behavior, but I can say that not one of the students in that class was in a fight at school that year.

And one more lesson for me: One afternoon after we had finished the unit, Travis and a friend came in after school. While I was helping Travis with class work, the friend starting messing around with the Gandhi dummy, which had now taken a place at the side of the room. The friend dropped into a mock boxing pose and fired off a couple of quick jabs at the foam-rubber head. Seeing this, Travis shot up and grabbed his friend's arm.

"Gandhi stands for nonviolence," he said, "so if you hit him again, I'm going to break your arm."

Some ideas, I suppose, take longer to sink in than others.

Works Cited

Adler, Mortimer. *The Paideia Proposal.*New York: Macmillan, 1982.

Bullard, Sara, ed. *Free at Last: A History of the Civil Rights Movement and Those Who Died in the Struggle.* Montgomery: The Southern Poverty Law Center, 1989.

King, Martin L. *Loving Your Enemies: Letter from a Birmingham Jail; Declaration of Independence from the War in Vietnam.* New York: A. J. Muste Memorial Institute, 1981.

Kuhn, Susan E. "Teenagers Talk about Life." *Fortune* 126.3 (1992): 54–61.

Post, Jory. *Into Adolescence: Stopping Violence.* Santa Cruz: ETR Associates, 1991.

Rich, John Martin. "Predicting and Controlling School Violence." *Contemporary Education* 64.1 (1992): 35–39.

Schmidt, Fran, and Alice Friedman. *Fighting Fair.* Miami: Peace Education, 1990.

Scholes, Robert. "An Overview of Pacesetter English." *English Journal* 84.1 (1995): 69–75.

18 Slam: Hip-hop Meets Poetry—A Strategy for Violence Intervention

Heather E. Bruce and Bryan Dexter Davis

Words make sense out of a world that won't.
Movie poster from Trimark Pictures Inc. for the film *Slam*

The violence escalating with fierce and frightening frequency in our nation's schools is sheer human tragedy. Our students are dying as an epidemic of violence on the streets and in some of their homes spills over into the schools. Students and teachers fear for their lives in the aftermath of so many dramatic and highly publicized school shootings. Teaching and learning numb, as many students and teachers daily face threats and bullying. In the face of this dangerous and menacing cultural climate, is it realistically possible to imagine how we might "teach English so that people stop killing each other," as Mary Rose O'Reilley asks of the nonviolent pedagogy she describes in her book *The Peaceable Classroom*?

We—Bryan, a twenty-something African-American male in his first year as a high school English teacher, and Heather, a forty-something white female English teacher educator—like many of our colleagues, are daunted by the increasingly hostile, disruptive, and violent culture intensifying in the schools in which we work. We are disheartened and perplexed by the woeful public rhetoric that heaps a good portion of blame for violence on teachers and public schools. Nevertheless, we choose to agree with Mary Rose O'Reilley that we can teach English so people stop hurting and killing each other. In this article we explain our thinking and share our experiences in attempting to develop a Hip-hop-influenced slam poetry curriculum that teaches for peace.

This essay appeared in *English Journal* 89.5 (2000) on pages 119–127.

Dislodging Violence in the English Classroom

We cannot brush aside the fact that our system of education has participated in both structural and systemic violence. It has closed down opportunities, especially for poor students, students of color, and students from limited English-speaking families (Stuckey). And yet, conversely, the English classroom can be a particularly productive site for "wording the world" (Freire and Macedo). The study of language and its effects on people is critical in changing that world. Words help to construct reality; they have powerful effects on real people. We believe that English teachers—experts in language use—can do a great deal to erase the inequality and discrimination that exists in the world. We can do a great deal to mitigate structural and systemic violence that has led to escalation of violent behavior. We can help to word the world more justly.

At the institutional level, we need to include and embrace the full diversity of society in our classrooms. We need to create a more just, inclusive, and nonviolent curriculum, which can contribute to a more just, inclusive, and nonviolent society. We need to examine more rigorously what we are doing in the name of English education and stop participating in procedures and promoting policies that can harm our students, even if it means breaking some rules.

At the individual level, we can work with our students to maximize their ability to express the complexity of their thoughts in words and to practice expressing those thoughts verbally, especially when it comes to emotions, rather than acting on angry, violent impulse. This is particularly crucial in our work with male students, who are much more likely than females to act in violent and aggressive ways (Gilligan). The role biology plays is by no means clear in the ways boys are characteristically different from girls in emotional expression and verbal facility; however, regardless of biological roles, the differences are magnified by a culture that has constructed femininity and masculinity in such ways that emotional development is supported for girls and discouraged for boys (Kindlon and Thompson 4). A consistent finding in the research is that there is a high correlation between lack of facility with verbal expression and aggression and delinquency (Kindlon and Thompson 275). Killings and other violent acts by emotionally troubled adolescent boys, along with the generally cruel ways boys tend to treat one another or girls, are indicative of the potentially dangerous and lethal ways boys exercise their "emotional illiteracy."

However, Gilligan suggests that it is indeed possible to prevent violence. Much of the therapy that he has done in prisons with violent male offenders consists of trying to facilitate their ability to think and talk about their thoughts and feelings "before and, instead of, committing impulsive, unreasoned, and unthinkable acts of violence" (58). Likewise, Dan Kindlon and Michael Thompson, psychologists who have worked with troubled and disruptive boys, indicate that a large part of their work is to help clients understand their emotional lives and develop an emotional vocabulary in order to increase their clarity about their feelings and those of others—recognizing them, naming them, and learning where they come from. Using words to talk about feelings releases emotional pressure and weakens the grip of anger and hostility. Once anger is raised to a conscious level, it loses some of its power (238). These mental health professionals try to teach violent boys and men, who have spoken through their actions, linguistic avenues for identifying, expressing, and channeling their thoughts and emotions before they erupt violently.

When girls experience the deep kind of shame and humiliation that is the root cause of violent behavior, they tend to do violence to themselves rather than to others. According to Pipher, girls experience the effects of structural and systemic violence when they come to realize the ways in which society has subordinated femininity to masculinity. They suffer unspeakably as objects of violence and abuse.

Everyone laughs at Alex's humorous poem.

However, girls are much more likely to internalize and repress the humiliating pain and shame that they feel rather than act outwardly violent. As Brown and Gilligan point out, they fall silent. They become depressed. They starve themselves. They eat compulsively. They vomit in response as a matter of course. They burn, cut, and mutilate themselves, but they generally do not go out and hurt and kill other people.

Although as a rule English teachers are not trained as counselors, we can help all our students—both male and female—find words that will in turn help them to identify, clarify, express, and channel thoughts and feelings rather than act either inwardly or outwardly violent. We can teach English so that people stop hurting and killing each other and themselves by embracing diversity, developing inclusive curriculum, and creating conditions in our classrooms that encourage our students to use the power of language rather than the force of fists or weapons of self-destruction to intervene symbolically in violence. To create such conditions, we need both a more humanizing pedagogy and multiple methods and strategies through which we can teach nonviolence nonviolently. One strategy that helps accomplish some of the goals of a peaceable curriculum is the poetry slam, a burgeoning pop cultural phenomenon.

Slam: Poets Intervene in Acts of Violence

Bryan: While I was student teaching in a diverse urban high school in the Pacific Northwest, I was responsible for *Julius Caesar* and a poetry unit. I worked hard to create lessons that would engage "below average" tenth-grade students and was disheartened when Hip-hop music and sports magazines appeared and circulated around the classroom while I was teaching. I conceded that I, too, would rather be reading the materials my students were studying in earnest than doing the required class work. Frustrated by curricular expectations that ignored the literacy skills my students brought with them and energized by my own identification with Hip-hop culture and familiarity with Hip-hop magazines such as *The Source* and *Vibe,* I began to think about how I might infuse the best of Hip-hop into my teaching as a way of both validating students' "home" languages and inspiring literacy development among students who were not expected to succeed.

At about the same time, I invited my advisor, Heather, to attend "a poetry reading" at the university. Saul Williams—a renowned Hip-hop poet, eclectic rock musician, star of the 1998 Sun-dance Film Festival's Grand Jury award-winning film *Slam,* and the 1996 national Grand Slam performance poetry champion—was "reading." Prior to

Williams's appearance, a number of college and high school students and I performed in a "slam," which is a combination of poetry and performance art. Slamming poets perform a "set" of two or three of their own poems. Randomly selected members of the audience judge the poetry spontaneously with a score of 1–10 immediately following each "reading." Slam poems are judged as much on content as on dramatic delivery. Slam is rather like an Olympics of poetry.

That night at the slam an emcee introduced the poets MTV vee-jay-style announcing, "Put your hands together for . . ." and *whua-whua-whuaed* Arsenio Hall-fashion. Each poet performed original works filled with electrifying imagistic language that danced with significant ideas about social justice. These poems spoke of love, anger, joy, and pain—of emotional and material poverty. The poems spit out powerful pleas for an end to violence, hatred, and discrimination. The judges shouted out ratings for each collection of poems performed. The audience—mostly high school and college students—cheered and applauded at the poets' renditions and consequent scores. Several swarmed the stage to "high-five" and otherwise congratulate the poets following their performances. Such is the poetry of slam.

Heather: Familiar with the eye-rolling groans "the poetry unit" typically receives in my classes, I was astounded by the energy, engagement, and vision of the poems written and performed by the young women and men who participated in the slam that night. Consequently, I saw the film *Slam* at Bryan's recommendation. *Slam* is a gritty, inspiring portrait of urban poverty and the redemptive power of art—of poetry and the power of performance. The film is set in a "warzone" housing project in Washington, DC, and in the DC city jail. *Slam* tells the story of Raymond Joshua (played by Williams), a gifted young poet who goes to jail on petty drug charges. In jail, Ray meets Lauren (Sonja Sohn), a volunteer teaching a writing class for the prisoners. Lauren encourages Ray to use his poetic talents to give voice to the anguish of a generation of young African-American men who have been locked away. In the climactic scene of the film—a moment in the prison yard when Ray is about to be attacked by members of a warring gang—he uses the word as a weapon and "saves his own skin by unleashing a barrage of verbal blows to the psyches of gang members poised to do battle" (Stratton 16). Ray Joshua's powerful poetry performance slams his would-be attackers and diffuses the pending violence.

Poetry has actually risen in status with our students since MTV aired its *Spoken Word: Unplugged* shows in 1992 and 1994. Says Stratton, "Rap music, the latest mutation of poetry, holds a generation in thrall, White and Black alike" (16). According to the *New York Times* News

Bryan reads Gil Scott Heron's "The Revolution Will Not Be Televised," a 1970s precursor to Hip-hop.

Service, the rise of rap music, the boom in stand-up comedy, and the proliferation of stage monologuists have all helped to make the spoken word an entertainment medium. The proliferation of open mike poetry readings and slam events in cafes and coffee houses from Chicago and New York to San Francisco and Santa Fe, the poetry movies *Slam* and *love jones*, the advent of spoken-word record labels such as Kill Rock Stars and Mouth Almighty/Mercury are signs that poetry is moving beyond the hype of rap and MTV into a central spot in the culture. All of this has expanded the popular notion of what poetry is and has brought "a wider, younger public to a form long associated with intimidating erudition" (The *New York Times* News Service). The melding of poem and performance is at the center of slam poetry's popularity. Young poets at slams are playing with words, texturing the language with rich rhythms and sounds. The result forms a palpable connection between poet and audience through the power of language.

As English teachers, we should catch our collective breaths, pay attention to poetry's resurgent vitality and strength outside of our classrooms, and think about how we might ride this current wave to serve our purposes. Contemplating the engaging dialectic and energy of slam/*Slam* and its raw power to quash potential acts of violence with words, we began to think about how Bryan might capitalize on both his and his students' Hip-hop acculturation and interests in performance poetry to develop slam as one strategy that builds on students' intrigue, bridges between students' home literacies and the literacies of high culture, and acts as violence intervention.

Hip-hop Meets Performance Poetry

Hip-hop is where many of our students live—the music they listen to, their traditions, the language they speak, the clothes they wear, the way they interact in the streets. Consequently, our students know a great deal about Hip-hop's evolution around concepts of flow, layering, ruptures in line, and repetition—perhaps more familiar to white teachers as poetic tropes and devices. With knowledge of Hip-hop's cultural elements, English teachers can more readily build on students' Hip-hop, rap, and poetic literacies and so intervene in the structural and systemic violence that has marginalized the knowledge they bring with them to our classrooms. A Hip-hop oriented pedagogy seeks first of all to reconstitute as subjects those who have been treated as objects. Home and academic literacies are thus not viewed as incompatible discourses but as mutually sustaining elements that traffic fluidly among home, street, and school.

There is a difference between Hip-hop culture and rap music, and many times the two are confused. Hip-hop is the term for urban-based creativity and expression of culture. Rap is the style of rhythm-spoken words across a musical terrain. While it is important to note that Hip-hop and rap are different, it is also important to understand their interrelationship. Hip-hop culture is structured around four fundamental cultural roles or elements: the DJ (deejay turntablist), the MC (Emcee), the graf artist (graffiti artist), and the B-boy and B-girl (breakdancers). Although each cultural element of Hip-hop has its own specific characteristics, they share certain "stylistic continuities" that coalesce around concepts of flow, layering, repetition, and ruptures in line. The perceived skill of MCs and DJs is unquestionably tied to their ability to connect with or create flow, even though the music is identified and defined by its break-beats. Rappers also layer meaning by using a repeated word with differing interpretations to signify a variety of actions and objects. B-boys and B-girls who "pop" or "lock" practice a style of dance that emphasizes quick jagged movements of their joints. However, fluidity is conserved because each snapping joint occurs one after the other along the body's natural line. In the production of graffiti pieces, sweeping and curving letters are broken with sharp angular breaks, but fluidity is maintained through the words' horizontal movement.

Many may be reluctant to recognize the connections among Hip-hop culture, rap music, and poetry because of the acrimonious debates over "Gangsta' Rap" that have played out in the public spaces of popular culture; the tendency to collapse Hip-hop into rap; and rap's reputation for explicit language use, violence, and sexism. However, we fail to do so at our students' peril. In any other context, English teachers comfortably argue that explicit, powerful, imagistic language is poetic material. We argue that taking the fewest words and making them mean the most is what poets expertly do. We argue that repetition, rhythm, and mimesis are important elements of poetry. We argue that poets manipulate the standard forms of English and use the language with license in terms of structure, rules, and meaning. We (especially those of us who are white teachers) need to acknowledge that these elements are also the material of Black Vernacular English or Ebonics in general (Holiday) and of rap in particular. Gilbert admonishes the reluctance to acknowledge these connections when he says, "Contrary to conventional absurdity, rap lyrics are poetry and rap is part of the African-American poetry continuum" (xxii). As we strive to create conditions in English classrooms that will allow our students widely to embrace both oral and written literacies, we need to broaden connections between our students' cultural literacies and the conventional English curriculum.

Promoting Slam in English Classrooms

"This ain't no metaphor. This is my life."

Ray Joshua

Students in our classes groan and roll their eyes during poetry instruction because somewhere along the way they have experienced poetry as esoteric and incomprehensible, and we apparently have not helped them much to see poetry otherwise. Many of our students nonetheless have managed to see the linguistic enchantment of poetry through rap music and slams without any help from us. More than anything, poetry is about words. Words and rhythms and sounds. Poetry is about texturing and punctuating the language. Poetry is about moving an audience with sound and image—with the magic of language.

Slam provides access to poetry for those who believe poems are impenetrable. Slams give students an outlet for the words, ideas, and sounds that circle inside them. Slams also provide Hip-hop poets with performance alternatives to rap. As slam promoter Bob Holman explains, slammers "liberate words from the dictionary and have them breathe in readers' minds." Young poets who hang out at slams want to fill the void "with language, entertainment, thought and love" (131).

In planning to use slam as a part of our English curriculum, we are guided by a curriculum entitled "Nonviolence and Leadership Poetry Workshops" developed by the Institute for Community Leadership, a Seattle-based nonprofit group whose founders and staff members are people who have worked over the past twenty years to promote nonviolence and civil rights (Cafazzo A1). The purposes for their curriculum are similar to our own: to show students the power of words in order to instruct them in nonviolence, leadership, character, and social change. "The goal is to improve literacy and public speaking skills, and at the same time, promote empathy" (Cafazzo).

We begin teaching slam-style poetry by inviting some local poets who have performed at coffee houses, bookstores, or at university slams to perform for and visit with the high school students. We also perform a number of our own poems for the students, reading as poets with two distinctly different voices and styles. We want them to have a number of models, voices, and rhythms in mind before we ask them to begin reading and writing poetry. There seems to be no end of performance poets in our area who are willing to "read" for our students and give them poetry pointers; however, we also introduce slam performance poetry by viewing video clips from the MTV *Spoken Word:*

Heather models the drama and emotion of a slam reading.

Unplugged series and from Bill Moyers's *The Living Language* PBS series. We have used clips of Quincy Troupe reading Blues-style poetry (Moyers), clips of slam poets performing Hip-hop poetry from the movie *Slam,* and a clip of Maya Angelou reading her gospel-style inaugural poem, "On the Pulse of Morning." We read a jazz-style poem that Bryan wrote and juxtapose it with the country-western twang of Utah Poet Laureate David Lee's "Pain" from *Day's Work* or the rock and roll voice of Bruce Springsteen in the lyrics of "Spare Parts."

Once our students have an idea about myriad poetry and performance possibilities, we begin with a mix of reading, discussing, and writing. We work with the words of a number of great poets and leaders. Our students read a mix of poems by Langston Hughes, Gwendolyn Brooks, Audre Lorde, Adrienne Rich, Donald Hall, Rita Dove, Jimmy Santiago Baca, Quincy Troupe, Li-Young Lee, Joy Harjo, Stanley Kunitz, Jane Kenyon, David Lee, Jessica Moore, and Saul Williams. We discuss the poets' ideas and word choices and compare them with the nonviolent ideas of Gandhi and Martin Luther King Jr. The students freewrite in response.

We use various prewriting exercises such as asking students to respond in writing to open-ended questions such as, "It makes me feel like screaming when . . ."; "I just don't get it when . . . "; "I get so angry when . . ."; "It made me laugh when . . ." or to cluster then freewrite around the word "pain" because it is a common emotion that surfaces in the poems we read. Students brainstorm and freewrite about dilemmas they have faced, mirroring another common theme in the poems we read. During all these freewrites, we encourage students to let words, any words that rise to the top of the brain, flow out. The object is for them to keep writing quickly for a few minutes about things that are in their thoughts, to get the words out so they can be crafted into images, lines, sounds, rhythms, poems. We adopt the Institute's term "target practice" for this writing warm-up in order to emphasize the aim of substituting word craft for violent outbursts. Writing tools— pens, pencils, word processors—are "weapons" acknowledging words' absolute power "to break someone's heart, free people from slavery, and stop wars" (Cafazzo A1). We encourage students to use their "weapons" to work for peace.

With the students' responses to ideas raised by the readings, discussions, freewrites, and their own life experiences for inspiration, they begin to shape their freewrites into drafts of poems through found-poetry exercises. During these exercises, poets cull the most meaning-laden words from their various freewrites. Students circle the most important words, single-slash clumps of word phrases into lines, double-slash groups of lines into stanzas. Poems begin to form as students write along a continuum about experiences that have made them angry and caused them pain—from fumbling a ball and losing a berth in the state football championships to dealing with the pressure for sex in a romantic relationship, from racial stereotyping to coming to terms with a parent's professed homosexuality. For the first time in the semester, every student writes continuously and makes the effort to revise.

We put names to poetry devices the students already know from Hip-hop lyrics they have memorized—similes, alliteration, metaphors, rhyming couplets. We encourage them to incorporate these devices into their poetry. We coach students on their writing and performances in pre-slam rehearsals, peer response sessions, and teacher conferences. During these coaching sessions, slammers learn how to stand straight and still, make eye contact, and show pride as they recite their poetic works to peer audiences. We teach our students to accept constructive criticism gracefully. Poets are applauded for their efforts during rehearsal sessions. Our students treat each other with dignity.

During peer response sessions, the students encourage each other to share, revise, and perform their words. They help each other find poetic devices that evoke the ideas behind the poem. Here is an example of one peer response session, as Jake prepares to perform his poem for the class:

"This is really something you should read," offers one classmate.

"I liked your poem, who is it about?" asks another.

"You were very dramatic when you read, but try to speak louder when you perform," says a third.

Jake thanks his critics. "I need a title. What do you think about 'I Apologize'"? he asks.

The room is silent as Jake performs a final version of his poem:

I Apologize

My whole life.
You said you'd be there.
No matter what I did.
You said I'd pay.
And I did.
I paid that day you sent me away.
I never understood why.
Those things I said. They made me hurt inside.
And after it was all over, it made me cry.
Dreams forgotten.
Hearts broken.
Love lost.
But not a word spoken . . .

Jake performs "I Apologize."

We work hard to electrify the room with the power of the word on slam days, which we organize once a week during this poetry unit. We want it to feel like the slam event we described earlier. The students vie affably for space, the opportunity to speak. Singing is allowed, props are not. The classroom resonates with applause, cheers, and mutual respect, as students take turns performing their poems. We see the students growing with confidence and pride as they experience their peers' appreciation.

Writing releases pent-up emotions, and performance brings acknowledgement and support, which urge healing and understanding. In these ways, student slammers find the experience of writing and performing poetry "life-transforming" (Cafazzo A1). As one slam student says, "Poetry helps get your mind and soul and heart together. It gives you a different view of life than you had before" (Cafazzo A1). Although we cannot yet speak for slam's long term or broad-reaching effects on our students, in our class they are demonstrating more tolerance and respect for each other and for us; and that, in itself, constitutes a laudable milestone.

Epilogue

Much that occurs in the name of multicultural education as a discourse for teaching a diverse student population is an emphasis on "What can we do for white teachers to prepare them to work with children different from themselves?" Inherent in this question is a notion that multicultural education constitutes learning tolerance for others unlike oneself. As Bartolomae and Macedo point out, framing multiculturalism as learning to tolerate others presupposes repugnance of those different from oneself. If the starting place of appreciating diversity is repugnance of "the other," the goal is always already out of reach. As teachers, we have everything to lose if we continue to think of so many of our students as somehow *other.* If we are to accomplish the goals for a more just, inclusive, and nonviolent English curriculum, which can contribute to a more just, inclusive, and nonviolent society, we must strive to see the *other* through empathic and celebratory eyes.

English teachers need to strive to recognize, understand, honor, and legitimize our students' linguistic and cultural identifications. We also need to provide resources and instructional support to all students—native, nonnative, and dialect speakers; African American, Latino, Asian/Pacific American, Arab American, Native American, and Euro-American—that will enable them to achieve oral and literate competence in conventional English, the language of wider communication (Smitherman) and economic success (Delpit). We need to figure out ways to sharpen and develop the knowledge and skills each student already possesses, while at the same time adding new knowledge and skills to that base. Delpit tells of a gifted white teacher who uses rap songs to develop a rule base for their creation. The students teach her their newly constructed "rules for writing rap," and she uses this knowledge as a base to begin a discussion of the rules Shakespeare used to construct his plays and the rules poets use to develop sonnets (67). We think about ways to travel from Hip-hop and slam to *Julius Caesar.* After slamming, we can better help our students connect with Shakespeare's use of Elizabethan language in his day through their shared understanding of the sheer power of the spoken word and temporal malleability of colloquial language. We can help our students better understand how anger, shame, and humiliation can lead to violence, how friend can betray friend, and how soliloquy, the rhetorical precursor of slam, might intervene. *Et tu, Brute?!*

Regrettably, far too few models exist for accomplishing humanizing goals in education. We had to make things up as we went along. We worked together across cultural boundaries to understand and appreciate our differently situated identifications so that we might each learn from and teach "the other." We continuously and fluidly shifted roles. At times, Bryan was the student and Heather the teacher; but more often than not, Heather was the student and Bryan the teacher. Bryan taught Heather about Hip-hop, rap, and slam; about rap's eloquent relationship with poetry; and about the structured loss of identity he experienced in training to become a black teacher in a white system, while Heather taught Bryan about becoming a high school English teacher. In our process, the traditional teacher-student hierarchy collapsed. Team teaching slam in Bryan's classroom, we arrived at an organic give-and-take among our different voices, experiences, and worlds to create curricula that draws in all the students. We think we may have much more to say about this in the future and plan to write together again.

"Democracy needs her poets, in all their diversity, precisely because our hope for survival is in recognizing the reality of one another's lives," writes Bill Moyers in the introduction to his book, *The Language of Life: A Festival of Poets* (xi). Opening up ways for Hip-hop literacies to travel into the English classroom in the form of poetry slams gives both our students and us spaces and opportunities to speak and to hear a more commodious language; language that makes room for our students' anecdotal, personal, and cultural reflections; language that helps to create a world, as Jim Corder has counseled, "full of space and time that will hold our diversities." Slam gives us a way "to make ourselves plain to all others, that reveals us as we're reaching for the others" (Corder 364). Slam gives us a space for teaching peace.

Works Cited

Angelou, Maya. "On the Pulse of Morning: The Inaugural Poem" Audio Cassette CSST Edition. New York: Random House, 1993.

Bartolomae, Lilia I., and Donaldo P. Macedo. "Dancing with Bigotry: The Poisoning of Racial and Ethnic Identities." *Harvard Educational Review* 67.2 (1997): 222–46.

Brown, Lyn Mikel, and Carol Gilligan. *Meeting at the Crossroads: Women's Psychology and Girls' Development.* Cambridge: Harvard UP, 1992.

Cafazzo, Debbie. "Poetic Lesson in Nonviolence." *Tacoma News Tribune* 24 Jul 1999: A1.

Corder, Jim. "Argument as Emergence, Rhetoric as Love." *Conversations in Context: Identity, Knowledge, and College Writing.* Eds. Kathryn R. Fitzgerald, Heather E. Bruce, Sharon Stasney, and Anna Vogt. Ft. Worth, TX: Harcourt Brace, 1998. 347–64.

Delpit, Lisa. *Other People's Children.* New York: The New Press, 1995.

Freire, Paulo. *Pedagogy of the Oppressed.* Trans. M. B. Ramos. New York: Continuum, 1970.

Freire, Paulo, and Donaldo Macedo. *Literacy: Reading the Word and the World.* South Hadley, MA: Bergin and Garvey, 1987.

Gilbert, Derrick I. M. *Catch the Fire.* Berkeley, CA: The Berkeley Publishing Group, 1998.

Gilligan, James. *Violence: Reflections on a National Epidemic.* New York: Random House, 1996.

Holiday, D. Alexander. "Street Corner Writing." Position paper ERIC NO: ED337776, 1991.

Holman, Bob. "Bob Holman Kicks the History of Slams." *Slam.* Eds. Richard Stratton and Kim Wozencraft. New York: Grove Press, 1998. 127–38.

Kindlon, Dan, and Michael Thompson. *Raising Cain: Protecting the Emotional Life of Boys.* New York: Ballantine Books, 1999.

Lee, David. *Day's Work.* Salt Lake City, UT: Copper Canyon Press, 1990.

Moyers, Bill. *The Language of Life: A Festival of Poets.* New York: Main Street Books, 1996.

———. *The Living Language.* Prod. David Grudin. Videocassette. Alexandria, VA: PBS, 1989.

New York Times News Service. "Interest in Poetry Reflects Rise of Slams, Readings and Rap." *Tacoma News Tribune* 22 Aug 1999: E3.

O'Reilley, Mary Rose. *The Peaceable Classroom.* Portsmouth, NH: Boynton/Cook, 1993.

Pipher, Mary. *Reviving Ophelia: Saving the Selves of Adolescent Girls.* New York: Ballantine Books, 1994.

Slam. Dir. Marc Levin. Perf. Saul Williams, Sonja Sohn. Trimark Pictures Offline Entertainment Group, 1998.

Smitherman, Geneva. "CCCC's Role in the Struggle for Language Rights." *College Composition and Communication* 50.3 (1999): 349–76.

Springsteen, Bruce. "Spare Parts." *Tunnel of Love.* Columbia Records, 1987.

Stratton, Richard. "SLAMMED in Dodge City." *Slam.* Eds. Richard Strattton and Kim Wozencraft. New York: Grove Press, 1998. 11–19.

Stuckey, J. Elspeth. *The Violence of Literacy.* Portsmouth, NH: Boynton/Cook, 1991.

Weber, Bruce (*New York Times* News Service). "National Poetry Slam Was Slam-bang Success with 3,000 People at Finals." *Tacoma News Tribune* 22 Aug 1999: E3.

19 Writing to Heal, Understand, and Cope

Vasiliki Antzoulis

All summer I had prepared, reading the novels and short stories I planned to teach. I tapped all of my resources—my imagination and what I had learned from my professors, books, and fellow classmates. My short story unit was finished and I had wonderful ideas for the entire semester. I was excited and nervous about teaching for the first time. To calm my nerves I had prepared and planned, but nothing could have prepared me for what I would encounter student teaching in the fall of 2001.

I began the semester with community-building activities. On the fourth school day, we instantly became a community, a community dealing with tragedy and coping with loss and a pervasive fear. On September 11, my students, along with the other 3,000 students of Stuyvesant High School, ran for their lives up the West Side Highway as they saw the twin towers come down. Our school was only a few blocks away; some had parents who would be in those towers. Everyone was scared and shocked, unable to understand how and why this could be taking place. Everything that they were sure of was to be questioned; everything that they took for granted—their freedom, their safety—now seemed all too fragile.

We were away from Stuyvesant and each other for a week and a half. I found myself feeling very isolated and longing for people to talk to, to share my feelings and fears with. I was sure that my students had the same need. I emailed all of them on the night of September 11, hoping and praying that they had all arrived home safely. Because Stuyvesant High School is a specialized school, students come from all five boroughs of New York City. Many of my ninth graders were still getting acquainted with Manhattan and now they had to find their way back to Queens and Brooklyn without public transportation.

This essay appeared in *English Journal* 93.2 (2003) on pages 49–52.

Some had to walk for miles over bridges; most took hours to get home. Luckily, all of my students and their families were fine.

Relocation and Dislocation

Stuyvesant was being used as a triage center, and the school and area around it were closed off to the public. We could not go back into the school to retrieve our belongings or books from the book room to teach our classes. All my preparation was pushed aside as we were relocated to a school in Brooklyn, with twenty-five-minute periods and no books. Everything that once seemed important now seemed so irrelevant. How could I go in and teach alliteration to students who had just witnessed people jumping out of the 110th story of the World Trade Center? How could I expect them to focus on style, mood, and theme when they were afraid of getting on the train to go to school because of terrorist threats of bombs and anthrax? The first day back was difficult, but I knew my students needed me as much as I needed them. They were thirsty for comfort and needed to be heard. All of them wrote about the event; all of them needed to talk about what had happened and what was going to happen.

Listening to my students talk, I fought to hold back my tears. One girl confessed how scared she was and claimed that she did not think we could ever be safe. She wondered how we would know who else was hiding, ready to attack us again. One boy told me privately how his best friend's mother was still missing; she worked on the 90-something floor. Some students went off on how we needed to go and bomb whoever did this to us. Then one girl raised her hand and said, "Ms. Antzoulis, I don't understand. I really thought I was going to die that day. I thought I would never see my parents or sister again. It was a horrible feeling. I wouldn't want our country to be the reason anyone else has to feel that way. No one should experience that, no one. There must be another way to solve this." Here was a group of ninth graders articulating what we all felt and feared. At that point I realized just how special my students were. I realized how important it is for us as teachers to listen and let ourselves learn from our students.

I wanted to tell them we would be fine and everything would be OK, but I didn't know that. I wish I could have given them a reason that this happened to us, but I was still trying to make sense of it myself. All I could do was be there for them and try to make every moment together in class a time where they could feel safe, help them realize they were not going through this alone, and provide them outlets to cope with all that they were feeling.

Designing for Relevance

Since I now had no books and only twenty-five-minute periods, I had to postpone the short story unit I had prepared over the summer. I turned to Dr. Rebecca Packer, my supervising professor from New York University. She supported me through this difficult time and provided me with poems and short stories I could use to help students cope with this horrific tragedy. Through my education, I was trained in the theories of constructivism. I always wondered how it would work in an actual classroom. How do we make literature relevant to our students? Here, early in my teaching career, I realized how important this is. Brooks and Brooks prioritize *emerging relevance* as the first principle of constructivism:

> Posing problems of emerging relevance is a guiding principle of constructivist pedagogy. However, relevance does not have to be pre-existing for the student. Not all students arrive at the classroom door interested in learning about verb constructs . . . but most students can be helped to construct understandings of the importance of these topics. Relevance can emerge through teacher mediation. (35)

Almost all of my students feared poetry. Some claimed they hated it, and most dreaded trying to figure out the "hidden" meaning. I knew if I had selected random poems for study they would probably continue to have these feelings. Instead I took Brooks and Brooks's advice and selected poems with themes of relevance for the students. I designed a poetry unit to help students deal with the grieving process and allow them a way to talk about what they were feeling through the analysis and discussion of poetry. Students read each poem closely and we analyzed and discussed them. Each poem was followed by a writing assignment, where students experimented with one or two stanzas of poetry. In the end, each student chose one poem to revise and compiled a portfolio of drafts, reflections, and one revised poem. Throughout the unit I saw students embrace poetry and take risks in their own writing. Many wrote in their reflections how their feelings about poetry had changed, and they realized it wasn't only about figuring out a meaning but also about feeling poetry and thinking about different issues.

Reading and Writing Poetry

The unit began with the lament, "Funeral Blues," by W. H. Auden. Students discussed the speaker's feelings of loss, grief, and despair. We looked closely at the poem and then students wrote their own laments.

Tom Romano notes that "getting students both to consume and to produce poetry is my strategy for moving . . . poetry into people's bones" (60). I agree, and throughout the semester reading and writing were closely intertwined. Students responded to the poetry they read by writing poetry. After reading Auden's lament, I gave the students the freedom to write about a serious topic or something more lighthearted, such as a lament for an object. I did not force them to continue talking about September 11 and the events that followed, but I wanted them to be able to if they wished. Laments ranged from a student who lost his favorite wallet, to a student who wrote about her experience on September 11 and the city's loss (see Figure 1).

I followed "Funeral Blues" with William Blake's "A Poison Tree," and we moved from grief to revenge. Students added a new stanza to Blake's poem and some wrote about the empty feelings that follow revenge. This led the class into a discussion of whether or not we would feel any better as a city or nation if we were to get revenge on the terrorists. What were we trying to accomplish? This discussion

---

The Horror Remains Forever On
by Marissa Galizia

The first plane hits, I can feel the quake;
I run to the window, this was no mistake.
The second plane hits, with barely a break;
I can't believe it, this must be fake.

We exit the building and walk uptown,
With millions of others I feel I might drown.
My eyes stay dry, but I can't help but frown;
upside down.

What will I do? Where will I go?
My mother at home must be filled with woe.
I'm frantic with calling everyone I know,
But the phone won't work, service is low.

We walk and walk as ambulances rush by,
"Marissa, Marissa," I hear Michael cry.
He is soaked with sweat like the middle of July.
Why did they do this? Oh why, oh why?

Back to his house on Houston Street;
The town is deserted, not a car do we meet.

We watch the news repeat and repeat;
Although I try, I can't even eat.

As we watch and wait I can feel the pain
Of all the kids who will never see parents again.
The thought is almost too much to sustain.
Finally, there is news of the train.

When at last I get home my parents just grin,
They were worried all day about losing their kin.
It takes days before the true horror sets in;
With thousands dead, the funerals begin.

The dark clouds of smoke finally leave N.Y.C.
The fight begins to keep the US free.
I know there are others far worse off than me,
Yet my heart still swims in a deep dark sea.

Although those beautiful twins are gone;
Their shadow remains forever on.
I'll never forget the events of that day,
Those horrific images, in my mind will stay.

Figure 1. Marissa Galizia used Auden's "Funeral Blues" as a model and wrote her own lament about September 11. This poem is a result of drafts, revisions, and workshops.

arose naturally, initiated by the students. We discussed what was on their minds, which helped the healing process, but we did it when they were ready.

I then introduced two more poems by William Blake—"Songs of Experience: A Divine Image" and "Songs of Innocence: The Divine Image." We compared the states of innocence and experience and closely analyzed Blake's wording, themes, and style. I felt that students had moved from a state of innocence before the towers were attacked, to a state of experience after they fell and their whole world was over-turned. Students responded by writing a stanza representing inno-cence and a stanza representing experience. One student wrote about a girl as a child adoring her mother and then a girl as an adolescent los-ing her mother. Another student wrote about the innocence of child-hood when the day was spent playing and the experience of adolescence with the realities of school and studying.

I ended the unit on an optimistic note by having students read and listen to John Lennon's "Imagine." Students speculated about what the perfect world would be. I was surprised to hear a student say that there should be no money so that people would not be greedy. One student felt that human beings would just spoil any utopia. Then one student raised his hand and said, "We could have a perfect world, or at least a much better world, if we all just took the time to really learn more and understand each other. Then maybe we would under-stand how people are, what they believe in, why there are conflicts— then we could see each other as humans and work our problems out and know where we are each coming from." I smiled at him and thought to myself, I hope these kids are running the country one day, and I hope that life doesn't make them too experienced and jaded. They are the ones who can truly make a difference. The students loved listening to the song and really got into the assignment of creating a poem that reflected what they would "imagine" for a perfect world. Their responses were touching and moving and reflected all that they feared about today's world and all that mattered to them.

Making Sense

From this unit, I felt that students learned a lot about poetry and at the same time were learning to cope with their mixed feelings of sadness, fear, and anxiety. Our discussions were not just about poetic tech-niques or abstract themes but about themes and issues that were rele-vant to their lives and their personal experiences. The writing the students produced was thoughtful and imaginative. They had more invested in it because it mattered to them. Brooks and Brooks claim, "When magnetic events occur that exert an irresistible pull on students' minds, continuing with pre-planned lessons is often fruitless" (105). I knew that I couldn't ignore what we were all experiencing. Had I continued with my scheduled short story unit I don't think students' writing would have been as powerful or engaging. Students needed to discuss their feelings, and by channeling their fears, grief, anger, and confusion into their writing they were able to begin the healing process and gain a new appreciation for the reading and writing of poetry.

I chose to teach because I wanted to make a difference in my students' lives. I felt that I could do that in English classes where I could learn about my students, discuss real issues, and help them learn from one another. Student teaching after September 11, 2001, affirmed my choices. I did not just teach students English; I taught them to channel their feelings into writing; I taught them that it is OK to be uncertain and to question; I taught them that nothing is too much for us to handle together. I was able to do this through reading and writing that was relevant.

The start of the twenty-first century has so far been a time of uncertainty, fear, and questioning. We have been made aware of our fragility in this world and have been forced to question all that we hear and see in the media, the way our government works, and all we have been taught to believe our whole lives. So what does it mean to be a teacher in the twenty-first century? We need to support our students. We need to give them a place where their fears and opinions can be heard and where they can be exposed to others' ideas and opinions. We need to give them outlets to deal with all that they are facing. But most of all, we need to be honest with them. They are aware of what is going on around them. We cannot hide behind our books and poems, but instead we must utilize such materials to make sense of the world. Now there is more reason than ever to read and educate ourselves, to learn about and understand different cultures. Now more than ever we need to write to discover our feelings, to have our voices heard, and to deal with our pain.

Works Cited

Brooks, Jacqueline Grennon, and Martin G. Brooks. *In Search of Understanding: The Case for Constructivist Classrooms.* Alexandria: ASCD, 1999.
Romano, Tom. *Writing with Passion: Life Stories, Multiple Genres.* Portsmouth: Boynton/Cook, 1995.

20 The Silent Classroom

Marion Wrye

When I see a corridor full of students clunking along under their fifty-pound backpacks, I wonder about the weight of our culture on their psychology and spirit. Do they, like *New York Magazine* film critic David Denby, feel that their minds have been invaded and taken over? In the fall of 1991, at the age of forty-eight, Denby went back to Columbia University, where he had been a freshman thirty years before, and sat down in the classroom with undergraduates. Denby confesses in *Great Books* to a midlife crisis, the most dramatic symptom of which was a deep emotional turmoil, even disgust, over the "modern state of living-in-the-media": the media with its blitz of fragmentary and inadequate information making Americans "half-mad with anxiety and restlessness," the media with its threat "to take over altogether and push literature out of sight. . . ." (15).

At the time, Denby was also keenly interested in the "curriculum wars" raging in the arena of education. So, rising to his wife's challenge to "put up or shut up," he bought his books and notebooks and went back to Columbia to ponder for himself what the controversy was all about. During the course of the year, he became a reader again and rediscovered the pleasures of concentration:

> . . . I had abandoned the pleasures of concentration to the pleasures of fantasy; that anguish of being lost in the media, a part of the swamp of representation, and therefore merely another producer and consumer of images and words without identity or form of my own—all of this was beginning to fade. It had been fading all year, I realized, and now I actually felt it going, and I saw a boundary. The man reading Kant and Hegel was not part of the pulsing electronic media. Not at that moment. (313)

It is certainly true that the contemporary individual in America is barraged with images and information and has to work harder than ever to eke out a space where the "pleasures of concentration"—both the discipline and the reward of reading—can be experienced and

---

This essay appeared in *English Journal* 89.5 (2000) on pages 79–83.

nurtured. Sven Birkerts in his essay, "States of Reading," sees the situation as more critical than we might ordinarily think:

> The one hope is that reading will, instead of withering away in the glare of a hundred million screens, establish itself as a kind of preserve, a figurative place where we can go when the self needs to make contact with its sources. (57)

It doesn't help the situation either that the hyperspace world of the media is seductive and mesmerizing, creating an atmosphere that can enlist the individual's own will often against his or her best interests. One of my students, a very bright high school junior, wrote a compelling personal narrative about a full-blown addiction to the cyberworld that brought her to the depths of pain and alienation and required psychiatric intervention and a grueling struggle before she was able to come back to the real world. The promises of technology can be bitterly ironic, ultimately robbing the human being of the powers that define and ennoble humanhood. Thoreau saw the complicated dangers when he said in "Walden:" "We do not ride on the railroad; it rides upon us" (1767).

Denby refound the "pleasures of concentration" in learning to read again and, in the year-long struggle, reclaimed his identity, proving that the "pleasures of concentration," like Nirvana, do not come easily. A host of adversaries in the form of distraction, fear, apathy, social and economic ills, personal tragedies, etc., provides for a mighty battle. It takes time, it takes discipline, it takes desire, and there is no magic formula. It's not easy to concentrate, especially in today's world. And it's certainly not easy to teach others how to do it.

If you are a teacher trying to teach others how to read, how to think, how to write—all of which require concentration—you have to learn to attend to the faintest signals in the student, and you have to be able to interpret them. You have to wrestle with all those factors that bedevil learning until that moment comes in your student's consciousnesss when the point of it all dawns. That moment when you see in the student's face the happy yielding to the "pleasure" is unmistakable. At that moment, you know the student has arrived and will be all right. You could both go home. Of all the success stories I have heard from my colleagues or have experienced myself, the most rewarding signal this theme. Those moments when students "get it" are always unique, even a bit transcendent, and they defy standardization and measurement. Somewhere in the student's mind a connection has been made, a circuit completed. One thing we know for certain is that the student has more power of understanding and appreciation for the endeavor than he or she had the moment before. Susan Ohanian in her essay

"Insults to the Soul" says, ". . . if I had the space, I could tell you a heart-warming story of each one of those kids making a connection with a book . . . I guess you have to be a teacher to realize the magic of this moment" (33).

David Denby was finally able to break free because he kept at it and because he finally "saw a boundary." What a moment. Held hostage to the insidious flotsam and jetsam of popular culture, Denby drew his line in the sand, escaped from the fantasy, and rescued his own mind. His internal reference point and power were restored; the sanctity of his identity and freedom was reasserted. Hard reading and thinking, as pleasure, had been refound.

Finding the "boundary." Isn't that what education, in the final analysis, is all about? Leading students to that line that circumscribes the zone of their own identity and power of intelligence. Where they can begin to read and to think and to write. Where they can begin to know that they want to. The boundary and the sacred space that it contains are not easy to find today, for Denby or for any of us, and the American school, sadly, is no exception. It is not the reliable safe haven of the late fifties and early sixties that I so fondly remember. Then, corridors and classrooms were fairly predictable and friendly. The engagement with challenge was, for the most part, in the area of learning, not wondering whether someone was going to open fire in the library.

Even the fifties fantasy supported the school effort. We believed in the ideal of the stable happy family depicted on leading sitcoms such as *Ozzie and Harriet, Father Knows Best, The Donna Reed Show,* and *Leave It to Beaver.* If our own family fell short of the ideal, there was still comfort in knowing that society was pointed in that direction. Genuine quality was still a prime value, whether in the engineering and manufacture of cars or the writing and production of television plays. Even dime-store items had a certain substance that has allowed them a second life as a kind of affectionate kitsch commentary on their era.

Today's fantasy, however, is less a benign assistant than it is a formidable adversary. A miasma of violence, pornography, cynicism, alienation, and vapid values, it leaches into our families, our schools, and our minds through every pore of our awareness. It is wily and seductive, ubiquitous and unrelenting. If the fantasy had so much power over Denby, a highly accomplished middle-aged writer educated at Columbia, that it took him a year to rescue his own mind, what chance does an eight or ten or fifteen-year-old coping with poverty, life in the inner city, or divorcing parents have?

Recently I spent an evening playing video games with an eleven-year-old who is usually restricted to one hour per day by a very present and responsible father. This evening was a holiday, an exception, and he was allowed to show his middle-aged aunts how it was done. I tried to hide and defend myself in the proliferation of Escher-like mazes on the screen, but I was no match for the reflexes of this kid. While I was still trying to figure out whether it was a tunnel, or staircase, or secret bridge coming up, he was already into the ammo cache, reloading and firing on me. By the time I had my bearings, I was shot and the screen wiped out with a wash of bright red blood. I imagined this smart kid one day piloting a spaceship, knowing just when and how to negotiate the horizons of black holes and singularities as he waltzed his way to galaxies on the other side of the universe. But I also imagined the less fortunate kids who play in this realm for many hours a day without the disciplining presence and love of the responsible parent who is always there to say, "That's enough, turn it off, do your homework." For them the lesson may be something far less helpful than the development of quick reflexes.

Indeed, the lesson for all our kids may be far more sinister than we can admit or even realize. As I write this essay, the news is breaking of yet another school massacre at Columbine High School in Littleton, Colorado. Travelling again down that video pathway with my young friend, I am suddenly aware of other places on the cyberspace map, names that I heard on the news this morning in stories covering the two perpetrators and what might have been influencing them, names such as *Matrix, Doom, Mortal Kombat, Basketball Diaries.* What can you think when you watch clips from these videos and films, when you see a handsome kid at the glorious peak of physical youth rush into a full classroom in a long black coat with guns blazing?

Surely we as a culture must know at this point that education is something so much bigger than our commonly held parameters indicate. We must know that every moment we are leading children to that which is worthy or that which is not. We must know that, for better or worse, every parent and adult in America is an educator, that every interest group and every business in America is in the business of education. Those of us who, like Susan Ohanian in the previously quoted essay, understand the complex nature of this responsibility and the wholesale weasling involved in keeping the finger pointed at the teacher and classroom must stay on this issue like terriers on a rat until everyone gets the point.

We also know that the media *per se* do not comprise the evil empire. Tools can be used wisely, or they can be used foolishly. It's the quantity of junk and the lightning-speed accessibility to that junk that are the major problems. For their part, the media—like all technologies, like the railroad in Thoreau's day—promise an easier life, and we stand in awe of their power to do so. But Thoreau cautioned us not to be bamboozled, not to lose sight of what is "essential." Reading, as opposed to the media, draws us inward, where we are able to experience not the external power of our tools, but the internal power of our being. Birkerts says, "It is an interesting speculation: that the cultural threats to reading may be, paradoxically, revealing to us its deeper saving powers" (57).

Denby's story is a dramatic illustration of this shift from external to internal power. He says, "I had risen from my back: the climber loves his conquerable rock which makes every muscle strain. It was the happiest moment of the year" (312). Only this realization of power as internal, as a faculty of self, can, in my opinion, provide a real antidote to violence predicated as it is on the belief that power is external. Therefore, it would seem to me that those factors that reinforce for students and teachers that power is external, those factors that lead them away from themselves, those factors that are blind to the void and anguish that powerlessness and alienation produce will ironically continue to yield results we do not really want.

Today our children and teachers lumber along like packmules under the weight of a culture of materialism, superficiality, and a rampant consumerism that is fueled by sex, drugs, and violence. The result of this mix is a miasma of overstimulation, compounded by increasing and increasingly contradictory expectations of everybody. On top of all this the culture piles a plethora of critiques—many of them debatable, superficial, or ill-conceived—as to how poorly teachers and students are doing and equally numerous suggestions as to how they can perform better. We strain at the gnats of scores and standards and curricula and methodologies and swallow the camels of wholesale demoralization and alienation. We need more than facile antidotes to profound malaise. We need something deeper and truer to hang our hat on.

We long for something more from education: We long to be liberated. From the waves of immigrants whose first order of business was to obtain an education, to David Denby, who needed to go back to see what it was that he had lost, education has about it the idea of transformation to a more desirable condition. We equate education with liberation, and we equate liberation with a chance for happiness.

Recently a group of cowboys called "horse whisperers" have come onto the popular scene. These men have revolutionized the horse training world, proving the brutal and terrifying old method of "breaking" horses to be entirely unnecessary, outmoded. Instead of roping, beating, and spurring the horse into despirited submission, these cowboys have learned to listen to the animal and understand its subtle language.

What we witness when man and horse come into the pen is a delicate ballet of communication consisting primarily of glances and body language. Understanding the horse as both flight animal and herd animal, the cowboy knows when to let go and when to invite. Understanding the meaning of cocked ears, exposed tongue, and lowered head, the cowboy knows how to interpret and how to respond. The outcome of training, or "gentling" as it is called, is quite predictable: In a remarkably short time and with virtually no distress the horse is saddled and takes the cowboy for a ride. I think it would be correct to claim that, for both cowboy and horse, the precinct of the corral is ground to yet another story of liberation, another "happiest moment of the year." It is also a story of education in which the educators have learned to put the horse before the cart: Methodology follows communication and understanding that are both deep and genuine.

One day a few years ago a group of seniors came into my room for English class. It was lunchtime, and they were tired and querulous, not up for *Hamlet.* They asked for a few moments of silence, and the room quieted down almost instantly. When I intended to begin the class after a few minutes, a voice in my head that was so emphatic it was almost audible said, "Listen." I did. When I looked around the room at the faces, I knew instinctively not to engage in eye contact, to let them have their space. I looked out the windows at the blue sky and the clouds skimming by. I looked at the bare grey winter trees. I looked at the bricks and windows of the building next door. A few moments turned into ten, twenty, and then forty. No one said a thing. Several times I had wanted to start class, but the voice persisted: "Listen."

While I listened in the silence, I noticed that the faces of the young people who sat in front of me were becoming transformed. When they had entered the room, the hard distorted lines of stress seemed to blur the faces into a mass, one virtually indistinguishable from the next. But the lines had faded and each face softened into its own quiet beauty. Each face seemed to find itself, and the person behind it shone through in a purity of identity. The faces almost glowed. Boundaries had been refound.

If the Standards Police had observed my class for the first forty minutes that day, I would probably have been arrested. But had they stayed for the second half of that day's class, they would have witnessed a discussion on the nature of art and consciousness the memory of which still sends shivers down my spine. For all of us in that room it was a moment of what is known in philosophy as the "greatest happiness."

Now when students want to have quiet time or read their journals aloud in class, which they do frequently, I am comfortable with the silence. I have learned that students need to assimilate each other's narratives and ideas, they need the space and time to weave each other's texts into their own experience. Sometimes it's just a second or two, sometimes five minutes. Sometimes they laugh, sometimes they cry, sometimes they just sit there and try to figure it all out. They always let me know when they're ready to move on.

I have also noticed that when I let students have their silences, they express more appreciation, both for each other's work and for the general tone in the classroom. I have seen whole classes arrive in September seething with tension and leave in June in a spirit of deep and genuine community.

Indeed the presence of silence in my classroom has had such a dramatically positive effect on students that I now consciously build it into my curriculum. Simple breath and relaxation exercises, guided visualizations for journal entries, and readings where students sit with their eyes closed while I read to them or spell and define vocabulary words, allowing for abundant pauses, are some of the ways in which I am exploring the dimension of silence and its place in the fabric of students' experience.

As the crisis in American education deepens and the debates as to cause and solution continue to swirl around us, we would do well to reorient ourselves to the True North of our real needs and most worthy values. Birkerts says, "The act of reading creates for us a world within a world—indeed, a world within a hollow sphere . . ." (53). Children are learning every moment how to create their own world. For teenagers, especially, it can be very difficult and complicated. For those teenagers who do not fit into the ready-made world of their peers or the larger culture, it can be critical. What students read and how they read are certainly very important issues, but beyond those factors that can be measured and standardized lies the realm of learning how to imagine a world for oneself.

If we can give credence and exploration to that "hollow sphere," where the invisibles and immeasureables dwell, that zone where students think their worlds before bringing them into being, perhaps we can find there a power to transform the undesirable and disheartening into something sublime to behold; to build—in the words of William Blake—"a heaven in hell's despair" (397). The human race loves its fictions and fantasies; but, in all his mythic winged glory, Pegasus was never as inspiring a vision as the real horse happily dancing around the ring with the enlightened cowboy in a cloud of luminous dust.

Works Cited

Birkerts, Sven. "States of Reading." *The Best American Essays 1998.* Eds. Cynthia Ozick and Robert Atwan. Boston: Houghton Mifflin, 1998. 49–58.

Blake, William. "The Clod and the Pebble." *Adventures in English Literature.* Eds. Leopold Damrosch et al. Orlando: Harcourt Brace Jovanovich, 1985.

Denby, David. *Great Books.* New York: Simon & Schuster, 1997.

Ohanian, Susan. "Insults to the Soul." *English Journal* 86.5 (1997): 32–35.

Roberts, Monty. *The Man Who Listens to Horses.* New York: Random House, 1997.

Thoreau, Henry David. "Walden." *The Norton Anthology of American Literature.* 4th ed., vol. 1. Ed. Hershel Parker. New York: W. W. Norton, 1994. 1719–1889.

Editor

Virginia R. Monseau is professor of English and secondary education at Youngstown State University, where she teaches graduate and undergraduate courses in young adult literature, children's literature, composition, and English methods. A former high school teacher, she is past editor of the *English Journal* and a past president of ALAN, The Assembly on Literature for Adolescents of the National Council of Teachers of English. The series editor of Boynton/Cook's Young Adult Literature Series, Monseau is the author of *Responding to Young Adult Literature* (1996) and *Presenting Ouida Sebestyen* (1995). With Gary M. Salvner she coedited *Reading Their World: The Young Adult Novel in the Classroom*, 2nd edition (2000), as well as the CD *A Complete Guide to Young Adult Literature* (2000). She is also coeditor, with Jeanne M. Gerlach, of *Missing Chapters: Ten Pioneering Women in NCTE and English Education* (1991).

Contributors

Editor's Note: The biographical entries below are based on information that was current when each author's essay was published in English Journal.

Vasiliki Antzoulis teaches seventh- and eighth-grade English at the Academy for the Intellectually Gifted in Queens, New York.

Rita Bornstein is head of the Department of Language Arts of North Miami Beach (Florida) High School.

Heather E. Bruce teaches in the Graduate School of Education at the University of Puget Sound, Tacoma, Washington.

Barbara R. Cangelosi teaches at Logan South Campus School, Logan, Utah.

Rosemarie Coghlan teaches English at Villa Maria Academy, Malvern, Pennsylvania, where she is also dean of students.

Elaine B. Coughlin teaches at Beaverton High School, Beaverton, Oregon.

Bryan Dexter Davis teaches English at Spanaway Lake High School, Spanaway, Washington.

David Gill teaches English education and young adult literature courses at the University of South Carolina, Wilmington.

Nancy Gorrell teaches at Morristown High School, Morristown, New Jersey.

Marsha Lee Holmes teaches composition and rhetoric at Western Carolina University, Cullowhee, North Carolina.

Jack Huhtala teaches at Beaverton High School, Beaverton, Oregon.

Larry R. Johannessen teaches at St. Xavier University, Chicago, Illinois.

Sara Dalmas Jonsberg teaches in the Department of English at Montclair State University, New Jersey.

Sandra Kowalczyk teaches at Montello Junior High School, Montello, Wisconsin.

Carolyn Lott teaches at the University of Montana, Missoula.

Daniel Mindich teaches English at Champlain Valley Union High School in Hinesburg, Vermont.

G. Lynn Nelson teaches in the Department of English at Arizona State University, Tempe.

Linda W. Rees is retired from St. Stephen's Episcopal School, Bradenton, Florida.

Joan Ruddiman is a reading teacher on an eighth-grade team at West Windsor Plainsboro Middle School in Plainsboro, New Jersey.

Colleen A. Ruggieri teaches English at Boardman High School, Boardman, Ohio.

Stephanie Wasta teaches at the University of Montana, Missoula.

Randal W. Withers recently received his master's degree in English education at Florida State University, Tallahassee.

Mary F. Wright teaches at Montello Junior High School, Montello, Wisconsin.

Marion Wrye teaches English at St. Mary Academy, Bay View, in East Providence, Rhode Island.

This book was typeset in Palatino and Helvetica by Precision Graphics.
Typefaces used on the cover were Charcoal, Trajan, and Usherwood Medium.
The book was printed on 60-lb. Accent Opaque paper by Versa Press.